COLLINS GCSE SCIENCES

Physics

Shirley Parsons
Ian Pritchard

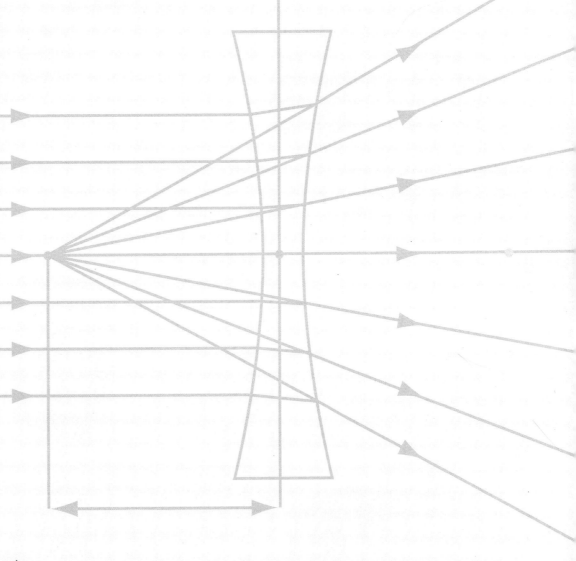

Collins Educational

An imprint of HarperCollinsPublishers

Contents

Managing energy

1	Energy transfer	1
2	Heat Energy	6
3	Work and power	16
4	Energy resources	23

Controlling matter

5	Matter and temperature	36
6	Pressure and hydraulics	46
7	Forces in liquids	51
8	Fluid flow	54
9	Pressure in gases	58

Controlling movement

10	Forces in action	64
11	Turning forces	70
12	Looking at motion	75
13	Forces and motion	85
14	Motion in two dimensions	96

Controlling electrons

15 Electrostatics 102
16 Current electricity 106
17 Resistance 113
18 Circuits and power 118
19 Using electricity 123
20 Magnets and electromagnetism 132
21 Electronics 144

Controlling waves

22 Oscillations 152
23 Sound 161
24 Light 171
25 Electromagnetic spectrum 184
26 Communication systems 191

Harnessing the atom

27 Inside the atom 199
28 Radioactivity 205

Beyond control?

29 Earth in space 213
30 Cosmology 219

Summary examples

Natural gas 224
Forces in a Fender Stratocaster 226
Car electrics 228
Colonising Mars 230

Glossary 232
Index 235

Acknowledgements

The publishers would like to thank the following for permission to reproduce photographs
(T = top, B = bottom, C = centre, L = left, R = right).

Ace Photo Agency/Lesley Howling 158TL; Ace Photo Agency/Mike Shirley 74L; Adam Hart-Davis/SPL 102B; Alex Bartel/SPL 136TL; Allsport 66B; Allsport/Ben Radford 80TL; Allsport/David Cannon 3; Allsport/Gray Mortimore 2C; Allsport/Mike Cooper 98CR; Allsport/Mike Powell 81BL; Allsport/Phil Cole 173TR; Allsport/Simon Bruty 75L, 98CL; Ann Ronan/Image Select 30CL, 85BR, 209CL; Associated Press Ltd 56L; BBC Natural History Unit/Mike Barton 37T; Betty Milon/SPL 213BL; BMW 61BR, 228T, 228B; Brad Nelson/Custom Medical Stock Photo/SPL 177TL; Brahm Public Relations/Theakston's Brewery 41BL; Bromilow, Chamberlain and Evans, IACR Rothamsted 206BL; Bruce Coleman/Jeff Foott Productions 87C; Bruce Coleman/Konrad Wothe 23R; C T R Wilson/SPL 207CL; CERN 105T, 199T, 199BL; CNRI/SPL 211C; David Parker/SPL 159TL, 177BR; David Redfern/Redferns Picture Library 47L; Department of Transport 20BL; Dick Luria/SPL 189CL; Dr Fred Espenak/SPL 218T; Dr Jeremy Burgess/SPL 188TL; Dr Ray Clark and Mervyn Goff/SPL 188CL; Edinburgh Photographic Library/Johnston 8; Ferranti Electronics/SPL 144L; Gary S Settles/Stephen S McIntyre/SPL 85TR; GCa/CNRI/SPL 190CL; George East/SPL 218B; Hamish Walker 160C, 168TL; Holt Studios/John Adams 23L; Holt Studios/Nigel Cattlin 212TL; Ian Pritchard 19TL, 42TL, 42TR, 43L, 43R, 46BL, 47R, 49BL, 49BR, 50TL, 50TR, 52, 71, 73C, 85CR, 92, 96BL, 96BR, 109BL, 112TL, 115, 116TL, 125TL, 129, 131TR, 133TL, 134TR, 135C, 143R, 171CR, 173TC, 226BL (2 images), 226CL, 227BL, 227BR, 227CR, 227TR; Image Select/Allsport/David Cannon 93TL; J A Cash 2R, 23C, 33TL, 54BL, 64, 66CR, 70T, 70B, 72TL, 75T, 81TL, 85T, 95L, 96T, 119BR, 153L, 160L, 161C, 176L, 177B, 187BL, 192TR, 216TR; James King-Holmes/SPL 166CL; Jerry Mason/SPL 135CL; John Birdsall 7L, 7R, 18, 20TR, 55L, 70C, 70L, 70R, 125BR, 135BR, 154CL, 171CL, 173B, 174; John Frassanito, NASA/SPL 100B; Julian Baum/SPL 214BL; Juilliard String Quartet/Redferns Picture Library 161CR; Mark Burnett/SPL 63; Martin Dohrn/SPL 211CL; Mattel UK Ltd 152CR; Mick Hutson/Redferns Picture Library 161CL, 167CR, 226T, 226CR; NASA/Image Select 215TL; NASA/SPL 100T, 190T, 132BC, 216TL, 230T, 230B; Nigel Francis/Robert Harding Picture Library 102T, 106T, 113, 118T, 119BC, 123T, 132T, 144T; NRAO/SPL 223; Nuclear Electric 25B; P Saada/Eurelios/SPL 170L; Pekka Parviainen/SPL 132BL; Peter Gould 13TL, 16L, 16R, 17, 48BL, 48CL, 48TR, 49, 51CL, 60TL, 105CL, 116CL, 126BL, 128, 132CL, 152T, 158TR, 161T, 161B, 182BL, 184T, 191T; Peter Menzel/SPL 33BL, 93BL; Rev Ronald Royer/SPL 220TL; Robert Harding Picture Library 4, 122, 192BL, 192TC, 192TL, 224T, 224T, 224CL; Robert Harding Picture Library/Adam Woolfitt 66C; Robert Smith/Redferns Picture Library 152C; Roger Ressmeyer, Starlight/SPL 36, 39L, 46T, 51T, 54T, 58T; Royal Observatory, Edinburgh/SPL 222BL; S.I.U./SPL 160R; Science Source/SPL 211CR; Shirley Parsons 1BL, 13BR; SPL 213T, 219, 220TR; St Bartholomew's Hospital/SPL 119BL, 132BR; Stephen Dalton/NHPA 51BL; The Science Museum/Science and Society Picture Library 103TL, 144C; Tony Craddock/SPL 1T, 6, 16T, 23T, 30B; Tony Hallas/SPL 213CL, 222BR; Tony Stone Picture Library 2L, 105BL, 152CL, 212CL; US Department of Energy/SPL 210BL.

Published by Collins Educational, an imprint of HarperCollins *Publishers* Ltd.
77–85 Fulham Palace Road, London W6 8JB.

First published 1996.

ISBN 0 00 322388 4

Original design by Moondisks Ltd, Cambridge

Edited by Gina Walker

Picture Research by Amanda Davidge

Artwork by Barking Dog Art

Printed and bound by Harper Collins (HK).

Energy transfer

Learning objectives

By the end of this chapter you should be able to:

- **define** energy
- **recall** that energy is measured in joules
- **understand** that energy can be used or stored

- **understand** that energy is required for anything to happen
- **list** the different forms of energy
- **recognise** energy transfers

1.1 Energy

What is energy?

It is very difficult to explain what energy *is* because you cannot see it or feel it. It is much easier to say what energy can *do*. Energy can heat things or make them move. Energy can make things give out light or sound. Energy can exist in many different forms (see figure 1). Energy is either stored, as potential energy, or it has an effect on other objects, as kinetic or electromagnetic energy. We can detect the *effects* of energy as it moves, or changes from one form to another.

Swimming is a popular way of transferring potential energy to kinetic energy.

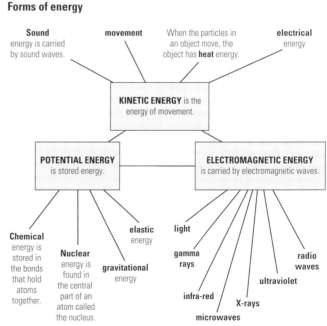

Forms of energy

Sound energy is carried by sound waves.

movement

When the particles in an object move, the object has **heat** energy.

electrical energy

KINETIC ENERGY is the energy of movement.

POTENTIAL ENERGY is stored energy.

ELECTROMAGNETIC ENERGY is carried by electromagnetic waves.

Chemical energy is stored in the bonds that hold atoms together.

Nuclear energy is found in the central part of an atom called the nucleus.

gravitational energy

elastic energy

light

gamma rays

infra-red

X-rays

microwaves

ultraviolet

radio waves

Figure 1

How do you measure energy?

You cannot measure energy directly but you can measure how much energy is transferred from one place or form to another. For example, you cannot see the energy in a battery or cell. But you can detect it when it moves in the circuits of a personal stereo as electrical energy, and you can hear it in the headphones as sound energy. Energy can have many different effects, but they are all measured in **joules** (J), kilojoules (kJ) or megajoules (MJ). 1 kJ is the same as 1000 J. 1 MJ is equal to 1 000 000 J, or 1000 kJ.

Having energy is a bit like having money. It is only useful to you when you exchange it for something you want. For example, energy in rocket fuel is only useful when the fuel burns to release hot gases. A transducer is a device that transfers energy. For example, an electric torch contains a series of transducers (see figure 2).

1 List the energy transfers in the photos below.

2 Write each energy transfer in a table with the headings 'Input energy', 'Transducer' and 'Output energy'. Add four more examples of your own.

Energy changes in an electric torch

chemical energy → electrochemical cell → electrical energy → torch bulb ⟨ light / heat

input ——→ transducer ——→ output/input ——→ transducer ——→ output

Figure 2

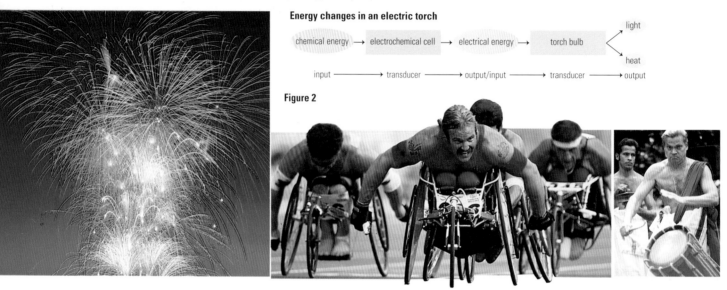

Energy is only useful when it is transferred from one form to another

How is energy stored in fuels and food?

Energy is stored in chemical bonds which hold atoms together. When the bonds break during a chemical reaction the energy is released. Food and fuels contain stored chemical energy. When they react with oxygen, energy is released. For example:

$$\text{methane (natural gas)} + \text{oxygen} \xrightarrow{\text{burns}} \text{carbon dioxide} + \text{water} + \text{heat and light ENERGY}$$

In your body, a chemical reaction called **respiration** releases energy from the food you eat. The energy transfers to your body cells, for movement, keeping warm or powering your body processes. You store excess energy in your body as chemicals such as fat and glycogen.

How else can energy be stored?

Batteries store chemical energy. A better name for a battery is an **electrochemical cell**. When the cell is connected in a circuit, chemical energy is transferred to electrical energy, which can be used to make all kinds of devices work (see chapter 16, *Current electricity*). Batteries are a convenient way of storing energy because they are portable.

When you lift an object, you give it **gravitational potential energy**. You can calculate the amount of gravitational potential energy an object has if you know its mass, the force of gravity and the height the object is lifted above the ground. On Earth, the force of gravity on every 1 kg of mass is 9.8 newtons (N). We usually round this up to 10 N/kg.

3 What forms of stored energy are there in a car?

$$\text{gravitational potential energy (J)} = \text{mass (kg)} \times \text{force due to gravity (N/kg)} \times \text{height (m)}$$

$$GPE = mgh$$

WORKED EXAMPLE

How much gravitational potential energy would you transfer to a 100 g pencil case if you lifted it up from the ground onto a desk 1 m high?

$GPE = mgh = 0.1 \times 10 \times 1 = 1 \text{ J}$

If the pencil case fell off the desk, the potential energy would be released as 1 J of kinetic energy.

Compressed springs and stretched materials store mechanical energy. When you stretch back the rubber band in a catapult, you give it **elastic potential energy**. When you let go, the band goes back to its original size and the pellet is fired forwards. Potential energy in the rubber band is transferred to kinetic energy in the pellet.

4 Cathy (60 kg) and her son, Jason (35 kg) walk 4 m up a flight of stairs in a shop.
a How much gravitational potential energy does each person gain?
b Cathy buys some books for Jason, which have a mass of 2 kg. She walks another 4 m up to the next floor in the shop, carrying the books. How much more potential energy does she gain?
c Jason offered to carry the books, but he dropped them down both flights of stairs. How much potential energy did the books lose?

An archer uses elastic potential energy in the bow to fire the arrow.

What makes bungee jumpers bounce?

When a person dives from a high board, once he reaches the pool, all his potential energy has been transferred to kinetic energy. He cannot collect the kinetic energy and use it to shoot back up to the high board. He must use chemical energy from his food to climb up again.

Bungee jumpers leap from great heights with strong rubber bungee ropes secured to their legs. When they reach the bottom of their fall, they bounce back up. As they fall, their kinetic energy is transferred to elastic potential energy, stored in the bungee. When the bungee is fully stretched, the elastic potential energy starts to convert back to kinetic energy, throwing the jumper back up again.

The bungee jumper used 16 000 J of her chemical energy to climb to the top of the tower. As she falls this energy is converted to kinetic energy.

5 a How much gravitational potential energy does the bungee jumper in the photo have at the top of the tower?

b When it is fully stretched, the bungee rope is only just shorter than the height of the tower. How much kinetic energy will the jumper have as she reaches the bottom of her fall?

c How much potential energy and kinetic energy will the bungee jumper have half way down?

d Bungee jumpers bounce up again at the bottom of each fall. Where does the energy come from to go up again?

Why don't bungee jumpers bounce forever?

As the bungee jumper in the photo bounces up and down, she collides with air molecules. Energy is transferred to the air molecules and makes them vibrate, so the air temperature rises slightly. The bungee jumper loses energy to the air, and the bungee rope also gets warmer. Each time she bounces up, the height she reaches is lower, because she has less energy to convert to gravitational potential energy. Eventually she does not bounce up again at all, and comes to a stop.

Each time energy changes to a different form, some energy is wasted. For example, in a food processor electrical energy transfers to kinetic energy in the blades, which chop the food. The energy in the spinning blades is useful. But the food processor also makes a noise and becomes warmer because of friction between its moving parts. This heat and sound energy cannot chop the food, so it is wasted. A transducer's energy inputs and outputs can be shown in a Sankey diagram, like the one in figure 3.

Sankey diagram for a food processor

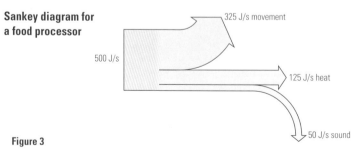

325 J/s movement

500 J/s

125 J/s heat

50 J/s sound

Figure 3

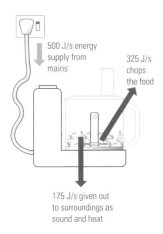

500 J/s energy supply from mains

325 J/s chops the food

175 J/s given out to surroundings as sound and heat

Figure 4 Energy changes from one form to another, but the total amount of energy always stays the same.

The **efficiency** of an energy transducer is a measure of how well it converts input energy into useful output energy (see chapter 4, *Energy resources*).

$$\text{efficiency} = \frac{\text{useful output energy}}{\text{input energy}} \times 100\%$$

We can make machines more efficient by reducing friction. Oil makes a car engine more efficient by helping the moving parts to slide past each other more smoothly, so less energy is transferred to heat and sound.

When energy is transferred from one form to another, the amount of useful energy drops, but the total amount of energy is unchanged (see figure 4). Energy can never be created or destroyed.

Whenever energy changes from one form to another, some energy escapes and spreads out into the surroundings. Most of this energy escapes as heat. It causes particles in the surroundings to vibrate a little faster than before, which raises the temperature of the surroundings (see chapter 2, *Heat energy*). It is usually too hard to collect this wasted heat energy and make use of it.

Summary of energy

- Energy can be stored (potential energy) or in motion (kinetic energy), or in electromagnetic waves.
- Energy is measured in joules (J).
- Energy can be transferred from one form to another, or from one place to another.
- A transducer transfers energy.

- When energy is transferred, it might have a different effect, but it is never created or destroyed. Total input energy = total output energy.
- Whenever energy is transferred, some is lost to the surroundings.

Investigation

Termutec Plc have designed a motor to lift building materials to the top of buildings under construction. They claim that the mass of the load will not affect the motor's efficiency. Your job is to plan an investigation to find out if the claim is justified.

These questions will help you decide what data to collect and how to use the data to find an answer.

a How will you measure the energy input of the motor?

b What will you have to measure so that you can calculate the energy transferred to the load?

c How will you use the answers to questions **a** and **b** to calculate efficiency?

d What do you need to record in your results table?

Heat *energy*

2

Learning objectives

By the end of this chapter you should be able to:

- **explain** the difference between heat and temperature
- **explain** how heat raises the temperature of materials
- **define** internal energy and specific heat capacity
- **calculate** the amount of energy required to increase the temperature of a known mass of a material

- **explain** how heat travels through materials and space
- **describe** ways in which heat energy can be kept in one place
- **evaluate** the effectiveness of different methods of insulation in the home
- **explain** heat transfer in terms of particles and waves

2.1 Heat and temperature

How can you make materials hotter?

You make things hotter by transferring energy to them. When you heat up soup on a cooker ring, heat flows from the hot ring to the cold saucepan and then to the soup. You can also make things hot by rubbing or shaking them (see figure 1). For example, rubbing your hands together helps to warm them up on a cold day. The kinetic energy of the movement is transferred to heat energy in your hands.

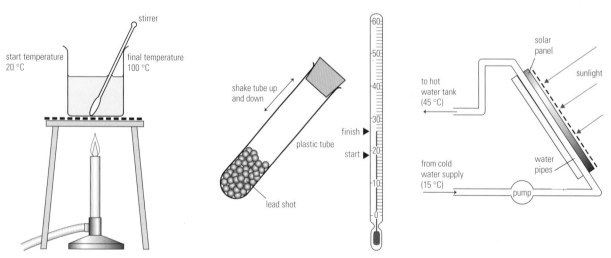

Figure 1 In each diagram energy is being transferred, and causing a temperature change.

6

1 Look at figure 1. Draw a table and fill it in, to show the initial and final energy forms, the initial and final temperatures, and the temperature change, for each energy transfer.
2 What is the effect of the energy transfer in each case?
3 Which units are used to measure temperature?

How hard is it to heat things up?

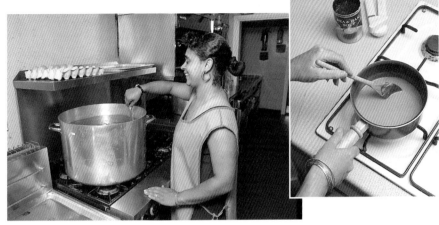

Soup is normally served at about 40 °C. Heating up soup for one takes a lot less energy than heating soup for a factory canteen to the same temperature.

You need more energy to heat up a large amount of material than a small amount. All materials are made up of tiny particles (see chapter 5, *Matter and temperature*). The larger the mass of the material, the more particles there are to share the added heat energy, so the smaller the temperature rise.

Some materials are harder to heat up than others. The amount of energy (in joules) needed to raise the temperature of 1 kg of a material by 1 °C is called the material's **specific heat capacity** (see table 1).

$$\text{specific heat capacity (J/kg °C)} = \frac{\text{energy used (J)}}{\text{mass (kg)} \times \text{temperature change (°C)}}$$

4 A kettle takes 67 seconds to boil enough water for one mug of coffee and 4 minutes 5 seconds to boil a full kettle. It uses 2200 J of energy per second.
a How much energy is used to boil a mugful of water?
b How much energy is used to boil a full kettle of water?
c If you just wanted a mug of tea for yourself, how much energy would you save by only boiling the water you need?
d How much time would you save?

Material	Specific heat capacity (J/kg °C)
Pure water	4200
Coal ash	900
Copper	390
Aluminium	910
Brick	800
Pyrex glass	780
Stainless steel	510
Concrete	3350
Magnetite (Fe_3O_4)	940

Table 1 *Specific heat capacities of different materials.*

WORKED EXAMPLE

A modern washing machine uses about 100 l of water for each load. If 1 l of water has a mass of 1 kg, and cold mains water is at about 10 °C, how much energy is needed to heat water for a hot wash at 90 °C?

energy used (J) = mass (kg) × specific heat capacity (J/kg °C) × temperature change (°C)

energy = 100 × 4200 × (90 − 10) = 33 600 000 J = 33.6 MJ

5 How much energy is needed to **a** make 1 kg of copper 1 °C hotter, **b** raise the temperature of 1000 g of steel by 1 °C?

6 Would you choose stainless steel, copper or Pyrex glass to make a saucepan? Explain your answer.

7 A hot bath is around 45 °C, and cold mains water is 10 °C in winter and 20 °C in summer.

a How much energy is needed to heat water for each bath design below? Assume the bath is filled, and it is summer.

Type	Plan view	Side view	Capacity (l)
Traditional			182
Shaped			164
Corner			225
Circular			555

b Estimate the amount of water you use when you have a bath. How much energy does it take to heat up in the summer?

c How much more energy do you use per bath in the winter?

d When you take a shower, you use about 20 l of water. How much energy do you save if you have a shower instead of a bath in summer?

e How much more energy would you save in winter?

Which materials make good heat stores?

Bed warming pans were filled with hot ashes, which acted as a heat store and gave out heat energy to warm the bedclothes.

Hot objects can be used to store heat energy. When hot objects cool, they give out heat to their surroundings. The amount of energy that can be released depends on the mass of material, its specific heat capacity and the temperature change.

WORKED EXAMPLE

How much energy is stored in a 0.5 kg block of iron which has been heated from 20 °C to 70 °C?

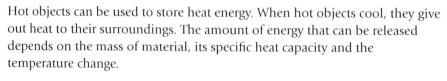

$$\text{energy needed to change temperature (J)} = \text{mass (kg)} \times \frac{\text{specific heat capacity (J/kg °C)}}{} \times \frac{\text{temperature difference (°C)}}{}$$

energy = 0.5 × 450 × 50

= 11 250 J, or 11.25 kJ

8 A hot water bottle contains 400 g of water at 80 °C. A bed warming pan contains 200 g of hot coal ash at 400 °C. A 1 kg brick is heated to 200 °C. When left in a empty bed, they all cool to 15 °C. Using table 1 on page 7, work out which is the best bed warmer.

9 In electric storage heaters, concrete blocks are heated up during the night when electricity is cheaper. During the day they slowly give out the stored heat energy.

a Why is concrete a good choice of material for storage heaters?

b Some storage heaters contain magnetite, instead of concrete. Which gives out the most energy per kilogram?

c A 1 kg block of magnetite takes up half the space of a 1 kg concrete block. Explain why many storage heaters use magnetite rather than concrete.

Which materials can be used for cooling?

10 Give as many advantages as you can for using water as a coolant.

Materials with high specific heat capacities can be useful for cooling other materials, because they can take in a lot of heat energy without getting very hot themselves. Water has a high specific heat capacity, and is relatively cheap and plentiful. Industries which generate excess heat often use water for cooling. For example, in dairies milk is heated strongly for about three seconds to kill harmful bacteria. Then pipes containing the hot milk run next to pipes of cold water. Heat energy transfers from the milk to the water, rapidly cooling the milk.

What is heat?

All materials are made of particles, which are always moving. You can observe this when you see the random movement of smoke particles in air. The smoke particles are pushed around by moving air particles. This movement is called Brownian motion after a Scottish botanist called Robert Brown, who first observed it in 1827. He was looking at pollen grains in water under a microscope, when he noticed the pollen grains moving around, pushed by moving water particles.

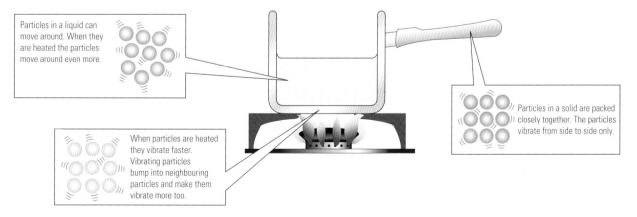

Particles in a liquid can move around. When they are heated the particles move around even more.

When particles are heated they vibrate faster. Vibrating particles bump into neighbouring particles and make them vibrate more too.

Particles in a solid are packed closely together. The particles vibrate from side to side only.

Figure 2 All materials are made up of particles in motion.

When a material is heated, the particles in it move faster (see figure 2), so they have more kinetic energy. So, strictly speaking, heat energy is kinetic energy. The particles in a hot object have more kinetic energy than those in a cool object. The term **internal energy** is used to describe the kinetic energy of the particles, to avoid confusion with the kinetic energy of the object itself.

Some particles need a lot of extra energy to make them move faster. The more energy the particles need to move faster, the harder it is to raise the material's temperature, so the higher the material's specific heat capacity is. Particles in a solid are packed closely together and are held in place by strong elastic forces. When a solid is heated, the particles vibrate more from side to side, but they cannot move from their fixed positions. Particles in liquids and gases are not held in such a rigid structure, and can move around freely when the material is heated.

11 In table 1 on page 7, do solids, liquids or gases have the highest specific heat capacities, in general? Try to explain this in terms of particles.

Are temperature and internal energy the same thing?

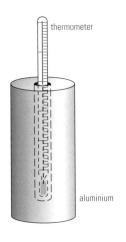

Figure 3 In this experiment, internal energy transfers from an aluminium block to water.

The temperature of an object gives a measure of how hot or cold it is, but it is not a measure of how much internal energy the object contains.

You cannot measure the internal energy of an object directly but you can measure its heating effect. The experiment shown in figure 3 was carried out using aluminium blocks of different sizes, which were all heated to the same temperature at the start. The results of the experiment are shown in table 2.

12 Using table 2, plot a graph to show the mass of the block against the temperature change in the water after two minutes. What pattern do you notice?

13 Explain why the largest aluminium block increased the water temperature more than the smallest one, even though the blocks were the same temperature at the start.

Mass of aluminium block (kg)	Initial temperature of water (°C)	Final temperature of water (°C)	Temperature change (°C)
0.16	20	30	10
0.31	20	38	18
0.54	20	47	27
1	20	55	35

Table 2 Results of an experiment to compare temperature and internal energy.

Summary of heat and temperature

- Heating can increase the temperature of a substance.
- Heating makes the particles in a material move faster. The particles have more internal energy.
- Internal energy is measured in joules (J).
- The amount of heat energy needed to raise the temperature of a material depends on the type of material and its mass.

- Heat energy = mass (kg) × specific heat capacity (J/kg/°C) × temperature difference (°C).
- The specific heat capacity of a material is a measure of how hard it is to heat up that material.

2.2 Heat transfer

How is heat transferred?

Heat is always transferred from a hot place to a colder place. Heat can be transferred in three ways — by **conduction**, **convection** or **radiation**.

Conduction

Conduction describes the way heat energy is transferred from one particle to the next in a material (see figure 4). As one particle gains internal energy, it vibrates more energetically, and bumps into the particle next to it. That particle starts to vibrate more energetically, and in turn forces its neighbour to do the same. It is a bit like passing parcels along a chain of people. The people stay in the same place but the parcels (the vibrations) move along the row.

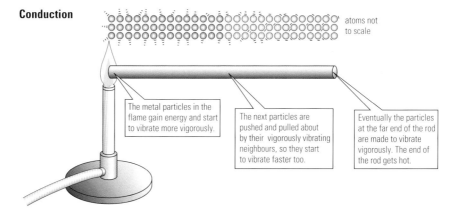

Conduction

atoms not to scale

The metal particles in the flame gain energy and start to vibrate more vigorously.

The next particles are pushed and pulled about by their vigorously vibrating neighbours, so they start to vibrate faster too.

Eventually the particles at the far end of the rod are made to vibrate vigorously. The end of the rod gets hot.

Figure 4 Heat energy passes from particle to particle in the metal rod.

Heat travels through some materials better than others (see figure 5 and table 3). These materials are good **conductors** of heat. A good conductor has a high **conductivity**. Metals are good conductors of heat. Non-metals and many compounds and mixtures, such as plastic and air, are poor conductors of heat. Liquids and gases are usually poor conductors because their particles are much further apart than in solids, so heat energy cannot pass easily from one particle to the next. Poor conductors are good **insulators**. A good insulator has a low conductivity.

Testing heat conductivity

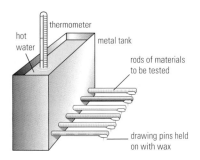

Figure 5 As heat moves to the end of each rod, the wax melts and the drawing pin falls.

Material	Time taken for pin to drop (s)
Wood	did not drop
Copper	14
Steel	73
Aluminium	16
Brass	20
Nylon	did not drop

Table 3 Results of the conductivity experiment.

14 List the materials in table 3 in order of conductivity. Put the best conductor first.

15 Why do you think some saucepans have copper bottoms?

16 Suggest a good material for saucepan handles. Give a reason for your choice.

If you take an aluminium foil container out of the freezer with your bare hands, you could get a nasty freezer 'burn'. Your skin may be damaged as heat quickly moves from your hand to the aluminium, which is an excellent conductor. The heat energy is conducted away so the bit of the foil you are touching stays cold. Heat energy continues to be transferred from your hand to the container.

If you take a polystyrene container out of the same freezer, it will not feel very cold even though it is at the same temperature as the aluminium container. Polystyrene is a poor conductor of heat. Heat from your hand passes into the polystyrene but it is not conducted away. Your hand warms up the polystyrene around your fingers, so it feels warmer than the aluminium.

17 Sonia found some coins and a plastic spoon in the freezer of her ice cream van. The coins felt colder than the spoon. Explain to Sonia why this was so.

Convection

Heat energy travels through **fluids** (liquids and gases) by convection. As the fluid is heated, particles near the heat source gain more internal energy so they move faster and further. As they move further apart, the fluid becomes less dense and rises. Colder, more dense fluid falls to take its place. This movement is known as a **convection current**.

Hot, coloured water in the bottle rises and forms a fountain in the colder surrounding water.

18 The first successful hot air balloon was made by two Frenchmen, in June 1783. It carried a sheep, a cockerel and a duck. Explain how hot air balloons work.

Convection currents

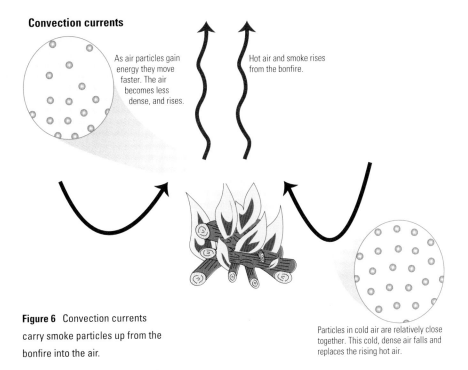

As air particles gain energy they move faster. The air becomes less dense, and rises.

Hot air and smoke rises from the bonfire.

Particles in cold air are relatively close together. This cold, dense air falls and replaces the rising hot air.

Figure 6 Convection currents carry smoke particles up from the bonfire into the air.

Radiation

When heat energy travels by radiation, it is not carried by particles but as electromagnetic waves. As it needs no particles, radiation can pass through a vacuum. The Earth is warmed by heat from the Sun, which radiates heat and light in all directions.

Radiant heat from the Sun raises the temperature of objects on the Earth. Dark surfaces absorb heat more than light colours. All warm objects radiate heat, but dull, dark surfaces are better radiators than light, shiny ones. This is why black tarmac feels hotter than pale concrete on a hot day. The hotter an object is, the more energy it can radiate.

When Misty has been sitting in the Sun, some parts of her fur feel hot, while others feel cooler.

19 Why does Misty's fur feel hotter in some places than others?

20 a When a space shuttle flies near the Sun, it gets extremely hot. How is the Sun's heat transferred to the shuttle?

  b Why are space shuttles covered in white tiles?

  c Space shuttles are well insulated. Give two reasons for this.

21 a Central heating 'radiators' do not radiate much heat. They warm the air around them, which then rises and circulates round the room. Suggest a better name for 'radiators'.

  b Draw a labelled diagram to show how central heating 'radiators' heat a room.

How do things keep warm?

Animals from cold climates often have a layer of fat under their skins to keep them warm. Fat is a good insulator. Mammals have fur as well. Some heat is transferred from the animal's body to the layer of air trapped by the fur, and warms it up. The heat is not conducted away because air is such a poor conductor.

Clothes keep you warm by trapping air, in the same way as fur. Many of the methods people use to keep their homes warm also use trapped air as an insulator (see figure 7).

Uninsulated house

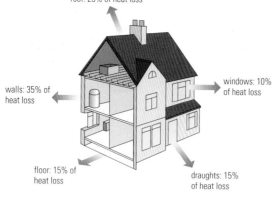

roof: 25% of heat loss

walls: 35% of heat loss

windows: 10% of heat loss

floor: 15% of heat loss

draughts: 15% of heat loss

total annual heating cost: £497
CO_2 emissions: 6300 kg

Insulated house

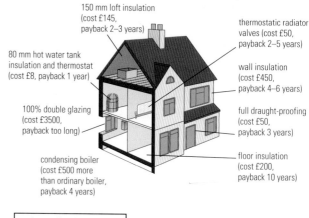

150 mm loft insulation (cost £145, payback 2–3 years)

thermostatic radiator valves (cost £50, payback 2–5 years)

80 mm hot water tank insulation and thermostat (cost £8, payback 1 year)

wall insulation (cost £450, payback 4–6 years)

100% double glazing (cost £3500, payback too long)

full draught-proofing (cost £50, payback 3 years)

condensing boiler (cost £500 more than ordinary boiler, payback 4 years)

floor insulation (cost £200, payback 10 years)

total annual heating cost: £150
CO_2 emissions: 1900 kg

Figure 7 It costs a lot of money to heat a house. You can save money and energy by using insulation to prevent heat loss.

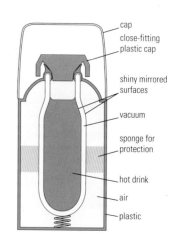

cap
close-fitting plastic cap
shiny mirrored surfaces
vacuum
sponge for protection
hot drink
air
plastic

22 Explain why you should fluff up your duvet in the winter but let the fibres become compressed in the summer.

23 a Look at the diagram on the right. Explain how each part of a vacuum flask keeps hot soup warm.

b James Dewar invented the vacuum flask in 1892, to keep liquid oxygen cold. How does a vacuum flask keep materials cold?

24 Look at figure 7.

a Which part of the uninsulated house loses the most energy?

b Which part loses the least energy?

c Which method of reducing heat loss is most expensive?

d Which method of keeping the house warm is the most effective?

e List the benefits of insulating a house to
i the owner, **ii** the environment.

Summary of heat transfer

- Energy is transferred from hot objects to colder objects.
- Energy can be transferred from one particle to the next in a material.
- Heat travels through solids by conduction, and through liquids and gases by convection.

- Energy can be transferred through a vacuum by waves, without involving particles. This is called radiation.
- Some materials are better heat conductors than others. Poor conductors are called good insulators.

Investigation

Householders are given a lot of advice on how to reduce their fuel bills. The Government recommends that people insulate their lofts with loft insulation. Hot water tanks should also be insulated to reduce heat transfer from the heated water to the surroundings. Companies recommend different materials, which are each available in different thicknesses. Design an investigation to find out what type of material, and what thickness of material, is best for insulating either a loft, or a hot water tank.

Work and power

3

Learning objectives

By the end of this chapter you should be able to:

- **define** work and power
- **calculate** the amount of work done
- **calculate** the rate at which work is done (power)
- **calculate** how much energy is transferred to an object when work is done
- **calculate** the increase in gravitational potential energy when work is done in lifting
- **calculate** the increase in kinetic energy when work is done in accelerating

3.1 Work

What is work?

Kassim did his work experience in a primary school. But is this work?

Fiona went to work in a supermarket. Is she doing work?

You need energy to do work. The amount of energy you transfer from one form to another tells you the amount of **work** you have done.

work done (J) = energy transferred (J)

Kassim and Fiona are on work experience. Kassim is helping out in a primary school, while Fiona chose to go to a local supermarket. They are arguing about who does the most work.

Kassim spends a lot of time listening to children read. He is not transferring energy as he listens, so according to the physics definition, he is not doing work. Fiona has to shift large boxes around the supermarket. To do this, she has to transfer chemical energy from her food to kinetic energy in the box. She is doing work.

1 **a** List the work you do in school.

   b Underline all those tasks which fit the physics definition of work.

   c In which lesson do you do the most work according to the physics definition?

How do you measure work?

When Fiona moves a box along the floor, she does work. If she moves the box further along the floor she does more work. The amount of work done depends on the distance travelled.

When Fiona moves a heavy box along the floor, she does more work than when she moves a light box. She needs to use a bigger push, or force, to move the heavier box. The size of the force applied affects the amount of work done.

Work is measured in joules, like energy. A joule is the work done when a force of 1 N is moved through a distance of 1 m.

$$\text{work done (J)} = \text{force (N)} \times \text{distance travelled in the direction of the force (m)}$$

WORKED EXAMPLE

How much work did Fiona do when she used a force of 20 N to move a box of washing powder a distance of 4 m?

work = force used × distance moved = 20 × 4 = 80 J

Fiona transferred 80 J of energy to the box of washing powder.

2 **a** Fiona had to move 150 cans 8 m across the store room. Each can needs a force of 5 N to push it along the floor. Calculate the amount of energy Fiona transferred to the cans.

   b How much work did Fiona do?

3 A force of 339 N is needed to push a full shopping trolley. Calculate the amount of work done in pushing the trolley 20 m from the supermarket to the car.

How much work do you do when you lift or pull?

The **weight** of the bottle in the photo will affect how big a force Fiona must use to lift it. The weight of an object depends on its mass and the force of gravity on each kilogram, g.

$$\text{weight (N)} = \text{mass (kg)} \times \text{force of gravity on each kilogram (N/kg)}$$

The force you must use to lift an object must be at least as big as the downward force of its weight. So the weight of an object affects the amount of work you do as you lift it. The height to which you lift the object also affects the amount of work done.

$$\text{work done in lifting (J)} = \text{mass (kg)} \times \text{force of gravity (N/kg)} \times \text{height (m)}$$
$$= \text{gravitational potential energy transferred to object, GPE}$$

So:
$$\text{GPE} = mgh$$

WORKED EXAMPLE

How much potential energy do you give to a 2 kg bottle if you lift it 1.5 metres onto a shelf?

GPE = 2 × 10 × 1.5
$\quad$ = 30 J

4 Firefighter Lesley Price took part in a sponsored ladder climb for charity. Lesley is 64 kg and the ladder reaches 13.5 m up a wall.
  a How much potential energy did Lesley have at the top of the ladder?
  b Lesley climbed the ladder 50 times. How much work did she do altogether?

The force you need to pull the springs apart on this bullworker changes the further you pull.

The amount of elastic potential energy stored in a catapult, or an archer's bow, or a bullworker, varies as you pull, because the size of your force varies. To calculate the work done against the springs, you use the average force.

$$\text{work done to pull the springs (J)} = \text{average force (N)} \times \text{distance (m)}$$
$$= \text{elastic potential energy transferred to the springs}$$

How can you make a small force bigger?

Sometimes you need a large force to do a job, but only a small force is available. For example, when you want to change a car wheel, you need a large force to lift the car, but you have only the small force your muscles can exert. To help, you can use a **machine** (see figure 1).

Gearwheels are used to make lifting jobs easier. The same amount of work is done as if there were no machine, but the input force required is smaller.

Machines uses a small input force to provide a large output force. The work done by the output force must be the same as the work done by the input force, because energy is conserved (although in practice the *useful* output work is always less than the input work, because some energy is wasted overcoming friction).

$$\text{input work} = \text{output work}$$

When a force moves through a certain distance:

$$\text{work done} = \text{force} \times \frac{\text{distance travelled}}{\text{in the direction of the force}}$$

So, in a machine, if friction is ignored:

$$\text{input force} \times \frac{\text{distance input}}{\text{force moves}} = \text{output force} \times \frac{\text{distance output}}{\text{force moves}}$$

This means that if the input force is small, it must move over a long distance to produce a large output force moving over a short distance (see figure 1).

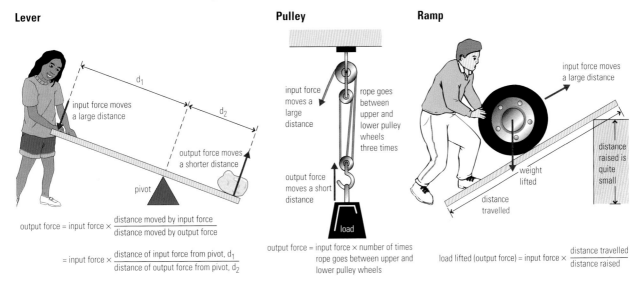

Lever

$$\text{output force} = \text{input force} \times \frac{\text{distance moved by input force}}{\text{distance moved by output force}}$$

$$= \text{input force} \times \frac{\text{distance of input force from pivot, } d_1}{\text{distance of output force from pivot, } d_2}$$

Pulley

$$\text{output force} = \text{input force} \times \text{number of times rope goes between upper and lower pulley wheels}$$

Ramp

$$\text{load lifted (output force)} = \text{input force} \times \frac{\text{distance travelled}}{\text{distance raised}}$$

Figure 1 In all machines that multiply forces, the small input force has to move a greater distance than the large output force.

WORKED EXAMPLE

A lumberjack uses a lever to lift some logs. He pushes down on the end of the lever pole with a force of 600 N and he moves it down 1 m. The other end of the pole moves up just 0.1 m. What size of force is produced by the lumberjack?

$$\text{input force} \times \text{distance input force moves} = \text{output force} \times \text{distance output force moves}$$

$$600 \text{ N} \times 1 \text{ m} = \text{output force} \times 0.1 \text{ m}$$

$$\frac{600 \times 1}{0.1} = \text{output force}$$

$$\text{output force} = 6000 \text{ N}$$

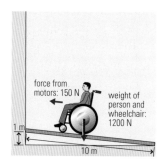

force from motors: 150 N

weight of person and wheelchair: 1200 N

1 m

10 m

5 **a** Calculate the work done by the wheelchair motors, in the diagram on the left.

b How much work would be done if the person and wheelchair were lifted directly onto the higher level without the ramp?

c Why do you think the ramp involves more work?

d If the ramp involves more work, why bother with it?

6 Mick must raise the car 20 cm to put the spare wheel on. The car weighs 1500 N, but the hardest Mick can push is 500 N.

a Work out the shortest distance Mick needs to move the end of the jack lever to lift the car.

b Mick actually had to move the end of the jack lever further than you calculated in **a**. Suggest two reasons for this.

Summary of work

- Work is done when energy is transferred, and is measured in joules (J).

- Work is done when a force moves over a distance.

  Work (J) = force used (N) × distance moved (m).

- When work is done to lift an object, gravitational potential energy, GPE, is transferred to the object.

  GPE (J) = mass (kg) × force due to gravity (N/kg) × height (m).

- When work is done to stretch a spring, elastic potential energy is transferred to the spring.

  Elastic potential energy (J) = average force (N) × distance moved (m).

- In a force-multiplying machine, the small input force moves over a larger distance than the large output force. The work done by both forces is equal, because energy is conserved.

3.2 Kinetic energy

Why is speeding so dangerous?

If a car travelling at 50 miles per hour (mph) hits a child, the child is likely to be killed. If a car travelling at 20 mph hits a child, there is a 9 out of 10 chance that the child will survive. This is because the slower car has less kinetic energy than the speeding car.

A pedestrian is more likely to be killed if she is hit by a lorry travelling at 20 mph than by a cyclist travelling at the same speed. The lorry's bigger mass means it has more kinetic energy.

The kinetic energy of a moving object depends on its mass and **velocity**. Velocity is a measure of how far something moves in a certain time, like speed, except that velocity always happens in a certain direction, while speed can happen in any direction. Velocity is normally measured in m/s.

$$\text{kinetic energy (J)} = \text{½ mass (kg)} \times \text{velocity}^2 \text{ (m/s)}$$
$$\text{KE} = \text{½ } mv^2$$

Vehicle	Mass (kg)
Mercedes-Benz 600SEL	2300
Citroen ZX Estate	1715
BMW 316i	1255
Fiat Tipo	1220

7 Look at the table on the left, and then answer the questions.

  a A Mercedes-Benz 600SEL, a BMW 316i and a Fiat Tipo were test driven into a wall at 20 km/h. Which one hit the wall with the most energy? Why?

  b A Citroen ZX Estate car was involved in an accident with a pedestrian. The car was travelling at 10 km/h. How much energy did the car have on impact? (Hint: remember to change km/h to m/s.)

  c How much more kinetic energy would the Citroen have had at 60 km/h?

How fast do bungee jumpers fall?

The bungee jumper in the photo on page 4 has a great deal of gravitational potential energy as she stands on the tower. As she falls, that potential energy transfers to kinetic energy, and then to elastic potential energy in the bungee rope. When she has fallen the length of the rope, just before it starts to stretch, all the gravitational potential energy she has lost so far has transferred to kinetic energy. At this point, before any energy is transferred to elastic potential energy, she is travelling at her fastest speed.

WORKED EXAMPLE

If a bungee rope is 9.8 m long when it is unstretched, what will be the bungee jumper's top speed, just before the rope begins to stretch?

decrease in GPE = increase in KE

$$mgh = \tfrac{1}{2}mv^2$$
$$gh = \tfrac{1}{2}v^2$$
$$v^2 = gh \times 2 = 10 \times 9.8 \times 2 = 196$$
$$v = \sqrt{196} = 14 \text{ m/s}$$

The bungee jumper's top speed will be 14 m/s, or 50.4 km/h.

8 A window cleaner in a pulley-cradle 12.8 m above the ground accidentally drops a 2 kg bucket.

  a How much kinetic energy does the bucket have as it falls to the ground?

  b At what speed does the bucket hit the ground?

Summary of kinetic energy

• When an object accelerates it gains kinetic energy, KE.

• KE (J) = ½ mass (kg) × velocity^2 (m/s).

3.3 Power

How fast do you work?

9 At what rate does a 100 W light bulb transfer electrical energy to light energy?

10 Sharonjeet weighs 57 N. She ran 5 m upstairs to her room 8 s.
   a How much work did Sharonjeet do?
   b How much power did her legs develop?

11 Firefighter Lesley Price (64 kg) climbed a 13.5 m ladder in 30 s. How much power did she develop?

The rate at which something does work is called **power** and is measured in watts (W). Power is a measure of how many joules of energy are transferred each second. One watt is equal to one joule per second. So, a 60 W light bulb transfers electrical energy to light and heat at the rate of 60 joules each second.

$$\text{power (W)} = \frac{\text{work done (J)}}{\text{time taken (s)}} \qquad \text{Or:} \qquad \text{power} = \frac{\text{energy transferred}}{\text{time taken}}$$

WORKED EXAMPLE

Kassim lifts 12 boxes of work cards onto a shelf 2 m high using a force of 40 N per box. It took him 40 s. How much power did Kassim develop?

work done $\quad = \text{force used} \times \text{distance travelled} = 12 \times 40 \times 2$

$\qquad\qquad\quad = 960 \text{ J}$

power developed $\quad = \dfrac{\text{work done}}{\text{time taken}} = \dfrac{960}{40}$

$\qquad\qquad\qquad = 24 \text{ W}$

Summary of power

- The amount of work done each second is called power.

- Power (W) = work done (J)/time taken (s)

Investigation

Investigate the factors that affect the kinetic energy of a moving vehicle. You can use trolleys and ramps to simulate moving vehicles. Consider the following questions as you plan and carry out your investigation.

Planning

a What factors might affect the kinetic energy of a moving vehicle?

b Which factor do you think will have the most effect? Why?

Obtaining evidence

c What will you have to measure to calculate the kinetic energy of the vehicle?

d How will you measure these factors?

e What must you do to make sure you have designed a fair test?

f How will you check that your results are reliable?

Analysing evidence and drawing conclusions

g What is the best way to present your results?

h What conclusions can you draw from your evidence?

i What scientific knowledge can you use to explain your findings?

Evaluating evidence

j Were your results accurate?

k How could you improve the accuracy of your experiment?

Energy resources

4

Learning objectives

By the end of this chapter you should be able to:

- **recognise** a variety of energy sources
- **recognise** different energy transfer technologies

- **assess** the suitability of different energy transfer technologies in a variety of situations
- **calculate** the efficiency of energy transfers

4.1 Energy for everyone

Why do we need energy?

People need energy to *do* things. We need energy from food or fuel in order to move around. Light energy enables us to see, and we use sound energy to hear.

People in the developed world use a great deal of energy every day, from a wide variety of sources. An **energy source** is any material or physical event that provides energy in a form that people can use. For example, coal burns in air to give out light and heat. The coal is the energy source, although the final energy forms are light and heat.

To get a reliable and safe supply of energy, engineers need to be able to:

- collect the energy effectively
- store the energy efficiently
- transport the energy easily

These photos show just a few of the energy sources people use.

1　**a** List as many energy sources as you can. The photos above might help.

　b Arrange your list in order, starting with those you think are the best energy sources. Explain how you decided on the order.

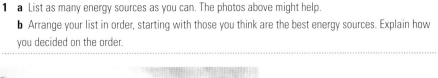

23

Why use electricity?

Energy sources rarely provide energy in the form people want to use. For example, fuels burn to release heat energy, but a lawnmower needs kinetic energy in the rotating blades to cut grass. Heat from the fuel cannot be used directly to make the blades turn. Energy must be transferred from the form provided by the source, to a more useful form.

Electrical energy is a very convenient form of energy. It is clean, efficient and relatively easy to transport. In power stations, huge amounts of energy from sources like fossil fuels, nuclear materials and moving water, are converted to electrical energy, which can then be carried over hundreds of miles and used to power all kinds of systems, from industrial machinery to hospital equipment.

Energy transfer wastes energy because not all of the energy from the source is changed into a useful form. Some is lost to the surroundings, often as heat or sound. The more energy changes there are, the more energy is lost overall. You can work out how well a power station transfers energy in the source to electrical energy by calculating the efficiency of the process. Efficiency is usually given as a percentage.

$$\text{efficiency} = \frac{\text{useful energy output}}{\text{total energy input}} \times 100\%$$

WORKED EXAMPLE

Calculate the efficiency of a coal-fired power station.

Input energy = 300 MJ in coal.

Output energy = 192 MJ heat loss in power station + 15 MJ heat loss in cooling towers
+ 9 MJ heat loss from power cables + 84 MJ electrical energy.

efficiency $= \dfrac{84}{300} \times 100\%$

$= 28\%$

2 **a** A nuclear power station generates 30 MJ of electrical energy for every 100 MJ of nuclear energy it uses. How efficient is this nuclear power station?

   b How much energy in the source material is wasted?

   c What do you think happens to the wasted energy?

3 As a car moves, chemical energy in the petrol is transferred to kinetic energy. In the average car, for every 100 J of energy in petrol, 50 J are used in overcoming friction between the car and the road, and 25 J are used overcoming air resistance.

   a Calculate the efficiency of petrol driven cars.

   b Draw a Sankey diagram to show the energy inputs and outputs for a petrol driven car.
   (Hint: You can read about Sankey diagrams in chapter 1, *Energy transfer*.)

How do power stations work?

All power station generators use energy from a source to turn a large electromagnet inside a coil of wire, which makes an electric current flow in the wire. The energy to turn the electromagnet can come from wind, waves, falling water or steam pressure. Steam pressure systems are powered by coal, gas, oil or nuclear fuel (see figure 1). Power stations that use steam pressure are called thermal power stations.

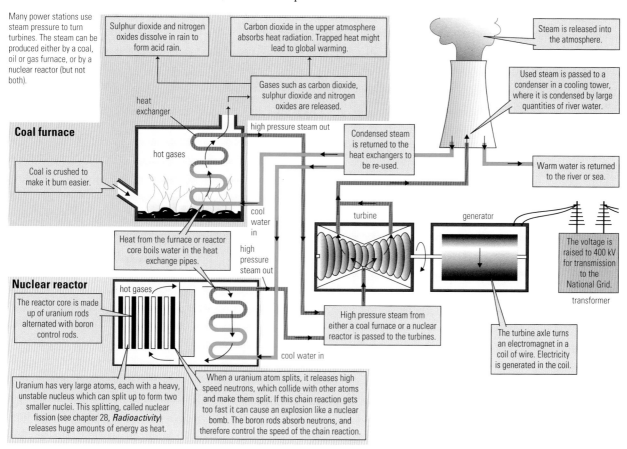

Many power stations use steam pressure to turn turbines. The steam can be produced either by a coal, oil or gas furnace, or by a nuclear reactor (but not both).

Sulphur dioxide and nitrogen oxides dissolve in rain to form acid rain.

Carbon dioxide in the upper atmosphere absorbs heat radiation. Trapped heat might lead to global warming.

Steam is released into the atmosphere.

Gases such as carbon dioxide, sulphur dioxide and nitrogen oxides are released.

Used steam is passed to a condenser in a cooling tower, where it is condensed by large quantities of river water.

heat exchanger

Coal furnace

high pressure steam out

hot gases

Coal is crushed to make it burn easier.

Condensed steam is returned to the heat exchangers to be re-used.

Warm water is returned to the river or sea.

cool water in

Heat from the furnace or reactor core boils water in the heat exchange pipes.

high pressure steam out

turbine

generator

The voltage is raised to 400 kV for transmission to the National Grid.

transformer

Nuclear reactor

hot gases

The reactor core is made up of uranium rods alternated with boron control rods.

High pressure steam from either a coal furnace or a nuclear reactor is passed to the turbines.

cool water in

The turbine axle turns an electromagnet in a coil of wire. Electricity is generated in the coil.

Uranium has very large atoms, each with a heavy, unstable nucleus which can split up to form two smaller nuclei. This splitting, called nuclear fission (see chapter 28, *Radioactivity*) releases huge amounts of energy as heat.

When a uranium atom splits, it releases high speed neutrons, which collide with other atoms and make them split. If this chain reaction gets too fast it can cause an explosion like a nuclear bomb. The boron rods absorb neutrons, and therefore control the speed of the chain reaction.

Figure 1 Both nuclear and coal-fired power stations are expensive to build, require a lot of land and use energy to transport fuels.

Sizewell B nuclear power station in Suffolk was opened in January, 1995. It cost £2 billion to build.

4 Use figure 1 to list some of the advantages and disadvantages of coal-fired and nuclear power stations.

Can we make power stations more efficient?

In a typical power station, nearly 70% of the input energy escapes as heat in water and steam. One way to solve the wasted energy problem is to capture and use the lost heat energy. Local Combined Heat and Power (CHP) stations can do this (see figure 2).

Conventional coal-fired power station

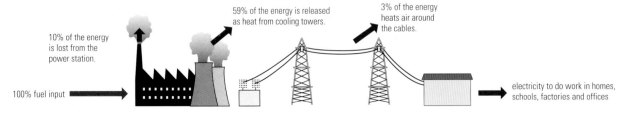

CHP station at Heathrow Airport

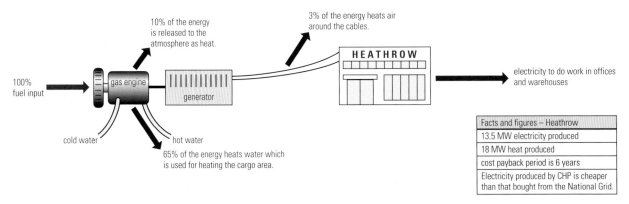

Facts and figures – Heathrow
13.5 MW electricity produced
18 MW heat produced
cost payback period is 6 years
Electricity produced by CHP is cheaper than that bought from the National Grid.

Figure 2 The conventional power station supplies very large towns. The Heathrow power station just supplies the airport buildings with electrical energy and heat.

5 a What proportion of the input energy is converted to electrical energy for each power station in figure 2?

b What proportion of the total input energy is useful output energy in **i** the coal-fired power station, **ii** Heathrow's CHP station?

c Why are CHP stations only used to supply heat across small areas?

d CHP stations use gas as a fuel. What else do you know that gas can be used for?

e What else can coal be used for?

f Give two advantages and two disadvantages of both CHP and conventional power stations.

g Suggest situations where CHP stations would be useful.

How can we get energy from the Earth?

Just under one per cent of the planet's energy can be found under the ground. The deeper down you go, the higher the temperature becomes. Heat energy from the Earth is called **geothermal energy**. It can be collected by pumping up water from deep below the Earth's surface (see figure 3).

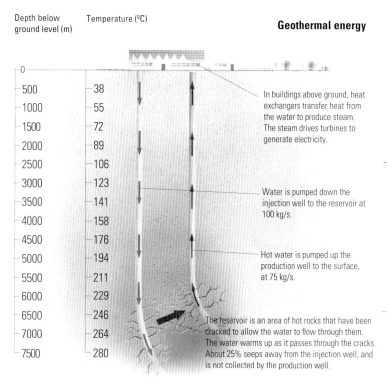

Depth below ground level (m) / Temperature (ºC)

Geothermal energy

Depth below ground level (m)	Temperature (ºC)
0	
500	38
1000	55
1500	72
2000	89
2500	106
3000	123
3500	141
4000	158
4500	176
5000	194
5500	211
6000	229
6500	246
7000	264
7500	280

In buildings above ground, heat exchangers transfer heat from the water to produce steam. The steam drives turbines to generate electricity.

Water is pumped down the injection well to the reservoir at 100 kg/s.

Hot water is pumped up the production well to the surface, at 75 kg/s.

The reservoir is an area of hot rocks that have been cracked to allow the water to flow through them. The water warms up as it passes through the cracks. About 25% seeps away from the injection well, and is not collected by the production well.

Figure 3 Some of the heat energy under the ground comes from the Earth's molten core. The rest comes from the radioactive decay of minerals such as uranium.

A geothermal plant in Svartsengi in Iceland supplies seven neighbourhoods, as well as the airport, with hot water for heating systems and washing (see figure 4). At the plant the water is at a temperature of 95 °C to 125 °C, but by the time it reaches homes, it has cooled to 80 °C. At peak times, 350 kg of hot water is needed every second. You would need 15 tonnes of oil each hour to produce this much hot water in an oil-fired boiler. Water leaves homes and offices at roughly 40 °C, and passes into the sewerage system and then into the ocean.

Geothermal energy in Iceland

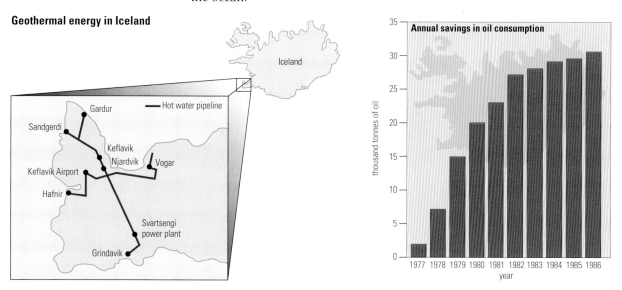

Figure 4 This map shows the geothermal energy plant and heat distribution system in Svartsengi, Iceland.

The total length of pipeline in the Svartsengi system is 300 km. Pipes above ground at the plant are insulated with rockwool and aluminium foil. Pipes near populated areas are underground so they do not cause an obstruction or spoil the environment. Underground pipelines are more expensive to lay and maintain than overground pipes.

6 **a** What are the costs and benefits of building a geothermal power system like the one in Iceland?

b Why must the pipelines be insulated?

c Do you think the Svartsengi pipeline system could be extended to supply the whole of Iceland? Give reasons for your answer.

d What do you think the effects might be of releasing water at 40 °C into the ocean?

e At the Svartsengi geothermal plant, high pressure steam is used to drive turbines and generate electricity. At a geothermal plant in Southampton in the UK water is pumped up at 70 °C and used to heat buildings, but not to generate electricity. Why do you think this might be?

How long will the Earth's energy resources last?

The deposits of fuel we know about are called **energy resources**. It may be too expensive or dangerous to extract all of these resources. The fuel we *can* extract at an economic price using today's technology is called our **energy reserve.** If circumstances change it might be worth tapping different resources. For example, it is expensive to extract oil under the sea so for many years the North Sea oil resources were not used, even though people knew about them. After the oil crisis in the early 1970s, oil from the Middle East became very expensive. This made the oil under the North Sea more valuable so it became a useful reserve.

Fossil fuels like coal, oil and gas are still being formed very slowly, but they are being used up much more quickly. In effect, fossil fuels cannot be replaced or used again once they have been extracted. Fossil fuels are **non-renewable** energy sources. Nuclear power is also non-renewable because uranium can only be used once. Even geothermal energy is not renewable. The water cools the rock more quickly than the Earth can re-heat it.

We do not know exactly how much fuel there is in the Earth's crust, but during the next century energy reserves will start to run out, and there might not be enough energy to supply the world's ever-increasing demand (see figure 5). When this happens there will be an **energy crisis**. No-one is sure when the energy crisis will occur but all are agreed that we need to look for ways of using new energy sources that will not run out.

Fuel	Known reserves ($\times 10^{21}$ J)	Estimated additional reserves ($\times 10^{21}$ J)
Coal and peat	24.7	53.6
Oil	2.0	27.7
Natural gas	0.7	7.6

Table 1 Estimates of fuel reserves.

Prediction of when non-renewable energy sources will run out

UK energy use

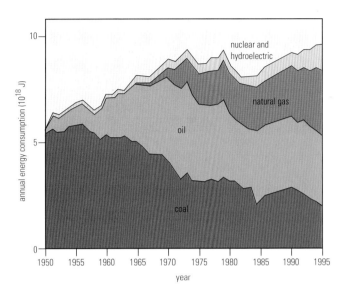

Figure 5 When reading graphs like these, remember that we don't know how much fuel remains undetected, or how quickly the fuels will be used up in the future.

7 Study table 1 and figure 5.
  a Which energy source is used most in developed countries like the UK?
  b A century ago, coal supplied 100% of the UK's energy demand.
    i Estimate the percentage of the UK's energy demand supplied by coal in 1995.
    ii Why do you think there has been such a change in the energy sources we use, over the last century?

8 Which energy source or sources are
  a likely to be in short supply when you are 70 years old?
  b likely to be readily available when you are 70 years old?
  c unlikely to be in short supply at any time?

9 What is meant by the term 'energy crisis'?

4.2 Renewable energy reserves

Renewable energy sources are sources which are replaced regularly. The most obvious renewable source is the Sun – no matter how much solar energy you capture today, the Sun will still rise tomorrow, and continue to radiate heat and light energy. The Sun also creates other renewable energy sources (see figure 6).

10 Solar energy is free, but few people in the UK fit solar panels to their houses. Suggest some reasons for this.

Renewable energy from the Sun

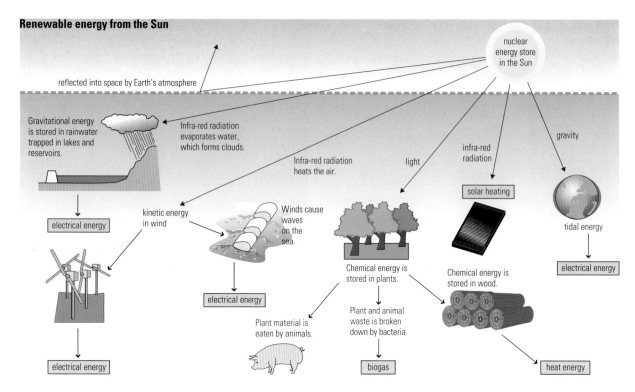

Figure 6 Many renewable energy sources originate from the Sun.

How can we use energy from the Sun?

This solar-driven printing press was invented by Monsieur Abel Pyre in 1882. It had 2.5 horsepower, and operated continuously for 4.5 hours.

The Sun is fuelled by a nuclear fusion reaction. Hydrogen atoms join up (fuse) to form helium atoms, releasing vast amounts of energy. If we could harness fusion reactions, we could satisfy our energy requirements for ever, without producing any polluting wastes.

In the meantime, we can use the energy from the Suns' fusion. The Sun provides 99% of the Earth's energy. It will be thousands of years before the Sun runs out. Solar energy is free, clean and does not cause pollution, so it might seem to be the answer to our energy needs. But trapping solar energy is expensive and making the equipment required can cause pollution.

Solar panels use energy from sunlight to heat water (see figure 7). The water can be used to heat houses directly, or preheat water for a central heating boiler. The preheated water needs less gas or oil to warm it for use in the central heating system.

This wall of mirrors in Odeillo, France, concentrates the Sun's rays onto a giant collector.

11 a List the factors that affect how well a solar panel collects sunlight energy.

b Plan an investigation to find out which of these factors has the greatest effect.

c How would the results of your investigation be useful to a designer of solar panels?

Homemade solar panel

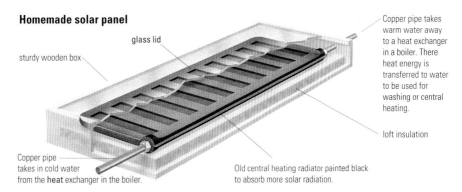

glass lid

sturdy wooden box

Copper pipe takes warm water away to a heat exchanger in a boiler. There heat energy is transferred to water to be used for washing or central heating.

loft insulation

Copper pipe takes in cold water from the **heat** exchanger in the boiler.

Old central heating radiator painted black to absorb more solar radiation.

Figure 7 Solar energy is captured by solar panels and transferred to heat energy in water. This home-made panel uses an old radiator, but it works in the same way as a commercially made panel.

Solar cells convert sunlight into electrical energy. A single cell produces a tiny amount of electricity, so they are only used when there is no alternative, or when a small amount of energy is needed. Many calculators use solar cells.

12 a Why do space satellites use solar cells for energy?

b Solar cells receiving 1000 J of sunlight energy produce 200 J of electrical energy. How efficient are these solar cells?

c Suggest a reason why satellites have such large banks of solar cells.

13 700 J/s/m^2 of energy reaches the Earth from the Sun. Of this, 30% is reflected back into space, and 23% causes water on the Earth's surface to evaporate.

a How many J/s/m^2 of the Sun's energy is absorbed by the Earth's surface?

b What is the minimum area needed to capture as much energy per second as is generated by a 1000 MW power station? (Hint: 1 MW = 1 000 000 W, and 1 W = 1 J/s.)

c There are proposals to cover 26 000 km^2 of the North American Desert with solar panels, to provide enough electricity for the whole of the USA. Are such power stations a practical proposition? Explain your answer.

Are biofuels renewable?

Biofuels are fuels produced by living organisms. Since living organisms are constantly growing, you might expect biofuels to be renewable, but it is not that straightforward. One of the earliest biofuels was wood. Although trees do grow back after wood has been cut, it takes time for them to grow to a reasonable size for harvesting. So wood is only renewable in the medium term. You have to wait years for wood supplies to be replenished.

Wood is a good fuel but can be difficult to transport and handle. The most convenient fuels to transport are gases or liquids. A **biodigester** can be used to convert plant materials and animal dung into gases. Bacteria in the digester tank break down the materials to produce methane gas. Methane can be used for cooking, heating, lighting, and even transport (see figure 8). Digesters are common in China, India and Africa.

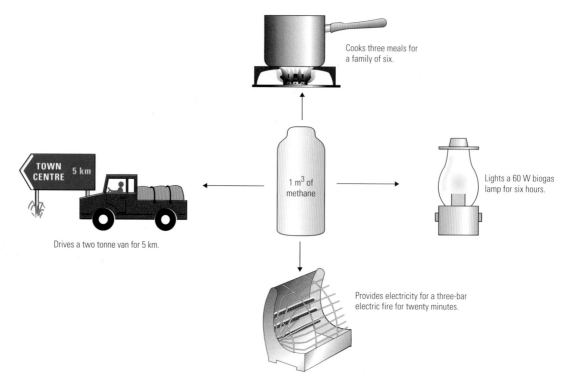

Cooks three meals for a family of six.

1 m³ of methane

Lights a 60 W biogas lamp for six hours.

TOWN CENTRE 5 km

Drives a two tonne van for 5 km.

Provides electricity for a three-bar electric fire for twenty minutes.

Figure 8 A cubic metre of methane can go a long way.

Harvested plant material can be fermented in large vats to make ethanol. Zimbabwe and Brazil use a mixture of ethanol and petrol to fuel their vehicles. The Brazil project began in the 1970s when petrol was in short supply. By 1986 one fifth of Brazil's cars ran on biofuel and they are hoping to use it in all cars by the year 2000.

14 A biodigester uses vegetable waste and manure from 6 pigs, to produce 3 m³ of methane every day.

   a What are the advantages of biodigesters?

   b Do families with a biodigester need other forms of energy? Explain your answer.

   c Look at figure 8. How many hours of light per day could one digester provide for a family with two 60 W lamps? Are they likely to use this much?

   d Why do you think so few petrol driven cars are converted to run on biofuel in Europe?

Can we use the energy in rainfall?

About 23% of the energy arriving on the Earth from the Sun is used up evaporating water. Eventually this water falls as rain and collects in rivers. Dams can be built to trap this water high up in hills, and force it to drive a turbine when it is released. Electricity produced when water flows through a turbine is called **hydro-electric power** or HEP (see figure 9).

Most of the UK's HEP stations are in Scotland. Their total power output is about 2000 MW – about the same as a single coal-fired power station. Over 70% of the potential sites for HEP have been used already.

About one fifth of the world's electricity comes from hydro-electric power.

Pumped storage HEP station

Rain falls and collects in rivers.

Water is pumped back up to the reservoir when electricity demand is low.

water evaporates

Sun's energy

River water is trapped by a dam.

sea

Water is released when electricity demand is high.

power house containing turbines, generators and pumps

Figure 9 At Europe's largest 'pumped storage' HEP station, at Dinorwig in Wales, approximately 4.9 kJ of energy is transferred for each kilogram of water falling 500 m from the top reservoir.

15 Use figure 9 to construct a flow chart of the energy changes involved in hydro-electric power stations.

16 List the advantages and disadvantages of HEP to:

a a city dweller in Glasgow   **b** a hill farmer in the Scottish highlands

17 At the moment HEP stations provide 1% of the UK's electricity. A large increase in the use of HEP in the UK is unlikely. Explain why.

18 Some people might say that using electricity to pump water up to the reservoir in an HEP station is a waste. Do you agree? Explain your answer.

How can you collect energy from the wind?

At different times of the day, or year, some parts of the Earth's surface become hotter than others. In areas which are heated, hot air rises. Colder air rushes in to replace the hot air and winds are created. The energy in wind can be used to turn an **aerogenerator**, which transfers kinetic energy from the moving air to electrical energy. A wind farm at Carmarthen in Wales feeds 130 kW into the UK National Grid – enough for a small village. The more electricity that is fed into the National Grid from renewable sources like wind, the smaller are the amounts of non-renewable resources needed to meet demands

There are some problems with using the wind as an energy source. For example, the wind is very unpredictable. Some days are calm, while others have winds in excess of 100 km/h. To generate electricity on a large scale large numbers of turbines are needed. The turbines are each 25 m in diameter, and are spaced 300 m apart. The environmental impact of such vast wind farms is considerable. Offshore wind farms, out to sea, may solve some environmental problems but they are more expensive to build and maintain.

19 a Draw a flow chart to show the energy changes when electricity is generated by a wind turbine.

b Imagine your District Council is considering a new wind farm in your area. Outline arguments for and against such a scheme.

Can you collect energy from the sea?

Energy from waves

Wave energy can be unpredictable but estuaries provide sites where the waves are within safe and useful limits. There are many ways to convert the kinetic energy of waves into electrical energy. One uses the waves to push air in and out of a concrete chamber to drive a turbine. The Osprey generators off the north coast of Scotland use this system. Another method uses 'nodding ducks' which convert the up and down movement of waves to circular movements in axles connected to a generator (see figure 10).

Figure 10 Kinetic energy in waves can be transferred to electrical energy by 'nodding ducks' like this one.

Using wave energy

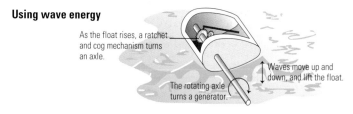

As the float rises, a ratchet and cog mechanism turns an axle.

Waves move up and down, and lift the float.

The rotating axle turns a generator.

Energy from tides

The gravitational pull of the Sun and Moon on the Earth cause huge movements in the world's oceans, called tides. If water is trapped in a reservoir during high tide, it can be released through a turbine when the tide goes out, and used to generate electricity (see figure 11).

Figure 11 Using tidal energy.

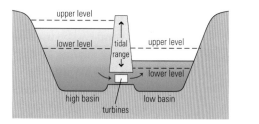

| Rising tide collects in reservoir. | Water is released once tide has retreated. | Flowing water turns turbines, which drive a generator. | Electricity is generated. |

potential energy ➡ kinetic energy ➡ kinetic energy ➡ electrical energy

20 Study figure 10. Use it to draw a flow chart to show all the energy changes involved in the nodding duck system.

21 Do you think the Severn Estuary barrage is a good idea? Give reasons for your answer.

There are proposals to build a tidal power station across the Severn Estuary, in the UK. It would take 20 years to build and be extremely expensive. Conservationists are concerned that the tidal barrage would change the marine habitat so much that some organisms would no longer be able to live there. The Renewable Energy Group claim that the Severn barrage could produce 7% of the electricity England uses today. This would mean 9 million tonnes of coal burned in conventional power stations could be saved every year.

Is the energy crisis inevitable?

All methods of harvesting energy have social, economic and environmental costs. An alternative to finding new ways to exploit the Earth's resources might be to use less energy. Increased energy efficiency would reduce consumption and fuel bills. Changing our lifestyles to demand less energy, by using public transport instead of private cars for example, will also help cut consumption.

Soar Valley College in Leicester began a policy in 1992, to see how much energy they could save using the following simple strategies. Table 2 shows the impact of their policy on electricity consumption. They also saved £20 on gas bills and £2464 on oil over the summer of 1992 compared to 1991 costs.

• They set room thermostats slightly lower than normal, at 19 °C.
• They encouraged teachers and students to switch off lights in unused areas.
• They installed low energy bulbs in areas which had to be lit at all times.
• They installed sensors to detect unoccupied areas and switch off power.
• They installed a zoning system to switch off heating in certain areas.

Table 2 Data from Soar Valley College's campaign to save energy.

Month	Electricity consumption (kWh)		Cost (£)	
	1991	1992	1991	1992
April	27 016	33 718	1712	2168
May	30 176	23 466	1900	1611
June	29 876	24 174	1892	1678
July	8 608	10 216	736	885
August	10 282	6 240	812	653

22 **a** Look at the strategies used in the Soar Valley College energy policy. Sort the list into 'energy-efficiency' strategies and 'changing-energy-use' strategies.
   b How could you tell which group of strategies had the greater effect on total energy consumption?
   c Draw a bar graph of electricity consumption in Soar Valley College in 1991 and 1992.
   d How much money did the scheme save on electricity in the five months shown?

Summary of energy resources

• Energy sources can be used to make electricity.
• When machines transfer energy some of the energy is wasted as heat.
• The efficiency of a transducer measures how well it converts input energy to useful output energy. Efficiency = (useful output/input energy) × 100%.
• Some energy sources are renewable, such as wind, waves, solar, wood and other biofuels.

• Some energy sources are non-renewable, such as coal, oil and nuclear fuel. There are limited amounts of non-renewable resources available.
• All methods of exploiting energy sources have social, economic and environmental effects.
• All methods of exploiting energy sources have advantages and disadvantages.

Matter and temperature change

5

Learning objectives

By the end of this chapter you should be able to:

- **describe** the different states of matter
- **explain** how liquids and gases mix without stirring
- **calculate** the energy needed to melt or evaporate a sample of material
- **calculate** by how much a sample of material will expand, as its temperature increases

- **discuss** some applications of saturated vapours and heat expansion
- **suggest** a suitable type of thermometer for a particular application

5.1 States of matter

What makes solids, liquids and gases different?

Almost all matter can be classified as solid, liquid or gas. These are called the three **states of matter**. Each state has different properties, determined by how strongly the forces are that hold particles in the material together.

Liquids and gases are called **fluids**. The particles in a fluid can change position, so the fluid takes up the shape of its container. Because the particles in a fluid can move about relative to each other, when two fluids are brought together, they tend to mix without being stirred or shaken. This mixing is called **diffusion** (see figure 1).

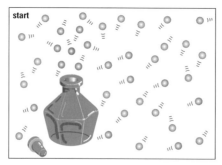

Figure 1 Scents and odours move through the air by diffusion. The 'scent particles' mix with the air particles as they move about relative to one another.

Particles in a solid are locked into position by strong forces between them. But even in a solid, the particles are not completely still. They vibrate constantly about their fixed positions. If the material is heated, it is given more internal energy, and the particles vibrate faster and further (see chapter 2, *Heat energy*).

Like all materials, water can exist as a solid, a liquid or a gas. These Japanese monkeys are warming themselves in a steaming hot pool, while ice settles on their fur.

There is one other state of matter, called **plasma**. In plasma, the particles have so much energy that the electrons, neutrons and protons in the atoms become separated, forming a 'gas' of charged particles (see chapter 27, *Inside the atom*). There are thought to be huge amounts of plasma in stars, nebulae and interstellar space (see chapter 30, *Cosmology*).

What happens when a material melts or freezes?

The temperature of a material depends on how quickly the particles in it are moving. Only at absolute zero (0 K, or –273 °C) are the particles in a material completely stationary. Above absolute zero, the particles start to vibrate, and at a certain temperature the vibrations may become so large that the forces between the particles are not strong enough to hold them in position. The particles may break free and move around relative to one another. At this point the solid melts and becomes a liquid (see figure 2). The temperature at which this happens is called the **melting point**, and is different for every material.

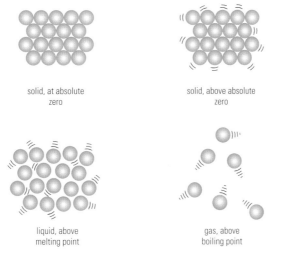

solid, at absolute
zero

solid, above absolute
zero

liquid, above
melting point

gas, above
boiling point

Figure 2 When a solid melts, the regular fixed arrangement of particles is destroyed, but weaker forces still act between the particles in the liquid. In most liquids, the particles are only slightly further apart that in the solid, but they are free to move.

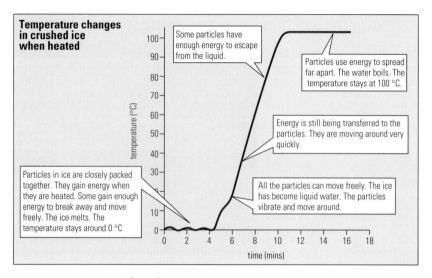

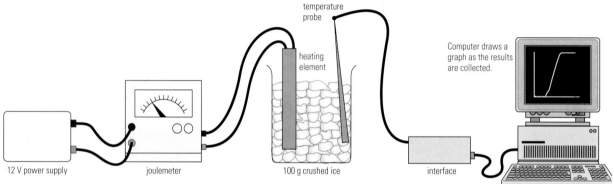

Figure 3 Investigating temperature change.

Overcoming the strong forces, or bonds, between particles in a solid requires energy. While a material is melting, even though energy is supplied as heat, the speed of the moving particles, and therefore the temperature of the material, does not change. The extra energy is used only for breaking bonds (see figure 3).

When a liquid cools to its freezing point, it becomes solid. As it freezes, strong bonds form between the particles, and energy is released. Because the speed of the moving particles does not change as the bonds form, the temperature of the liquid stays constant as it freezes, even though the material is losing heat energy.

What is latent heat of fusion?

The energy that is given out as a material freezes without temperature change, is called **latent heat of fusion**. The same amount of energy is taken in when that material melts without temperature change. It is measured in joules per kilogram (J/kg).

1 The specific latent heat of fusion of water is quite large. Explain why this makes ice so effective at cooling drinks.

Material	Lead	Copper	Water	Soft solder
Specific latent heat of fusion (J/kg)	26 000	210 000	334 000	1 900 000

Table 1 Each material has its own specific latent heat of fusion value.

$$\text{energy needed to melt a sample (J)} = \frac{\text{specific latent heat}}{\text{of fusion, SHLF (J/kg)}} \times \text{mass (kg)}$$
$$= \text{energy released as sample freezes (J)}$$

WORKED EXAMPLE

How much energy will it take to melt 100 g of copper, when it is warmed to its melting point?

energy needed = SLHF of copper × mass

$= 210\,000 \times 0.1$

$= 21\,000$ J

What happens when materials boil or condense?

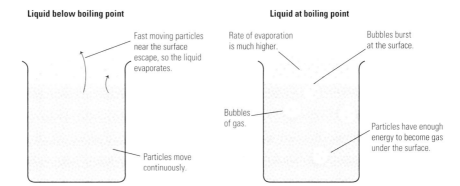

Liquid below boiling point

Fast moving particles near the surface escape, so the liquid evaporates.

Particles move continuously.

Liquid at boiling point

Rate of evaporation is much higher.

Bubbles burst at the surface.

Bubbles of gas.

Particles have enough energy to become gas under the surface.

Figure 4 When particles in a liquid have enough kinetic energy they escape as a gas.

In many power stations, water is made to evaporate to form steam, which has such a large volume that it is forced to spread out along tubes containing turbines like this. The movement of the turbines is used to generate electricity.

If particles moving near the surface of a liquid have enough energy, they can overcome the forces of attraction from other particles, and **evaporate** as a gas (see figure 4). When a liquid is heated, it has more internal energy, so the particles move faster and further. If the particles are given enough kinetic energy, bubbles of gas form within the liquid and rise to the surface. The liquid is boiling. Liquids that need more energy to make them boil have a higher **boiling point**. Water boils at 100 °C. Cooking oil boils at temperatures over 200 °C.

2 Explain why boiling chip oil causes more serious skin burns than boiling water.
3 Salt raises the boiling point of water. Do you expect potatoes to cook quicker in pure water or salty water? Explain your answer.

When a liquid boils and becomes a gas, there are no forces pulling the particles together. The particles move much greater distances apart, so the gas takes up a much larger volume than the liquid. At normal air pressure, 1 kg of steam takes up a volume about 1250 times larger than 1 kg of liquid water at the same temperature. This huge expansion means large forces are exerted on the container holding water as it becomes steam. This effect was used to drive steam engines and machinery in the nineteenth century, and is still used to drive steam turbines to produce electricity in most power stations today.

When a gas is cooled, it has less internal energy so the particles move more slowly, and become closer together. At the material's boiling point, the particles are close enough for strong forces between them to pull them much closer together, and the gas condenses to form a liquid. Because the speed of the moving particles does not change as the bonds form, the temperature of the material stays constant as it condenses, even though it is losing heat energy.

What is latent heat of vaporisation?

The energy taken in when a liquid boils and becomes a gas (and released when a gas condenses) is called **latent heat of vaporisation**.

$$\begin{array}{c}\text{energy needed to} \\ \text{evaporate a sample (J)}\end{array} = \begin{array}{c}\text{specific latent heat} \\ \text{of vaporisation, SLHV (J/kg)}\end{array} \times \text{mass (kg)}$$

$$= \text{energy released as sample condenses (J)}$$

Material	Specific latent heat of vaporisation (J/kg)
Helium	25 000
Air	214 000
Benzene	400 000
Water	2 260 000

Table 2 *Each material has its own specific latent heat of vaporisation value.*

WORKED EXAMPLE

How much energy is needed to evaporate 10 g of benzene, when it is at its boiling point?

energy needed = SLHV of benzene × mass

= 400 000 × 0.01

= 4000 J

The specific latent heat of vaporisation value for water is very high, so a scald from steam is really dangerous. The steam releases some energy as it cools, but also releases a great deal of energy as it condenses. The heat energy released is therefore greater, and more harmful, than from boiling water.

4 Calculate the heat energy needed to carry out the following tasks. In each case the temperature does not change. (Hint: remember that 1 g = 0.001 kg.)

a melt a 20 g ice cube

b evaporate 200 g of boiling water

c melt a 1 000 000 kg iceberg

d turn 100 kg of water into steam in a power station

5 The graph shows the temperature of sample of gold as it was heated. Which parts of the graph correspond to:

a gold as a solid

b gold as a liquid

c gold as a gas

d gold melting

e gold boiling?

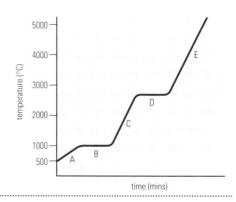

Summary of states of matter

- There are four states of matter – solid, liquid, gas and plasma.

- Liquids and gases are fluids. Particles of fluids can mix by diffusion.

- When materials change state, there is no temperature change until all the sample has changed state. Energy exchanged with the surroundings is used to overcome or form bonds between particles.

- Energy needed to melt a sample at its melting point = specific latent heat of fusion × mass.

- Energy needed to vaporise a sample at its boiling point = specific latent heat of vaporisation × mass.

5.2 Heat expansion

Why do materials expand on heating?

To make a barrel, the cooper slides hot metal bands around wooden slats. As the metal cools, it contracts and pulls the slats tight together.

As materials become warmer, the particles move more quickly, so they move further and take up more space. Materials expand as their temperature increases, and contract as their temperature decreases.

In fluids, the particles are free to move relative to one another, so fluids expand a great deal on heating. Because their volume increases, but their mass stays the same, fluids become significantly less dense when heated. Warmer, less dense regions in the fluid rise up, and cooler, more dense regions fall to replace them. This movement sets up convection currents (see chapter 2, *Heat energy*).

Like other liquids, water contracts as its temperature falls, and its density increases. Unlike other liquids, when its temperature falls below 4 °C, water begins to expand again, and becomes less dense. This is called the anomalous expansion of water. The density falls even further as it freezes, because the water molecules form an open crystal structure in the solid state. So ice is less dense than water, while almost all other materials are more dense in the solid state than as a liquid.

6 Why can freezing water cause rocks to crack apart?

How can the expansion of materials be useful?

Almost all solids expand as the temperature rises, and contract as the temperature falls. This can cause problems. For example, bridges and railway lines have to be designed to allow for this expansion and contraction.

This canal bridge has been built in sections with flexible joints between them, to allow for its expansion and contraction as the temperature changes through the seasons.

However, the effect can also be useful. Metals expand at different rates as their temperatures rise. So if strips of two metals are bound closely together, and are warmed, they bend as one metal expands more than the other. **Bimetallic strips** like this can be used to control the temperature in a heating system, such as an electric iron (see figure 5).

Bimetallic strip

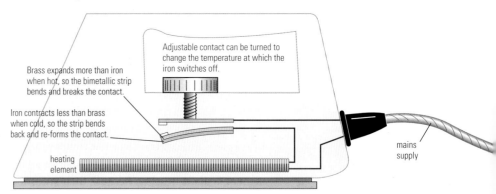

Brass expands more than iron when hot, so the bimetallic strip bends and breaks the contact.

Adjustable contact can be turned to change the temperature at which the iron switches off.

Iron contracts less than brass when cold, so the strip bends back and re-forms the contact.

heating element

mains supply

Figure 5

Mercury thermometers use the heat expansion effect to provide a measure of the temperature. The thermometer has a glass bulb at the bottom, filled with mercury, which narrows into a fine glass tube marked with a scale. You place the bulb where you want to measure the temperature. The higher the temperature, the more the mercury expands, and the further up the scale it moves. Using a larger bulb of mercury and a narrower tube improves the sensitivity. Alcohol often replaces mercury in school thermometers, because mercury is so toxic. With alcohol thermometers, the whole length of the alcohol has to be placed in the substance to be tested to get an accurate reading, rather than just the bulb.

7 A device is needed to switch on a light when the temperature rises above a certain point. Design a system to carry out this task, which uses the heat expansion effect.

How can you measure how much a solid expands?

You can predict the amount that a material will expand when it is heated using a value called **linear expansivity** (see table 3). This is the proportion by which a length of the material expands for a change in temperature of 1 °C.

$$\text{expansion (m)} = \text{old length (m)} \times \frac{\text{linear expansivity}}{\text{(per °C)}} \times \frac{\text{temperature}}{\text{change (°C)}}$$

Material	Linear expansivity (per °C)
Diamond	almost 0
Concrete	0.000 012
Steel	0.000 015
Ice	0.000 051
Rubber	0.000 220

Table 3 *Linear expansivity values for some materials.*

WORKED EXAMPLE

The Forth Railway Bridge is made of steel and is 1042.0 m long when the temperature is 0 °C. How long will the bridge be on a day when the temperature is 25 °C?

expansion (m) = old length (m) × linear expansivity (per °C) × temperature change (°C)

    = 1042.0 × 0.000015 × 25

    = 0.4 m

new length = old length + expansion

    = 1042.0 + 0.4 m

    = 1042.4 m

8 A steel railway line is 400 m long when the air temperature is 10 °C. Calculate the length at 30 °C.

9 Plastics and glass expand when they get warm, and are poor conductors of heat. Glass is more brittle than plastic.

 a A Fortune Fish is meant to tell you something about your personality by the way it curls in your hand. Explain why a Fortune Fish, which is made from thin plastic, curls up like this.

 b Explain why a wine glass can shatter if you put boiling water into it.

10 A mercury in glass thermometer has a narrow tube, and thin glass around the bulb. Explain how these features make the thermometer 'work well'.

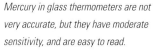

Mercury in glass thermometers are not very accurate, but they have moderate sensitivity, and are easy to read.

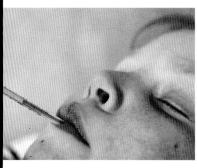

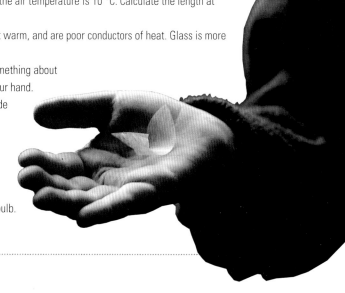

Summary of heat expansion

- Most materials expand as they get warmer.
- Expansion of material = old length × linear expansivity × temperature change.
- Water expands when it cools below 4 °C. This is called the anomalous expansion of water.

- Heat expansion can be used in temperature controls, thermometers and manufacturing processes. It must be allowed for in construction.

5.3 Vapours, gases and liquids

What is saturated vapour pressure?

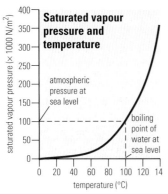

Figure 7 This graph shows how the saturated vapour pressure of water varies with temperature.

The particles in a liquid are always moving. The particles moving fastest have the most kinetic energy. If a liquid is placed in a vacuum, the most energetic particles may escape into the empty space. They form a **vapour**. These particles move around in the space colliding with the sides of the container, with each other, and with the surface of the liquid.

These collisions cause **vapour pressure**, which tends to push down on the liquid, stopping less energetic particles from escaping. When the vapour pressure is large enough to stop any more particles evaporating, the vapour is said to be saturated. The saturated vapour pressure of a liquid is higher if the temperature is higher, because the liquid has more internal energy: the particles are moving faster, so more will escape into the vapour state.

If the volume of the space above the liquid is increased, the vapour pressure falls. It is no longer saturated, so more particles can escape from the liquid, until the vapour pressure returns to the saturated level. At the new saturation point, there will be less liquid left than before (see figure 6).

The volume of the space above the liquid could be increased again and again, until all the liquid has evaporated, and there is none left in the container. The vapour is then unsaturated, since it would be possible to have more particles in the vapour if some were available.

Vapour pressure and temperature

Vapour pressure and volume

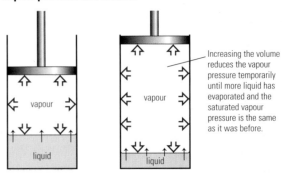

Figure 6 At the same temperature, the saturated vapour pressure of a material is always the same, whatever the size of the space above the liquid. At a higher temperature, the saturated vapour pressure is higher.

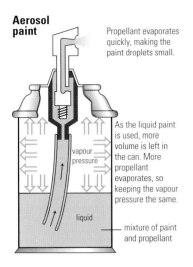

Aerosol paint

Propellant evaporates quickly, making the paint droplets small.

As the liquid paint is used, more volume is left in the can. More propellant evaporates, so keeping the vapour pressure the same.

vapour pressure

liquid

mixture of paint and propellant

Figure 8 Vapour pressure has many important applications.

If the space above the liquid in a sealed container is reduced, the saturated vapour is compressed. Vapour particles return to the liquid state, until the vapour reaches the same saturation pressure once more. A vapour is a gas that can be changed back to a liquid just by compressing it without cooling. A gas that is not a vapour must be cooled before it will return to its liquid state.

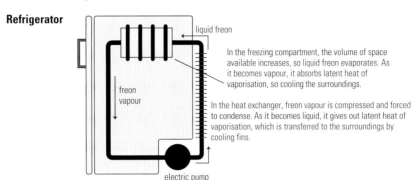

Refrigerator

liquid freon

In the freezing compartment, the volume of space available increases, so liquid freon evaporates. As it becomes vapour, it absorbs latent heat of vaporisation, so cooling the surroundings.

In the heat exchanger, freon vapour is compressed and forced to condense. As it becomes liquid, it gives out latent heat of vaporisation, which is transferred to the surroundings by cooling fins.

freon vapour

electric pump

How do pressure cookers make food cook faster?

When a liquid is near boiling point, bubbles containing saturated vapour form at the bottom of the liquid. If the atmospheric pressure pressing on the liquid surface is higher than the vapour pressure inside the bubbles, the bubbles will be compressed and the vapour forced back into the liquid state. The liquid will not boil. If the atmospheric pressure is equal to the saturated vapour pressure inside the bubbles, the liquid will boil.

So, if the outside pressure is higher or lower than normal, a liquid will boil at a higher or lower temperature from normal. For example, at high altitudes atmospheric pressure is lower, so water boils below 100 °C.

At higher than normal atmospheric pressures, the saturated vapour pressure of water must reach a higher level before the water will boil, so the water must reach a higher temperature before it will boil. This effect is used in pressure cookers to make food boil at temperatures above 100 °C, and therefore cook more quickly (see figure 10).

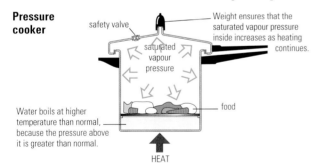

Pressure cooker

safety valve

saturated vapour pressure

Weight ensures that the saturated vapour pressure inside increases as heating continues.

food

Water boils at higher temperature than normal, because the pressure above it is greater than normal.

HEAT

Figure 10

Summary of vapours, gases and liquids

- When the vapour above a liquid is saturated, the number of particles evaporating matches the number condensing.
- At a higher temperature, the saturated vapour pressure for a liquid is higher.

- When the vapour pressure of bubbles forming within a liquid is equal to the external pressure, the liquid will boil.
- A liquid boils at a higher temperature when the pressure acting on its surface is higher.

Pressure and hydraulics

6

Learning objectives

By the end of this chapter you should be able to:

- **define** pressure
- **calculate** the pressure on an object from measurements of the force and the area the force affects
- **describe** how pressure affects a gas
- **measure** the pressure of gases

- **describe** the factors that affect pressure in a liquid
- **explain** the principles behind hydraulic and pneumatic systems
- **apply** ideas about pressure in different situations

6.1 Pressure

Why doesn't a bed of nails hurt?

Figure 1 Lying on a bed of a thousand nails is not nearly as painful as you might think.

A spike hurts because it makes a force act over a tiny area. It exerts a large pressure.

If you've ever stepped on a drawing pin, you will know how much it hurts – so why does the person in figure 1 look so comfortable? If she was sitting on just one nail all her weight would act through it. This large force would push the nail deep into her body. If she used two nails, her weight would be shared between the nails – so the force acting through each nail would be halved, though still large enough to puncture her skin. When the person lies on a bed of a thousand nails, each nail supports one thousandth of her weight. The force acting through each nail is small so the bed is quite comfortable.

The total force acting on the magician's body is the same whether she sits on one nail, or a thousand nails. The force is her weight, which does not change. To describe the change in the way the nails act, you can use the idea of **pressure**. The pressure depends on the force *and* the area it affects.

$$\text{pressure} = \frac{\text{force}}{\text{area}} \qquad P = \frac{F}{A}$$

Note

Force is measured in units called newtons. Area is usually measured in m^2 (square metres). So pressure can have the units N/m^2 (newtons per square metre). The unit N/m^2 is also known as a pascal, after Blaise Pascal, a seventeenth century French mathematician.

$1\ N/m^2 = 1\ Pa$

Often, it is more convenient to use cm^2 or mm^2 for area, instead of m^2. This means pressure sometimes has the units N/cm^2 or N/mm^2. To avoid confusion, always make it clear which units you are using when you do calculations about pressure.

WORKED EXAMPLE

A woman weighing 600 N lies on a bed of 5000 nails. What is the pressure on her body, if the tip of each nail has an area of $1\ mm^2$?

$$P = \frac{F}{A} = \frac{600\ N}{1 \times 5000}$$

$$= 0.12\ N/mm^2$$

The pressure on the woman's body is just 0.12 N for each nail, which is not enough to puncture her skin.

1 Use the idea of pressure to explain why:

a a surgeon's scalpel needs to be sharp.

b when rescuing someone who has fallen through the ice on a lake, the rescuer lays a plank of wood over the ice before crawling along it to reach him.

c it is more comfortable to press on the blunt end of a drawing pin than the sharp end.

2 If snow can withstand a pressure of $2000\ N/m^2$ before it collapses, what area of track surface is required on a 3000 N snow vehicle, to make sure it does not sink?

3 Building Regulations state that a normal building brick should be able to withstand a pressure of $2.76\ N/mm^2$ before it is crushed.

a Predict how high a building could be before the bricks at the bottom were crushed by the weight of those above.

b In fact, the regulations say that this sort of brick should only be used on single storey, or two storey buildings. Suggest reasons why they are not to be used for higher buildings.

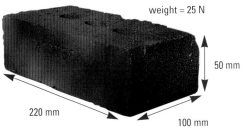

weight = 25 N

50 mm

220 mm

100 mm

The strings of musical instruments like violins exert a great pressure on the body of the instrument. To reduce the pressure, stringed instruments are designed to spread the pulling force across a larger area of wood.

Summary of pressure

- A force acting on a small area causes a high pressure. A force spread over a large area produces a low pressure.

- Pressure, force and area are related by the formula $P = F/A$.

- The unit of pressure is the pascal (Pa).
  $1\ Pa = 1\ N/m^2$.

6.2 Fluid pressure

What is fluid pressure?

Fluid pressure

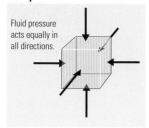

Fluid pressure acts equally in all directions.

Figure 2

The air has been sucked out of this can, using a vacuum pump. With nothing inside to push back against it, the air pressure outside pushes against the can's outer surface and makes it collapse.

When a skier stands on snow the pressure acts in one direction – downwards, in this case. When an object is submerged, **fluid pressure** acts inwards from *all* directions equally (see figure 2). The opposite is also true. If you press on a fluid, it presses out in all directions with equal force. This observation was first made by the French mathematician Blaise Pascal (1623–1662), and is known as Pascal's Law.

You are living under fluid pressure all the time. The air presses in on you with a pressure of about 101 325 N/m^2. That's like lying down with about 10 000 large bags of sugar piled on top of you! Luckily, unlike the can in the photo, you have liquid and gas inside you pressing out, which stop you from collapsing inwards.

As this musician pushes air into the bagpipes, air is forced out in all directions.

4 A thin plastic lemonade bottle feels firm and hard when you buy it. When half of the lemonade has been drunk, the same bottle feels very flimsy. Why?

How can you calculate fluid pressure?

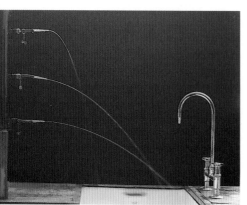

The pressure in a fluid is greater the deeper you go.

The air pressure you feel depends on the weight of air pushing down on you. If you go underwater, the extra weight of the water also presses on you to increase the pressure you feel. The deeper you go, the greater the weight of water and so the greater the pressure you feel.

When something presses on a surface, the pressure depends on the weight or force pressing on each square metre of the surface. In fluids, the weight of the fluid resting on a particular area depends on the depth of the fluid, and the density of the fluid.

$$\text{pressure} = \frac{\text{density}}{\text{of the fluid}} \times \frac{\text{force}}{\text{due to gravity}} \times \frac{\text{depth}}{\text{below surface}}$$

$$P = \rho g h$$

ρ is the Greek letter rho (pronounced 'ro'), which stands for the density of a fluid.

WORKED EXAMPLE

This aquarium is 4 m deep in parts. The designers had to work out the pressure on the view-tunnel to make sure it was safe. If the density of water is 1000 kg/m^3, and there is a force of gravity of 10 N/kg, how high is the pressure?

$P = \rho g h = 4 \times 1000 \times 10$

$= 40\ 000$ N/m^2 $= 40\ 000$ Pa $= 40$ kPa

5 Calculate the pressure on a North Sea diver's face mask when he is working 50 m below the surface. How many times larger than atmospheric pressure is this?

6 The Aswan dam in Egypt traps water to a depth of 114 m.

a Predict the sideways pressure the bottom of the dam must withstand.

b Engineers want to increase the height of the dam, to generate more hydro-electric power from the trapped water. Why would it be unwise just to build on top of the current dam?

What use is fluid pressure?

Because fluids press outwards in all directions when you squeeze them, they can pass a force from one place to another. **Pneumatic** systems use air to transmit a force. Pneumatic systems are useful to move a force from one place to another very quickly, or over short distances. When larger forces or distances are involved, **hydraulic** systems are used, which use oil or water.

7 In a theme park, animatronic characters are operated by compressed air at 400 000 N/m^2.

a A cylinder in a dragon's leg has a piston with an area of 8 cm^2. Predict the maximum force that this system can produce.

b A much smaller force is needed to move the dragon's eyelids and eyes. In what ways would the cylinders be different from those in the legs?

Animatronics

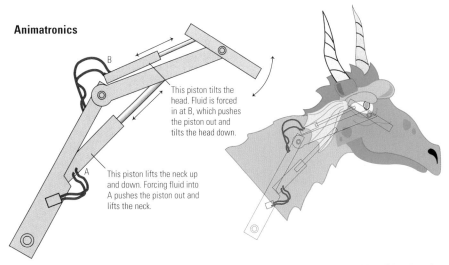

This piston tilts the head. Fluid is forced in at B, which pushes the piston out and tilts the head down.

This piston lifts the neck up and down. Forcing fluid into A pushes the piston out and lifts the neck.

Figure 3 Next time you see an animatronic display like this dragon, listen out for the hiss of the air as it escapes from the pneumatic cylinders.

How can fluids magnify forces?

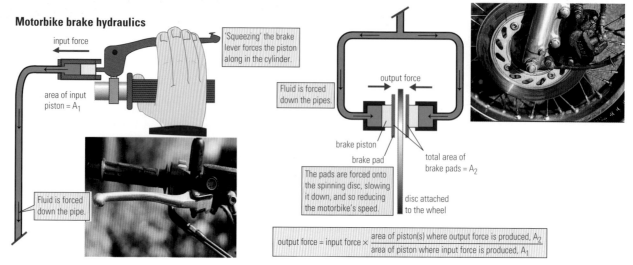

Motorbike brake hydraulics

input force

'Squeezing' the brake lever forces the piston along in the cylinder.

area of input piston = A_1

output force

Fluid is forced down the pipes.

Fluid is forced down the pipe.

brake piston

brake pad

total area of brake pads = A_2

The pads are forced onto the spinning disc, slowing it down, and so reducing the motorbike's speed.

disc attached to the wheel

output force = input force × $\dfrac{\text{area of piston(s) where output force is produced, } A_2}{\text{area of piston where input force is produced, } A_1}$

Figure 4 A hydraulic system magnifies the force applied by the rider, so the force applied by the brake disc is much larger.

WORKED EXAMPLE

In figure 4, the area of the input piston is 1 cm^2, the total area of the brake pad is 8 cm^2, and the input force is 50 N (although the lever means the rider only has to squeeze with a force of about 10 N). Calculate the force on the motorbike brake pads.

$$\text{output force} = \frac{\text{input force} \times \text{area of piston where output force is produced, } A_2}{\text{area of piston(s) where input force is produced, } A_1}$$

$$= 50 \times \frac{8}{1} = 400 \text{ N}$$

8   The master cylinder on a hydraulic car braking system has an area of 4 cm^2. A driver presses the brake pedal down with a force of 600 N.

   a What pressure does the driver's pedal-press produce in the braking system?

   b Calculate the force produced by a brake cylinder with an area of 6 cm^2.

   c Fluids are used in braking systems because they transmit the pressure equally to all the wheels. What might happen if a car braked with a different force on each wheel?

Summary of fluid pressure

- Pressure in a fluid increases the deeper you go.
- The pressure at any depth in a fluid can be calculated using the formula $P = \rho g h$.
- Fluids transmit pressure equally in all directions.

- Pneumatic systems use air to transmit small forces over short distances.
- Hydraulic systems use oil or water to transmit high forces over long distances.

Investigation

Two plastic syringes can be linked by a tube to make a simple hydraulic or pneumatic system.

Compare the efficiency of using water or using air in the tubes of such a system. Try to explain any difference you find.

Forces in *liquids*

Learning objectives

By the end of this chapter you should be able to:

- **explain** the difference between cohesive and adhesive forces
- **describe** what causes surface tension
- **describe** factors which affect surface tension
- **explain** how surface tension is used in a variety of applications

7.1 Cohesive forces

What keeps a liquid together?

Forces of attraction between particles hold these rounded droplets together.

All particles in a liquid feel **cohesive forces** of attraction towards other particles, which pull the particles together. If there were no cohesive forces, liquids could not exist, since they would simply evaporate and become gas even at low temperatures. The strength of the forces between the particles varies from liquid to liquid, but they are always due to electric attraction between oppositely charged parts of the particles. Cohesive forces pull a drop of liquid together, and if no other forces act, they make the drop spherical.

A particle within a volume of liquid feels cohesive forces of attraction towards every other particle around it. For every force in one direction, there is a force pulling the particle in the opposite direction, so the forces effectively cancel each other. This leaves the particle free to move around within the liquid as if no forces acted on it at all (see figure 1).

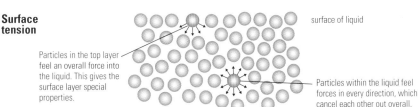

Surface tension

Particles in the top layer feel an overall force into the liquid. This gives the surface layer special properties.

surface of liquid

Particles within the liquid feel forces in every direction, which cancel each other out overall.

Figure 1

Surface tension means that pond skaters can rest on water without getting wet.

Particles at the edge of the liquid feel an overall force of attraction into the liquid, because there are no liquid particles outside to balance the cohesive forces from the particles within it (see figure 1). So the outer surface layer of particles behaves almost like a skin, which can be stretched and can support small loads without breaking. The property that allows the surface of a liquid to act in this way is called **surface tension**.

Can surface tension be changed?

1 Liquid helium boils at −268.91 °C. Liquid hydrogen boils at −252.81 °C. What does this suggest about the cohesive forces in these liquids?

2 Predict how adding detergent to water might affect its boiling point. Justify your answer.

Small amounts of impurities (such as soap, detergents or hydrocarbons) reduce the strength of surface tension in a liquid. For example, soapy water has a surface tension about a quarter of the strength of that of clean water. Particles of the impurities gather in the surface layer, weakening the cohesive forces between liquid particles. It is useful to be able to weaken surface tension in water using detergents, when you are cleaning clothes for example. The reduced surface tension means the water soaks more easily into the cloth fibres.

Soaps and detergents can have devastating effects on whole aquatic ecosystems, if they are allowed to pollute rivers and ponds, because of their effects on surface tension. If you go camping in the countryside where there are no washing facilities, you should never wash with soap directly in a pond or stream.

Summary of cohesive forces

- Cohesive forces act between particles in a liquid.
- Cohesive forces cause a liquid's surface to behave like a weak, stretched skin, producing surface tension effects.

- Cohesive forces cause liquid droplets to be spherical, if no other forces act.
- Impurities can reduce the strength of cohesive forces, and reduce the surface tension.

7.2 Adhesive forces

What are adhesive forces?

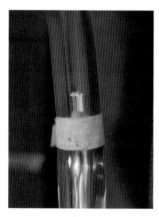

The meniscus of mercury in glass curves downwards at the edges, because the adhesive forces between mercury and glass particles are not as strong as the cohesive forces between particles within the mercury.

As well as cohesive forces between particles in a liquid, there are **adhesive forces** of attraction between particles in a liquid and particles in any solid that the liquid comes into contact with. Adhesive forces are also due to electrical attraction between charged parts of the particles.

The adhesive forces between some liquids and solids are stronger than the cohesive forces within the liquid. For example, the adhesive forces between water and glass particles are stronger than the cohesive forces in water. In other liquids and solids, such as mercury and glass, the cohesive forces in the liquid are stronger than the adhesive forces between the solid and the liquid.

If water is poured into a glass container, adhesive forces cause the liquid to be pulled up at the sides. The surface of the water meets the glass in an upward curve, rather than as a completely flat surface. This curving surface is called a **meniscus**.

Why does water climb up narrow gaps?

When water is in a narrow **capillary tube**, the adhesive forces between the water and solid particles can pull the water up the tube. The narrower the tube is, the higher the liquid is pulled before its weight balances the strength of the adhesive forces. This effect is known as capillary rise or **capillarity** (see figure 2).

Capillarity

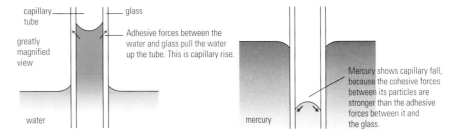

Figure 2

Capillary rise is used in chromatography. Filter paper contains many tiny holes and gaps, so when one end of a strip is placed in water, the liquid rises up the paper. If a pigment is placed at the bottom of the strip, it gets carried upwards with the water. The water moves more slowly as it gets further up the paper, and leaves particles of pigment behind. The height a pigment reaches depends on the weight of its particles. The particles of different dyes weigh different amounts, so you can use chromatography to separate a coloured pigment made from a mixture of dyes, and see what was in it. This technique is very useful in forensic and medical science for testing blood and for DNA profiling.

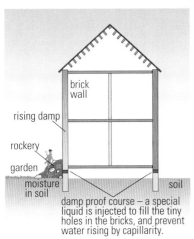

damp proof course – a special liquid is injected to fill the tiny holes in the bricks, and prevent water rising by capillarity.

3 When a towel is washed in fabric conditioner, the conditioner coats the fibres. The towel feels fluffier, but does not absorb moisture as well as before. Use the idea of adhesive and cohesive forces to suggest why this happens.

4 The diagram on the left shows a house which is suffering from rising damp, even though it has a damp proof course. Suggest what could be done to solve the problem.

Summary of adhesive forces

- Adhesive forces act between particles in a solid and those in a liquid.

- If the adhesive forces are stronger than the cohesive forces, a liquid will rise up a narrow tube. This is called capillarity.

Investigation

Water rises in narrow tubes due to capillary action.

Investigate how the height that the water reaches depends upon the diameter of the tube.

Fluid *flow*

Learning objectives

By the end of this chapter you should be able to:

- **discuss** the factors that affect how rapidly a fluid flows through a pipe
- **explain** what viscosity is, and how it affects the flow of fluids
- **explain** the differences between Newtonian, thixotropic and dilitant fluids

- **explain** the difference between laminar and turbulent flow
- **state** Bernoulli's principle, and describe some of its applications

8.1 Viscosity

What is viscosity?

As a river flows, the water moves faster on the surface and in the middle than at the edge or on the river bed.

A fluid is a material that can flow, and take the shape of any container. Gases and liquids are fluids. The way fluids flow affects all aspects of our lives.

When a fluid flows smoothly, the fluid in contact with the sides of the container gets slowed down by friction. Fluid away from the sides slides over the slower layers, and so flows more quickly. The more **viscous** the fluid is, the less easily the layers can slide over each other (see figure 1). Syrup and treacle are fluids with high **viscosity**. Air has a low viscosity.

Figure 1 A flowing fluid acts like layers, sliding over one another.

Viscosity

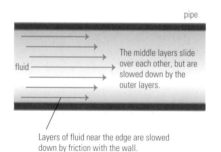

pipe

The middle layers slide over each other, but are slowed down by the outer layers.

fluid

Layers of fluid near the edge are slowed down by friction with the wall.

Table 1 *Viscosities of fluids, compared to water.*

Fluid	Relative viscosity, compared to water
North sea gas	0.01030
Air at 20 °C	0.01813
Carbon dioxide	0.015
Water at 20 °C	1.00
Mercury	1.55
Engine oil	≈ 800

1 The table shows how the speed of water flow in the Mississippi River, USA, depends on the depth below the surface. All the measurements were taken in the middle of the river.

Speed (m/s)	0.994	0.992	0.984	0.972	0.955	0.934	0.907	0.876	0.839	0.798	0.753
Depth (m)	0 surface of river	0.27	0.54	0.81	1.08	1.35	1.62	1.89	2.16	2.43	2.7 river bed

a Plot a graph to display the data in the table.

b Describe in words how the speed of flow is related to the depth of the water.

c These measurements were taken in the middle of the river. How might the results be different if they had been taken from near the river bank? Justify your answer.

What factors affect viscosity?

2 Many household paints are designed to be thixotropic.

a Why is this a useful property for a paint to have?

b Describe what it would be like to paint using a 'dilitant' paint.

The viscosity of a fluid usually decreases as its temperature rises. This can be a problem in many situations, such as car engines. If the engine oil becomes too thin (with low viscosity) as the engine heats up, it cannot protect the components of the engine. If the oil is too thick (with high viscosity), the engine components may not move at all. To help solve this problem, engine oil is made from several different types of oil. Some of the oils increase in viscosity as they get hotter, while for others the viscosity decreases. The aim of this 'multigrade' oil is to produce a fluid which has about the same viscosity over a wide range of temperatures.

The speed of flow of a fluid can affect its viscosity. Some fluids have a viscosity that is almost constant, no matter how fast the fluid flows. These are called Newtonian fluids. Air and water are **Newtonian fluids**.

For other fluids, viscosity increases when the fluid flows quickly. These are called **dilitant fluids** (see figure 2). 'Super putty' behaves like a dilitant fluid. If you pull it out gently, super putty flows and stretches a long way, as layers slide over each other. If you tug it quickly, the layers do not slide easily. The material becomes more viscous, and actually snaps instead of flowing.

Thixotropic fluids are more common than dilitant fluids. The faster a thixotropic fluid flows, and the stronger the force making it flow, the lower its viscosity is (see figure 2).

Non-drip paint is a thixotropic fluid. When you press on the paint with a brush, its viscosity decreases, and the paint flows into place. When the brush is removed, the force causing the flow is removed, so the viscosity increases.

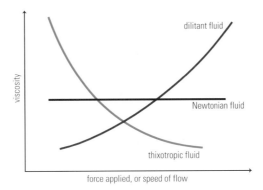

Figure 2 The viscosity of some fluids changes with the speed at which they flow.

Summary of viscosity

- Liquids and gases are fluids. They can flow from one place to another.
- Viscosity is a measure of how easily a fluid flows. Fluids with a high viscosity do not flow easily.
- The viscosity of a Newtonian fluid is fixed.

- The viscosity of a thixotropic fluid decreases when the rate of flow is faster, or when the force causing the flow is larger.
- The viscosity of a dilitant fluid decreases when the rate of flow is slower, or when the force causing the flow is smaller.

8.2 Flow

What is turbulent flow?

As winds blew across the Tacoma Narrows Bridge in Washington USA, in 1940, air turbulence caused it to collapse.

Sometimes, fluids flow in straight lines. This is called **laminar flow**. Sometimes flow is **turbulent**, with a swirling motion (see figure 3). When a large lorry moves, air is pushed out of the way at the front, and swirls in to fill the space at the back. This can cause traffic accidents, as other road users are pushed sideways in an unpredictable way by the swirling air.

As winds blow around buildings and wires, air turbulence can cause them to sway to and fro, even though the air is moving at a steady rate. This effect makes overhead wires 'sing,' and has caused buildings to collapse.

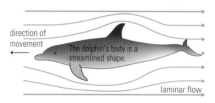

Figure 3

What affects the speed of fluid flow in pipes?

- **Pressure.** The larger the difference in pressure between the two ends of the pipe, the faster the rate of flow.
- **Size of pipe.** The larger the cross-sectional area of the pipe, the faster the rate of flow. The longer the pipe, the slower the rate of flow. One pipe with twice the diameter of another will allow fluid to flow 16 times faster.
- **Viscosity and smoothness.** The lower the viscosity of the fluid, and the smoother the inside of the pipe, the faster the rate of flow.

The effects of all these factors on fluid flow can be summarised like this:

rate of flow (m^3/s) = constant × pressure difference (N/m^2)

The constant takes into account the smoothness and size of pipe, and the viscosity of fluid. This equation does not apply to very narrow capillary tubes.

What is Bernoulli's Principle?

Daniel Bernoulli (1700–1782) was the first person to apply the idea of conservation of energy to fluid flow. He argued that the total energy in a flowing fluid was really in two parts: kinetic energy, because the fluid is moving, and potential energy, which is linked to the pressure of the fluid. If a fluid is made to flow faster, without any extra source of energy, the potential energy must be reduced. This means that the pressure must also be reduced.

This idea became known as Bernoulli's principle and it has a great many applications. Figure 4 shows two of them.

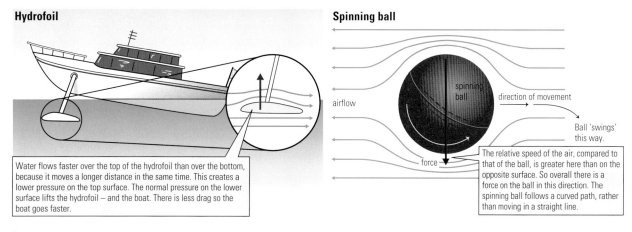

Hydrofoil

Water flows faster over the top of the hydrofoil than over the bottom, because it moves a longer distance in the same time. This creates a lower pressure on the top surface. The normal pressure on the lower surface lifts the hydrofoil – and the boat. There is less drag so the boat goes faster.

Figure 4a

Spinning ball

airflow

spinning ball

direction of movement

Ball 'swings' this way.

force

The relative speed of the air, compared to that of the ball, is greater here than on the opposite surface. So overall there is a force on the ball in this direction. The spinning ball follows a curved path, rather than moving in a straight line.

Figure 4b

Summary of flow

- Factors that affect how rapidly a fluid flows through a pipe include:
  1 the viscosity of the fluid
  2 the length of the pipe
  3 the diameter of the pipe
  4 the smoothness of the pipe
  5 the pressure difference between the ends of the pipe.

- Laminar flow is smooth and straight. Turbulent flow is disturbed and swirling.
- When fluids are made to flow more quickly without any extra input of energy, their pressure drops. This is called Bernoulli's principle.

Investigation

1 Top swimmers wear swimsuits that are too small for them. The swimmers believe that the stretched fabric allows water to flow through more easily, enabling them to swim faster. Investigate how the stretching of a fabric affects the flow of water through it.

2 Many holidaymakers fit 'top boxes' onto their cars for extra luggage. Such boxes must allow air to flow over them easily, but the driver could have problems if the box produces an overall upward force. Investigate how effective the shapes of top boxes are in terms of air resistance and producing unwanted lift.

Pressure in gases

Learning objectives

By the end of this chapter you should be able to:

- **describe** some of the features of an ideal gas
- **describe** what Boyle's law, Charles's law and the pressure law mean

- **apply** these gas laws in a variety of situations
- **describe** the importance of absolute zero and the absolute scale of temperature.

9.1 Gas pressure

What causes gas pressure?

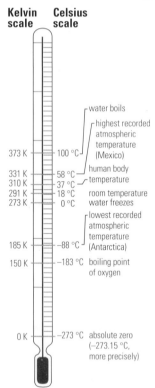

Figure 2 Absolute zero (0 K) forms the starting point for the absolute, or Kelvin, scale of temperature.

Gases are made of molecules or single atoms, which are fast moving and in constant motion. The particles travel in straight paths and at steady speeds, only changing speed and direction when they collide with the walls of their container, or with each other (see figure 1). It is these collisions that cause gas pressure.

The speed of the particles in a gas depends on their temperature and mass. More massive particles travel more slowly than lighter particles at the same temperature. The hotter the gas, the faster the particles move.

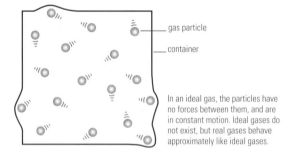

Gas pressure

gas particle

container

In an ideal gas, the particles have no forces between them, and are in constant motion. Ideal gases do not exist, but real gases behave approximately like ideal gases.

Figure 1 Gas pressure is caused by millions of tiny particles colliding with the walls of the container.

If the temperature is low enough, the pressure is zero because the particles have no kinetic energy, and so do not move at all. This temperature is known as **absolute zero**, and is the lowest possible temperature (see figure 2).

The way a particle in a gas moves is random and unpredictable, because of the way it repeatedly collides with other particles and with its container. However, the overall behaviour of a gas can be predicted, using three main rules which link its temperature, pressure and volume.

Summary of gas pressure

- The particles in an ideal gas have no forces between them, and are in constant motion.
- At absolute zero, or −273.15 °C, the particles in a material are stationary.

- The absolute scale of temperature starts at absolute zero and is sometimes called the Kelvin scale.

9.2 The gas laws

What is the link between pressure and temperature?

As the temperature increases, the gas particles move more quickly and strike the sides of the container more often. The greater number of collisions each second increases the pressure of the gas. If the temperature (measured in Kelvin) doubles, the pressure also doubles.

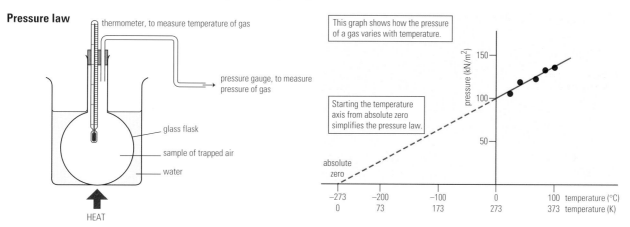

Pressure law

thermometer, to measure temperature of gas

pressure gauge, to measure pressure of gas

glass flask

sample of trapped air

water

HEAT

This graph shows how the pressure of a gas varies with temperature.

Starting the temperature axis from absolute zero simplifies the pressure law.

absolute zero

Figure 3 This apparatus can be used to test the pressure law.

The pressure law

For a fixed amount of gas, the pressure is proportional to the temperature, if it is measured on the Kelvin or absolute scale. This is the pressure law.

$$P \propto T$$

This means that, for a fixed volume of gas:

$$\frac{P_2}{P_1} = \frac{T_2}{T_1}$$

where P_1 = initial pressure, P_2 = final pressure, T_1 = initial temperature and T_2 = final temperature.

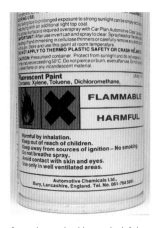

Aerosol cans should never be left in direct heat, because the expansion of the pressurised gas inside could cause an explosion.

WORKED EXAMPLE

The pressure of a gas sample is 100 000 N/m³ at 27 °C. What will be the pressure at 127 °C?

First convert the temperatures from °C to K, by adding 273. So 27 °C is 300 K, and 127 °C is 400 K.

$$\frac{P_2}{P_1} = \frac{T_2}{T_1}$$

$$\frac{P_2}{100\ 000} = \frac{400}{300}$$

$$P_2 = \frac{400 \times 100\ 000}{300}$$

$$= 133\ 333 \text{ N/m}^2$$

1 A car tyre is pumped up to a pressure of 300 000 N/m², when the temperature is 7 °C.

  a At what pressure will the tyre be when the temperature is 27 °C?

  b Why might it be dangerous to allow the tyre to get too hot?

  c In the pits on a formula 1 race track, spare wheels are warmed ready for when a driver comes in for a pit-stop. Why are they warmed?

What is the link between pressure and volume?

To investigate the relationship between the pressure and volume of a gas, you could gradually compress a sample of gas, recording the pressure and the volume. The temperature of the gas, and the number of particles in the gas, have to be kept constant during the experiment.

Boyle's law

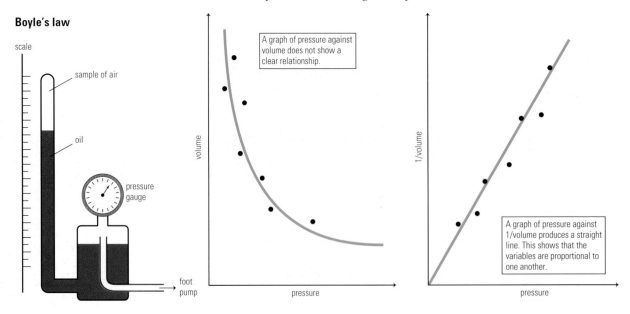

Figure 4 You could use this apparatus to explore the link between pressure and volume of a gas.

Why Boyle's law works

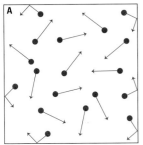

Each container holds the same number of gas particles, but in B, whose volume is twice that of A, the pressure is half that in A.

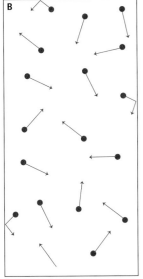

The particles in B have further to travel between collisions than in A. Because collisions with the sides of the container are less frequent, the pressure in B is lower.

Figure 5

Boyle's law

Figure 4 shows that, provided the temperature and the amount of gas are not changed, the pressure of a gas is **inversely proportional** to its volume. This means that the pressure increases, the volume decreases. This is Boyle's law.

$$P \propto \frac{1}{V}$$

Boyle's law can be expressed in other ways:

$$PV = \text{constant} \quad \text{or} \quad P_1 \times V_1 = P_2 \times V_2$$

where P_1 = initial pressure, P_2 = final pressure, V_1 = initial volume and V_2 = final volume.

Robert Boyle carried out experiments to investigate the link between the pressure and volume of a gas, and published his discoveries in 1660. The rule linking pressure and volume is known as Boyle's Law in the UK and USA.

WORKED EXAMPLE

A bicycle pump contains 300 cm^3 of air at a pressure of 100 000 N/m^2. You put your finger over the end of the pump and compress the gas to 75 cm^3. What is the new pressure?

$$P_2 \times V_2 = P_1 \times V_1$$
$$P_2 \times 75 = 100\,000 \times 300$$
$$P_2 = \frac{100\,000 \times 300}{75}$$
$$= 400\,000 \text{ N/m}^2$$

2   Many modern cars now have air bags, which use compressed air to inflate quickly if the car crashes, to cushion the impact felt by the driver. Use the table to estimate the pressure inside the cylinder used to store the compressed air

	inflated bag	cylinder
volume of air (m^3)	0.1	0.001
pressure (N/m^2)	300 000	?

What is the link between volume and temperature?

A sample of gas expands to fill a larger volume when it is heated. In 1787 the French scientist Jacques Charles worked out the exact relationship between volume and temperature.

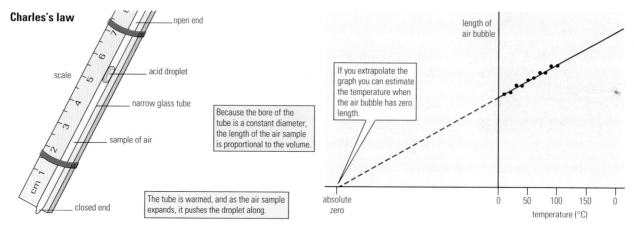

Charles's law

open end

scale

acid droplet

narrow glass tube

Because the bore of the tube is a constant diameter, the length of the air sample is proportional to the volume.

sample of air

cm 1

closed end

The tube is warmed, and as the air sample expands, it pushes the droplet along.

length of air bubble

If you extrapolate the graph you can estimate the temperature when the air bubble has zero length.

absolute zero

0   50   100   150   0

temperature (°C)

Figure 6 This apparatus can be used to test Charles's law.

Charles's law

Figure 6 shows that equal changes in the temperature of a gas cause equal changes in volume. In this case, each increase of 10 °C caused a change of 3 mm in the length of the air pocket. The volume of the sample is proportional to the temperature, if the temperature is measured on the Kelvin, or absolute scale. This is Charles's law.

$$V \propto T$$

Charles's law is sometimes expressed like this:

$$\frac{V_2}{V_1} = \frac{T_2}{T_1}$$

where V_1 = initial volume, V_2 = final volume, T_1 = initial temperature and T_2 = final temperature.

Charles's law only works if the pressure and the mass of the gas stay constant. One common problem with the air pocket apparatus in figure 6 is that some of the liquid in the droplet evaporates into the air pocket, adding extra molecules to the sample and making the volume larger than it should be. This is a particular problem when the tube is very hot.

WORKED EXAMPLE

200 cm^3 of a gas is warmed from 67 °C to 217 °C. Find the new volume, if the pressure is unchanged.

First, convert the temperatures from °C to K, by adding 273. So 67 °C is 350 K, and 217 °C is 500 K.

$$\frac{V_2}{V_1} = \frac{T_2}{T_1} \qquad V_2 = \frac{500 \times 200}{350} = 285.7 \text{ cm}^3$$

3 In a solar powered engine, the Sun warms the air in a cylinder from 17 °C to 37 °C. As the air expands, it forces out a piston, so the pressure remains constant. Before each stroke, there is 0.01 m^3 of air in the cylinder. What will be the volume at the end of each outward stroke?

Can the gas laws be combined?

4 A meteorological balloon is partly inflated, until its volume is 5 m^3. The air pressure at ground level is 100 000 N/m^2 and the temperature is 17 °C. How large will the balloon be when it rises to a height of 9 km, where the pressure is 600 N/m^2, and the temperature is −53°C?

The pressure law, Boyle's law and Charles's law can be combined into a single law. They can be combined in two ways.

1

$$PV = nRT$$

R is a constant called the universal gas constant, and n is the number of moles of gas particles in the sample. (A mole is simply a fixed, very large number of particles.)

2

$$\frac{\text{initial pressure} \times \text{initial volume}}{\text{initial temperature}} = \frac{\text{final pressure} \times \text{final volume}}{\text{final temperature}}$$

$$\frac{P_1 \times V_1}{T_1} = \frac{P_2 \times V_2}{T_2}$$

Strictly speaking, the gas laws apply only to 'ideal gases', which have no forces between the particles, even at high pressures. In practice, real gases are never completely ideal, but they *do* approximately obey the gas laws. The rules do not work well at high pressures, or at very low temperatures, or when the gas contains water vapour.

Summary of the gas laws

- Ideal gases obey the gas laws.
- Boyle's law says that the pressure of a gas is inversely proportional to its volume, at constant pressure: $PV = $ constant, or $P \propto 1/V$.
- The pressure law says that the pressure of a gas is proportional to the temperature, measured on the absolute scale, if the volume is kept constant: $P \propto T$.

- Charles's law says that the volume of a gas is proportional to its temperature, measured on the absolute scale, if the pressure is constant: $V \propto T$.
- The gas laws can be combined to produce one rule, for a fixed mass of gas: $PV = nRT$, where R is the universal gas constant, and n is the number of moles of gas.

Investigation

Thermometers can be difficult to read if they are too small. One design for a thermometer could use the volume of air contained in a small syringe as a measure of temperature. The position of the plunger would indicate the temperature. Investigate how feasible such a thermometer would be.

Learning objectives

By the end of this chapter, you should be able to:

- **describe** some of the effects forces have on objects

- **compare** how different materials stretch

- **describe** the necessary conditions for an object to be stationary

- **apply** ideas about forces to a wide range of situations

10.1 Forces

What are forces?

A force is a push or a pull. The way an object moves or behaves depends on the combined effect of all the forces acting on it. To describe a force clearly, you should always state:

- the size of the force
- the direction in which the force is acting, or trying to move an object

The size of a force is usually measured in newtons (N). The direction can be described in many different ways, such as 'left to right', 'upwards' or 'Northwards'. Sometimes it is useful to describe all the forces in one direction as positive, and all the forces in the opposite direction as negative. For two forces to be equal, they need to have the same size *and* the same direction.

What is friction?

Whenever you try to slide two surfaces over each other you need to overcome a resistive force called **friction**. Friction is caused by forces between atoms in the two surfaces pulling towards each other (see figure 1). Smooth surfaces allow the atoms in the two surfaces to get closer, often causing greater friction than between two rough surfaces.

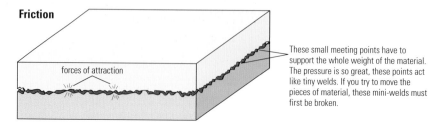

Friction

forces of attraction

These small meeting points have to support the whole weight of the material. The pressure is so great, these points act like tiny welds. If you try to move the pieces of material, these mini-welds must first be broken.

Figure 1

In some situations, friction is a problem. For example, friction makes machines less efficient. Some of the kinetic energy of the moving components has to be used to overcome friction between the surfaces, and gets converted to heat. Less of the input energy is therefore left to be converted to useful output energy. Friction can be reduced by lubricating surfaces with oil.

In other situations, friction is useful. Nails, screws and bolts rely on friction to hold objects firmly together. Cars, bikes and wheelchairs rely on friction between their tyres and the ground to move forwards. People could not even walk without friction between their feet and the ground to stop them slipping.

Note

When you describe a force, you give the direction as well as the size. Forces are **vector** measurements. Other examples of vectors are velocity and acceleration. On diagrams, arrows show the directions in which vectors act, while their lengths show the relative sizes of the vectors.

If you add two vectors that have the same size but opposite directions, they cancel each other out.

In level flight, there is no net force up or down.

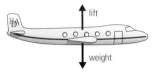

Measurements such as energy, temperature, distance and speed have size, but no direction. These are **scalar** measurements.

The direction of the frictional force depends on which way the object is 'trying' to move. Friction always acts in the opposite direction.

direction of movement

applied force

friction

If an object is not moving, the forces acting on it must be balanced. The frictional force must be the same size as the force trying to move the object.

friction

tendency to move in this direction

Figure 2

1 Sketch a simple version of each of the diagrams below. Show clearly where the frictional force is acting, and in which direction.

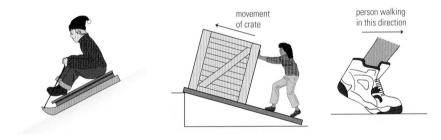

movement of crate

person walking in this direction

What is gravity?

Gravity is the force that makes all objects pull towards each other. The size of the force depends on the masses of the objects and the distance between them.

On Earth, a 1 kg mass is pulled by a force of 9.81 N towards the Earth's centre. This is the force you detect as the **weight** of an object. On Earth, a mass of 1 kg weighs 9.81 N. (This is often rounded up to 10 N to make calculations easier.)

weight of object (N) = mass of object (kg) × force due to gravity (N/kg)

$$W = mg$$

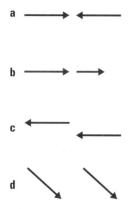

2 Which diagrams on the left show two forces that are equal to each other?

3 Draw a diagram to show what is happening in each of the following situations.

a An ice hockey puck is pushed to the left with a force of 10 N.

b A 0.1 N force acts downwards on an acorn falling from a tree. A 0.2 N force acts sideways as the acorn is pushed by the wind.

c As a firework rocket shoots up into the air, it feels an upward push of +4 N. Air resistance acts with a force of –1 N. Gravity acts with a force of –2 N.

d A plane in level flight feels an upward force (lift) equal to its weight of 10 000 N. The 3000 N thrust of its engines is matched by the air resistance.

4 Calculate the weight in newtons of a 750 kg astronaut as she visits parts of our Solar System.

Site	Mercury	Venus	Earth	Moon	Mars	Neptune
Force due to gravity (N/kg)	4.0	8.2	9.8	1.6	3.8	11.2

What do forces do?

Effects of forces

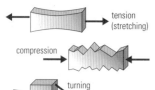

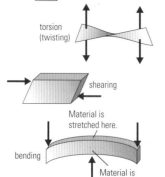

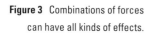

A force is a push or a pull, but when forces combine they can have far more complicated effects than simply pushing or pulling. If two forces act on an object along the same line, the object might be squeezed or stretched. If the forces don't act along the same line, the object will be sheered, or turned. At least three forces are needed to bend an object (see figure 3). When forces act to stretch an object they cause **tension**. When forces act to squeeze an object they cause **compression**.

Figure 3 Combinations of forces can have all kinds of effects.

Combinations of forces are acting in these photos, causing objects to be turned, squeezed and stretched.

5 Look at the list of actions below, and describe the effects of forces acting on the objects in *italics*. Choose your answers from the following list of words:

pushing	pulling	compression (squeezing)	tension (stretching)
turning	torsion	(twisting)	sheering	bending

a cutting *paper* with scissors

b using a screwdriver to put in a *screw*

c wringing water out of a wet *sponge*

d prising the *lid* from a can of paint

e preparing to use a *bow* to fire an arrow

f striking a *snooker ball* with a cue

Do forces always make things move?

It is easy to think that an object that is not moving has no forces acting on it. But this could only be true if the object was infinitely far away from everything else in the Universe. Everywhere else in the Universe, forces are acting on all objects, all the time, even when they are completely still.

An object is stationary when all the forces on it are balanced against each other. The upward forces on the object are matched by downward forces. The forces to the left are matched by those to the right (see figure 4).

Balanced forces

pull

reaction

Figure 4 The forces are balanced, so there is no movement overall.

Summary of forces

- A force is usually measured in newtons. It is a type of vector.
- Combinations of forces can produce tension (stretching), compression (squeezing), sheering, bending, turning and torsion (twisting).
- Objects are stationary because the forces acting on them are balanced, *not* because there are no forces on them.

- Mass is different from weight. Mass and weight are linked by the equation weight = mass × force of gravity on each kg, or $W = mg$.
- On Earth, g is about 10 N/kg.
- Friction is caused by forces of attraction between atoms in surfaces that are in contact. Friction tends to oppose movement, which is a nuisance in some situations but essential in others.

10.2 Stretching forces

What happens when things stretch?

Many objects and materials have to withstand being stretched. The plastic tape inside a cassette feels stretching forces each time you play it. When you brake on a bicycle, the brake cable feels stretching forces. Knowing how an object or material will cope with stretching forces is vital in designing safe and effective products.

To compare how materials stretch, you could gradually change the stretching force on different samples (see figure 5). If you measure the length of the sample each time you change the force, you can calculate the **extension**. This is the difference between the original length and the length when stretching forces are acting (see figure 6).

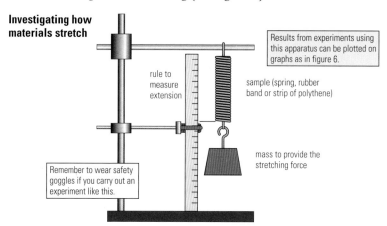

Investigating how materials stretch

Results from experiments using this apparatus can be plotted on graphs as in figure 6.

rule to measure extension

sample (spring, rubber band or strip of polythene)

mass to provide the stretching force

Remember to wear safety goggles if you carry out an experiment like this.

Figure 5

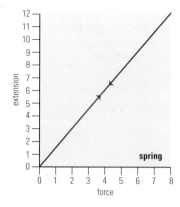

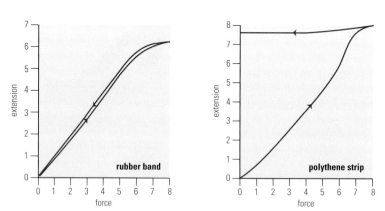

Figure 6 The spring stretched and sprang back in an even way, but the rubber band and polythene strip behaved less predictably.

A material that returns to its original size and shape after it has been stretched is called **elastic**. In figure 6, the spring and the rubber band behaved elastically, but the polythene strip did not. Polythene is called **plastic** because it does not return to its original size and shape after stretching.

An elastic material can be overstretched, so that it does not return to its original size and shape. The point at which it stops being elastic is called its **elastic limit**.

What is Hooke's Law?

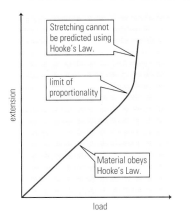

Stretching cannot be predicted using Hooke's Law.

limit of proportionality

Material obeys Hooke's Law.

extension

load

Figure 7

Around 1676, Thomas Hooke was investigating how materials stretched. With some materials, he noticed that when he doubled the stretching force, or **load**, the extension of the sample doubled too. He found that the extension was proportional to the force applied. This rule is known as Hooke's Law.

Many materials obey Hooke's Law, but not all. Even those materials that do obey the rule only follow it up to a limit (see figure 7).

6 From the list below, choose the objects most likely to behave elastically. Which will behave plastically?

| Plasticine | steel rule | guitar string | putty | wooden ruler |

7 Look at figure 6. Which of the materials tested obeys Hooke's Law?

8 The table shows some data from two experiments. Some data are missing.

Load (N)	0	1	2	3	4	5	6
Extension of sample 1 (cm)	0	2.0	4.0	?	?	10.0	?
Extension of sample 2 (cm)	0	1.0	2.0	3.1	4.3	5.6	snaps

a Assuming that sample 1 obeyed Hooke's Law, suggest values for the missing data.

b Plot a graph of the two sets of data.

c Which sample could withstand the largest force?

d Which sample was hardest to stretch?

9 Look at the markings on a spring balance. Are they spaced at regular intervals? Use this information to argue whether or not the spring inside the balance obeys Hooke's Law.

Summary of stretching forces

• For some materials, over a certain range of loads (stretching forces), the extension is proportional to the load applied. This rule is known as Hooke's Law.

• Elastic materials return to their original size and shape after they have been stretched. Plastic materials become permanently deformed.

Investigation

1 A large force is needed to lift a heavy weight. Pulling an object up a ramp or slope usually makes it easier. Investigate how much easier a ramp makes it to raise an object.

2 There are performers who demonstrate their strength and endurance by pulling large objects attached to their hair. Do people with a certain colour of hair have an advantage in performing such feats? Investigate whether the strength of hair depends on the colour.

Turning forces

Learning objectives

By the end of this chapter you should be able to:

- **describe** how forces make an object turn
- **describe** the conditions necessary for an object to be balanced and stable
- **explain** what is meant by centre of mass
- **describe** some ways of increasing the size of a force

11.1 Moments

What makes something turn?

If an object is fixed at a single point, or **pivot**, it can be turned or rotated around that point. A force on the object that does not act through the pivot will tend to make the object turn. The turning effect is larger if the force acts further from the pivot, and if the force is larger (see figure 1). The turning effect has many applications. It is the principle that makes spanners, bottle openers, levers and electric motors work. The turning effect of a force is called the turning moment, or sometimes just the **moment**.

turning moment = force × distance from pivot

Because force is measured in newtons and distance is measured in metres, the turning moment of a force is normally measured in newton-metres (Nm).

Each photo shows an object turning about a pivot, because a force is acting on it.

Moments and couples

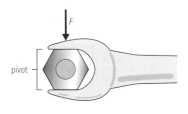

When a force acts in line with the pivot, there is no turning effect, or moment.

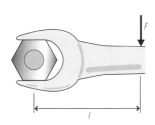

When a force acts out of line with the pivot, the object will turn.

moment = $F \times l$

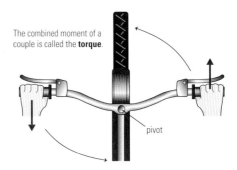

The combined moment of a couple is called the **torque**.

A **couple** is a pair of forces with moments of equal size, acting to turn an object the same way.

Figure 1

What happens when two moments act in opposite ways?

1 Look at the photos on page 76. Who is likely to be producing the greatest moment?

Sometimes an object feels several forces that together result in two moments acting in opposite directions. If the moment trying to turn the object in one direction is the same as the moment trying to turn the other way, the object is balanced. Remember, it is not the *forces* which have to be the same size, but the *moments* of the forces. When the system is balanced:

clockwise moment = anticlockwise moment

WORKED EXAMPLE

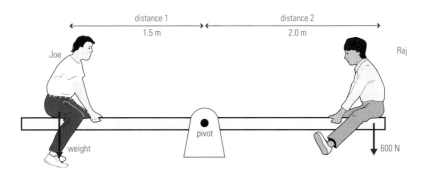

The turning moment in one direction may be the result of several forces.

For the see-saw to balance, the moment acting clockwise must equal the moment acting anticlockwise.

clockwise moment = anticlockwise moment

weight of Joe × distance 1 = weight of Raj × distance 2

weight of Joe × 1.5 m = 600 N × 2 m

weight of Joe = $\dfrac{1200}{1.5}$

= 800 N

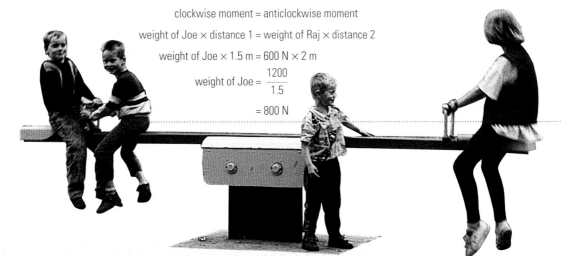

The weight of a load on your head acts downwards in line with your back, so it does not cause a twisting effect that could strain your back.

2 a Look at the diagram showing an athlete's arm. If the biceps muscle is capable of exerting a force of 400 N, calculate the moment produced.

b What is the heaviest load the person could lift without straining the muscle, assuming the lower arm is 35 cm long?

c Some athletes have a longer distance between their elbow joint and the position where the biceps muscle joins. Suggest how that could be an advantage in some ways, and a disadvantage in other ways.

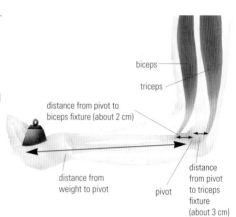

biceps

triceps

distance from pivot to biceps fixture (about 2 cm)

distance from weight to pivot

pivot

distance from pivot to triceps fixture (about 3 cm)

Summary of moments

- The turning effect, or moment, produced by a force is found using the formula:
  moment = force × distance from pivot.

- A couple involves two equal moments acting to turn an object in the same direction.

- A balanced object has equal moments acting upon it clockwise and anticlockwise.

11.2 Centre of mass

What is an object's centre of mass?

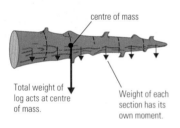

centre of mass

Total weight of log acts at centre of mass.

Weight of each section has its own moment.

Figure 2

When you are looking at moments, you must take into account the turning effect of the object's weight, as well as those of other forces acting on it. Imagine the object is divided into many different parts (see figure 2). There is a place on the object where the total of the moments of all of the parts on one side is exactly equal to the total of the moments of all the parts on the other side. This is true no matter how you turn the object. This place is called the **centre of mass** of the object, or sometimes the centre of gravity. The total weight of the object acts at the centre of mass.

When pivoted and allowed to swing freely, an object moves until its centre of mass is directly below the pivot. You can also balance an object with the centre of mass directly above the pivot, but the smallest knock will unbalance it. When the centre of mass is directly above or below the pivot, the total weight of the object acts in line with the pivot, and has no turning effect. So, provided an object is pivoted directly above, below or actually at its centre of mass, the weight of the object can be ignored in all calculations of moments.

If an object is not pivoted in line with the centre of mass:

$$\text{turning moment} = \frac{\text{total weight}}{\text{of beam}} \times \frac{\text{distance of centre of mass}}{\text{from pivot}}$$

Note

To find the centre of mass of an object, follow these steps:

1 Hang the object from any pivot point. Use a plumb line to draw a vertical line beneath the pivot point. The centre of mass is somewhere along that line.

2 Hang the object from another pivot point. Use the plumb line to draw another vertical line. The centre of mass is at the point where the lines cross.

3 Check the position by repeating with a third pivot point.

Another way of estimating the position of the centre of mass is to let the object spin freely. It will spin around its centre of mass.

WORKED EXAMPLE

If the counterweight on this car park barrier weighs 600 N, and the barrier is the same thickness all the way along, how heavy is the barrier?

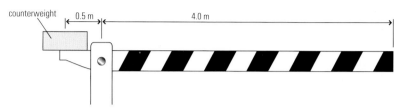

clockwise moment = anticlockwise moment

$$\text{weight of barrier} \times \frac{\text{distance of centre of mass}}{\text{from pivot}} = \text{weight of counterweight} \times \text{distance from pivot}$$

Distance of centre of mass of barrier from pivot is 2 m, because barrier is the same thickness all the way along so centre of mass is in the middle. So:

$$\text{weight of barrier} \times 2.0\,\text{m} = 600\,\text{N} \times 0.5\,\text{m} = 300$$
$$\text{weight of barrier} = \frac{300}{2} = 150\,\text{N}$$

3 Draw diagrams to show the approximate position of the centre of mass in:
   a a plastic coathanger   **b** a wheel nut   **c** a drinks can when it is **i** full, **ii** half full, **iii** empty

4 The crane in the photo lifts a 1000 N load. The jib (the long horizontal arm) is the same thickness all along its 40 m length, and and weighs 2000 N. The counterweight (on the short arm) is 10 m from the vertical shaft.
   a What is the turning moment produced by the load?
   b What is the turning moment produced by the jib on its own?
   c Calculate the turning effect provided by the counterweight.
   d Calculate the weight of the counterweight.

When is an object stable?

Imagine a person gradually tilting backwards in his chair, while holding onto the desk. (You should *never* actually do this as it can be extremely dangerous.) Each time he lets go of the desk, he falls forwards again. But, at some point he tilts so far back that if he let go he would fall backwards, because his centre of mass had moved beyond a vertical line drawn upwards from the pivot. In this case, the pivot is where the legs of the chair touch the floor (see figure 3).

Stability

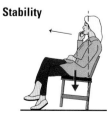

Figure 3 When the centre of mass moves towards a vertical line through the pivot point, the object becomes unstable.

Because the weighted ends of the pole bend down, the centre of mass of the high wire artist and pole together is lowered. The artist is more stable and becomes unbalanced less easily.

An object is stable if it has to be tilted a long way before it tips over on its own. Unstable objects tip over when they have been tilted just a little way. An object is more stable if it has:

- a wide base
- a low centre of mass

5 A European Standard states that traffic cones should just topple over if a constant force of 7 N is applied to the top.

a If a cone topples over when a smaller force is applied, how could it be redesigned to meet the specification?

b If a cone needs a much larger force to make it topple over, how could it be redesigned?

c Suggest a design for a 'self-righting' cone, which turns upright after being knocked over.

d Self-righting cones have been tried on motorways, but have caused some accidents. Can you suggest reasons why?

6 A netball goal is mounted on a structure of steel tubes. Suggest ways of making the structure as stable as possible, without it getting in the players' way.

7 Think of some reasons why a formula 1 racing car is more stable than a normal family car of the same mass.

Summary of centre of mass

- The centre of mass of an object is:

1 the point where it seems the object's mass is concentrated

2 the point around which an object will spin if free to do so

3 directly below the pivot when the object is suspended freely from any point

- The stability of an object is increased if its centre of mass is lowered, or its base is widened.

Investigation

Using what you have learned in this chapter to help you, design and make a device to measure the weight of a very large or a very small object. Test your device for accuracy and reliability.

Looking at motion

Learning objectives

By the end of this chapter you should be able to:

- **distinguish** between velocity and speed
- **distinguish** between displacement and distance
- **interpret** graphs of distance against time, and displacement against time, to find out speeds and velocities

- **interpret** graphs of velocity against time to find out accelerations and displacements
- **calculate** the velocity, displacement or acceleration of an object, using the equations of motion

12.1 How far and how fast

What is the difference between distance and displacement?

Sophie is training to swim across the English Channel. She trains by doing lengths in a swimming pool. In both the pool and the Channel, Sophie travels a distance of 27 km. In the pool, her displacement is zero, because she ends up where she started. In the Channel, her displacement is 27 km, because she ends up 27 km from the starting point. The displacement of a moving object is the distance between the starting and finishing points.

Distance and displacement are both measured in metres, but while distance is always a positive measurement, displacement can be negative or positive. For example, a step forward and a step back might both move you a distance of 1 m. But if the step forward displaces you +1 m from your starting position, a step back displaces you –1 m. A displacement of +1 m (a step forward) followed by a displacement of –1 m (a step back) makes your overall displacement zero. You are back where you started.

Because distance and displacement are different, graphs of distance against time, and displacement against time, have to be interpreted differently. For example, figure 1 on page 76 shows the displacement of a ferry as it crosses a river and comes back. Because of the way the river flows, the ferry is slower in one direction than in the other. Figure 2 shows how the distance travelled varies with time, for the same ferry crossing.

Displacement/time graph

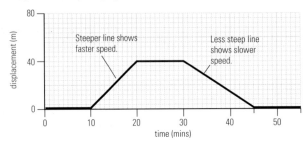

Figure 1 When the ferry has crossed the river and come back, its displacement is zero.

Distance/time graph

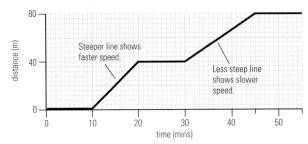

Figure 2 The total distance the ferry has travelled after the return crossing is 80 m.

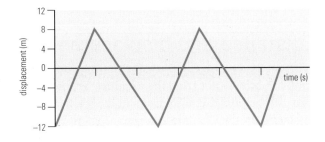

1 Andy and Kalpesh are playing tennis. The graph shows the ball's displacement during a rally, measured from the net. Andy hits first.
   a Who is standing furthest from the net? How can you tell?
   b Who is making the ball go fastest? How can you tell?
   c How many times is the ball hit?
   d Who wins the rally?
   e Sketch a graph of distance against time for the same rally.

How do you work out an object's speed?

The greater the distance a car covers in a certain time, the faster the car is travelling. Traffic speed is often measured in miles per hour (mph) or kilometres per hour (km/h). In physics, speed is usually measured in metres per second (m/s).

$$\text{average speed} = \frac{\text{distance travelled}}{\text{time taken}}$$

WORKED EXAMPLE

a A motorcyclist travels 8.4 km in 7 minutes. What is her average speed in m/s?

$$\text{average speed} = \frac{\text{distance}}{\text{time}} = \frac{8400 \text{ m}}{7 \times 60 \text{ s}}$$

$$= 20 \text{ m/s}$$

Notice that the time taken is converted into seconds, and the distance is converted into metres, because the speed is needed in m/s.

b How far will she travel in one hour?

distance travelled = average speed × time taken = 20 m/s × (1 × 60 × 60 s)

$$= 72\,000 \text{ m} = 72 \text{ km}$$

2 The British Grand Prix at Silverstone is a race around 60 laps of the 4.8 km track. The race finishes at the start line.

    a About what distance is travelled by each car that completes the race?

    b What is the final displacement of the cars as they finish?

    c If a car wins after exactly 2 hours, what was the winner's average speed?

3 Fast reaction times are important in many sports. Use the table to work out which top class sportsperson needs the fastest reaction time.

Sportsperson	Distance	Speed
Tennis player	length of court: 24 m	top class serve: 60 m/s (126 mph)
Football goalkeeper	penalty spot to goal line: 11 m	top class kick: 25 m/s (50 mph)
Cricketer in bat	length of pitch: 20 m	top class bowl: 45 m/s (91 mph)

How do you describe motion when the speed is changing?

Usually when an object moves it does not travel at the same speed from start to finish. Instead, the speed varies (see figure 3).

Distance/time graph

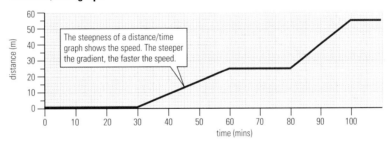

Speed/time graph

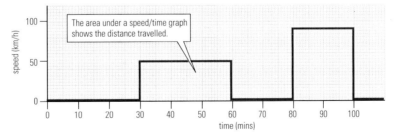

Figure 3 These two graphs look different but they both record the same motion, and they can both be used to work out how fast and how far the object travelled.

The steepness of the distance/time graph in figure 3 shows the speed of the object. The steeper the graph is, the faster the object is moving. The steepness of the graph is called its **gradient**.

The total area under the speed/time graph in figure 3 shows the distance the object travelled.

Measuring gradient

You find the gradient of a line by dividing 'how much the line goes up' by 'how far the line goes along' (see figure 4).

$$\text{gradient} = \frac{\text{change in Y value}}{\text{change in X value}}$$

Gradient

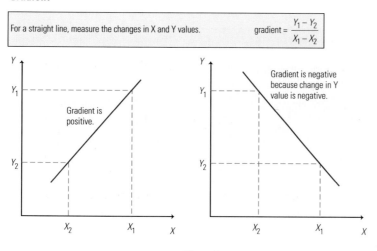

For a straight line, measure the changes in X and Y values.

$$\text{gradient} = \frac{Y_1 - Y_2}{X_1 - X_2}$$

Gradient is positive.

Gradient is negative because change in Y value is negative.

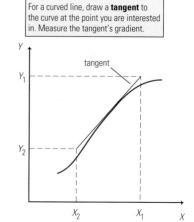

For a curved line, draw a **tangent** to the curve at the point you are interested in. Measure the tangent's gradient.

tangent

Figure 4

Measuring area under a graph

The area under a speed/time graph gives you the distance travelled, because distance = speed × time (see figure 5). Always make sure the units are consistent – if speed in km/h, you must use time in hours too.

Area under a graph

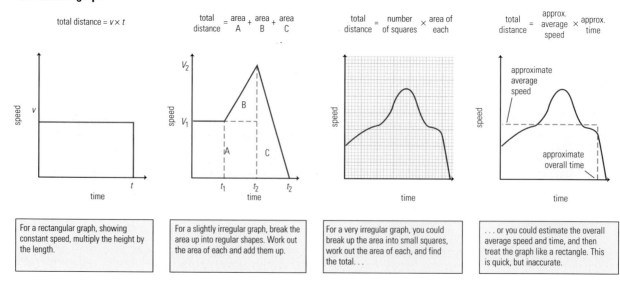

total distance = $v \times t$

$$\frac{\text{total}}{\text{distance}} = \frac{\text{area}}{A} + \frac{\text{area}}{B} + \frac{\text{area}}{C}$$

$$\frac{\text{total}}{\text{distance}} = \frac{\text{number}}{\text{of squares}} \times \frac{\text{area of}}{\text{each}}$$

$$\frac{\text{total}}{\text{distance}} = \frac{\text{approx.}}{\text{average}} \times \frac{\text{approx.}}{\text{time}}$$
$$\text{speed}$$

approximate average speed

approximate overall time

For a rectangular graph, showing constant speed, multiply the height by the length.

For a slightly irregular graph, break the area up into regular shapes. Work out the area of each and add them up.

For a very irregular graph, you could break up the area into small squares, work out the area of each, and find the total. . .

. . . or you could estimate the overall average speed and time, and then treat the graph like a rectangle. This is quick, but inaccurate.

Figure 5

How do you measure changing speed?

To record the motion of small vehicles in the lab, you can attach a long strip of paper to the vehicle and, as it moves, use a 'ticker-timer' to mark a dot on the paper every 0.02 s. After the experiment, you can cut the ticker tape into lengths which have 10 gaps between dots. When the lengths of tape are stuck down next to each other, they form a speed/time graph (see figure 6).

Ticker timer

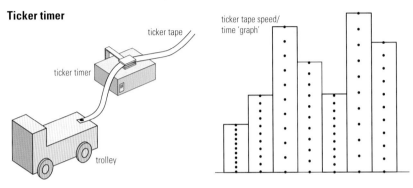

Figure 6

Tachographs like the one in figure 7 are used in buses and lorries to record their speeds. The record includes a speed/time graph, made on circular graph paper. The graph can be used to check that the vehicle did not go above the speed limit and that the driver had enough rest time between drives.

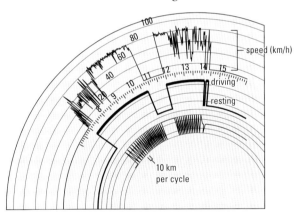

Figure 7

4 When a hot air balloon takes off, one person has to drive a car to follow the balloon, and see where it lands. Using the car's milometer, the driver records the distance the balloon travels over certain times.

Time	6:00	6:10	6:20	6:30	6:40	6:50	7:00	7:10	7:20	7:30	7:40
Distance (km)	0	5	10	15	18	20	20	22	25	28	31

a Sketch a distance/time graph for the balloon's journey. Label on your graph where you think the wind was strongest.

b Mark on your graph when the wind dropped so much that the balloon stopped.

c Work out the average speed of the balloon during its flight.

d From your graph, work out the maximum speed of the balloon.

What is the difference between speed and velocity?

The cricketer who hit this ball was pleased with its speed, but not with its velocity.

To say that an object has a speed of, say, 10 m/s is not enough to fully describe its motion. You must also say what direction the object is moving in. When your description gives the object's speed, *and* its direction, it is called the **velocity**, rather than the speed. When you talk about motion in a straight line, you can describe it as positive (a forwards motion) or negative (a backwards motion). For example, +10 m/s and –10 m/s are the same speeds, but they are different velocities. Velocity is a vector quantity, while speed is scalar (see page 65).

$$\text{average velocity} = \frac{\text{total displacement}}{\text{time}}$$

When an object is always moving in the same direction, a velocity calculation gives the same numerical answer as a speed calculation. However, if the object changes direction, the two calculations give very different results.

WORKED EXAMPLE

A child on a swing moves forward 3 m in 1.5 s, and then swings back through the middle 1.5 s later. After 1.5 s:

$$\text{average speed} = \frac{\text{total distance}}{\text{time}} = \frac{3\text{ m}}{1.5\text{ s}} \qquad\qquad \text{average velocity} = \frac{\text{displacement}}{\text{time}} = \frac{3\text{ m}}{1.5\text{ s}}$$
$$= 2\text{ m/s} \qquad\qquad\qquad\qquad = 2\text{ m/s}$$

After 3 s:

$$\text{average speed} = \frac{6\text{ m}}{3\text{ s}} = 2\text{ m/s} \qquad\qquad \text{average velocity} = \frac{0\text{ m}}{3\text{ s}} = 0\text{ m/s}$$

How do you describe motion when the velocity is changing?

Figure 8 These graphs describe the motion of a piston inside a car engine.

When the velocity of an object varies, velocity/time graphs and displacement/time graphs are a convenient way to describe the motion. The velocity/time graph and displacement/time graph for an object's motion are linked, just as its speed/time graph and distance/time graph are linked (see figure 8).

This graph shows how the displacement of a car engine piston varies over time, measured from the middle of the cylinder.

At any point in time, the gradient of a displacement/time graph is equal to the velocity.

This graph shows how the velocity of the piston varies over time.

Over any time interval, the area under the velocity/time graph gives the displacement during that interval.

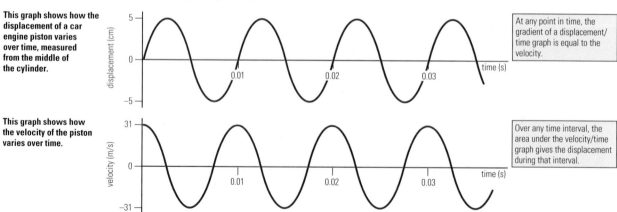

5 The graph below shows how the velocity of a person on a skateboard varied as he went backwards and forwards on a section of U-shaped track.

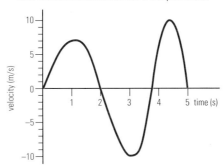

a How many lengths of the track did the skateboarder do?

b Explain how you decided on your answer to **a**.

c Which of the lengths was covered fastest?

d In what two ways does the graph show this?

e Sketch a rough displacement/time graph for the skateboarder, measuring displacement from the middle of the track (the lowest point).

Summary of how far and how fast

- Velocity and speed describe how fast an object is moving.
- Displacement and distance describe how far an object has travelled.
- Displacement and velocity can have negative values, because they are vectors.
- Speed and distance are always positive, because they are scalars.
- Average speed = distance travelled/time taken.

- Average velocity = displacement/time taken.
- The gradient of a displacement/time graph for an object moving in a straight line equals the velocity. The gradient of a distance/time graph equals the speed.
- The area under a velocity/time graph shows the displacement. The area under a speed/time graph shows the distance.

12.2 Acceleration

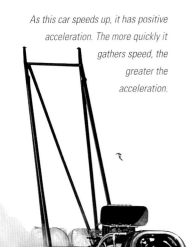

As this car speeds up, it has positive acceleration. The more quickly it gathers speed, the greater the acceleration.

When the velocity of a moving object changes, the object is **accelerating**. For example, as a car speeds up it has a positive acceleration, and as it loses speed it has a negative acceleration – or **deceleration**.

$$\text{average acceleration} = \frac{\text{change in velocity}}{\text{time taken}}$$

$$= \frac{\text{final velocity} - \text{initial velocity}}{\text{time taken}}$$

$$a = \frac{v - u}{t}$$

or: $v = u + at$

where v = final velocity, u = initial velocity, t = time taken and a = average acceleration.

Because acceleration is the rate of change of velocity, it has the units m/s/s, or m/s^2 (metres per second squared).

81

WORKED EXAMPLE

Car	Time from 0 to 30 m/s
Austin Maestro	12.8
Porsche Turbo 3.3	5.1

Look at the table on the left. What are the average accelerations of the Porsche and the Maestro?

For the Porsche:

$$a = \frac{v-u}{t} = \frac{30-0 \text{ m/s}}{5.10 \text{ s}}$$

$$= 5.88 \text{ m/s}^2$$

For the Maestro:

$$a = \frac{30-0 \text{ m/s}}{12.8 \text{ s}}$$

$$= 2.34 \text{ m/s}^2$$

The formula for average acceleration only gives an accurate answer for the acceleration at a point in time if the velocity changes at a steady rate between the initial and final velocities. When the velocity of the object varies in an irregular way, as in figure 9, you can find the acceleration at a point in time by drawing a tangent to the graph and finding its gradient (see page 84).

Finding the acceleration

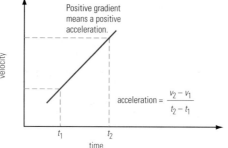

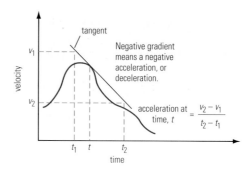

Figure 9

When the velocity varies at a steady rate, there are several formulae that you can use to find the acceleration, known as the equations of motion:

$$v = u + at$$
$$v^2 = u^2 + 2as$$
$$s = ut + \tfrac{1}{2}at^2$$

To use the equations of motion to solve problems involving moving objects, follow these steps:

1 Write down the data you know.
2 Choose the equation which includes the things you have values for, and the thing you want to find out, and *nothing else*.
3 Put the data into the equation, and solve it.

WORKED EXAMPLE

A monkey hanging from a tree branch lets go, and falls to the ground 4.0 m below. Assuming the acceleration due to gravity is 10 m/s^2, how fast is the monkey travelling when it reaches the ground?

1 Write down the data you know:

a = acceleration due to gravity = 10 m/s^2 u = initial speed of monkey = 0 m/s

s = distance travelled = 4.0 m

2 Choose an equation:

You want to find v, the velocity of the monkey. The equation which uses v, u, a and s, and no other variable, is:

$$v^2 = u^2 + 2as$$

3 Put in the data, and solve the equation:

$$v^2 = 0 + 2 \times 10 \times 4.0 = 80$$

$$v = 8.9 \text{ m/s}$$

How can you measure the acceleration due to gravity?

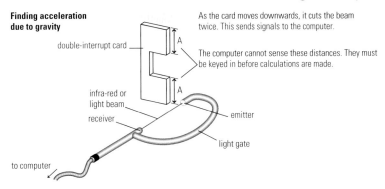

Finding acceleration due to gravity

double-interrupt card

infra-red or light beam

receiver

to computer

As the card moves downwards, it cuts the beam twice. This sends signals to the computer.

The computer cannot sense these distances. They must be keyed in before calculations are made.

emitter

light gate

Figure 10

To measure the acceleration of an object due to gravity, you could attach a 'double interrupt card' to the object and use a light gate connected to a computer to monitor the object's motion as you drop it (see figure 10). Using appropriate software, the computer measures time T_1 when the light beam is first broken, and time T_2 when the light beam is restored. It then registers time T_3 when the light beam is broken again, and time T_4 when the light beam is restored once more.

The computer can be programmed to do the following calculations:

average velocity as first section passed, $v = \dfrac{A}{(T_2 - T_1)}$

average velocity as second section passed, $u = \dfrac{A}{(T_4 - T_3)}$

time between v and u, $t = \dfrac{(T_3 + T_4)}{2} - \dfrac{(T_1 + T_2)}{2}$

acceleration, $a = \dfrac{\text{change in velocity}}{\text{time}} = \dfrac{v - u}{t}$

Time (s)	Velocity (m/s)
0	10
2	14
4	18
6	22
8	26

6   The velocity of a car was measured at several times in a journey. The table shows the results.
  a If the car keeps speeding up in the same way, how fast will it be going at 10 s and 12 s?
  b What is the acceleration of the car?
  c What was the velocity of the car 2 seconds *before* these measurements were taken (i.e. at a time of −2 s)?

7   The World Trade Centre in New York is 412 m high.
  a If a worker knocks a stone from the top, how long will it take to hit the ground? (Assume that acceleration due to gravity, *g* is 9.8 m/s^2, and that there is no air resistance.)
  b At what speed will the stone hit the ground? (Assume there is no air resistance.)
  c Is there any point in the worker calling out to warn people below? (Assume the speed of sound in air is 340 m/s.)
  d In fact, air resistance will affect the object. In what ways would your answers to **a**, **b** and **c** be different if its effect is considered?

Summary of acceleration

- The gradient of a velocity/time graph for an object moving in a straight line equals the acceleration.
- Acceleration = change in velocity/time taken.

- For objects moving at a steady velocity, or changing velocity at a steady rate:

$$v = u + at$$
$$v^2 = u^2 + 2as$$
$$s = ut + \tfrac{1}{2} at^2$$

where s = displacement (m),
u = initial velocity (m/s), v = final velocity (m/s),
a = acceleration (m/s^2) and t = time (s).

Investigation

The acceleration of objects is often compared to that of gravity. If an object accelerates or decelerates at a rate 5*g* it means the object accelerates or decelerates five times faster than it would if it were simply moving up or down through the air under the effect of gravity. The USA's first spaceman, Alan Shepard, endured 5*g* in his first flight. In experiments, monkeys have survived accelerations of 15*g*. Find out how the acceleration of a spring loaded toy vehicle, or a slot-car, compares to these examples.

Forces and *motion*

Learning objectives

By the end of this chapter, you should be able to:

- **state** Newton's three laws of motion
- **calculate** the forces and accelerations involved in collisions
- **understand** what is meant by momentum, and how it is different from kinetic energy

- **predict** what will happen to objects in some collisions and explosions
- **discuss** the effects of air resistance and friction on moving objects
- **apply** ideas about forces and motion to a wide range of situations

13.1 Motion, momentum and inertia

How do forces affect motion?

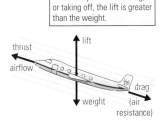

When the plane is climbing, or taking off, the lift is greater than the weight.

In level flight, the lift from the plane's aerofoil wings balances the plane's weight.

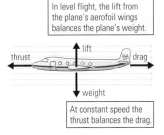

At constant speed the thrust balances the drag.

Figure 1 For the plane to take off, the forces acting on it must be unbalanced.

When the forces acting are equal and opposite, there is no motion.

In 1889, a tug of war contest between two companies of soldiers in India lasted two hours and 41 minutes! Until then, both teams were pulling with the same force, so the system was balanced. The two forces cancelled one another, so there was no change in the motion of the rope.

When a plane takes off, airflow over the aerofoil wings causes an upward lifting force (see chapter 8, *Fluid flow*), while the force of gravity pulls the plane down. If all goes to plan, the lift is larger than the plane's weight, and the plane climbs upwards. The forces are unbalanced, so there is an overall **net** force in one direction, that makes the plane's motion change. In this case, the plane speeds up in the upward direction. In other situations, unbalanced forces can make an object slow down or change direction.

Braking distances

When a car driver brakes, a force is exerted to slow the moving vehicle down. One reason that speeding is dangerous is that the brakes can only exert a limited force. The faster the car is moving, the longer the time and therefore the distance it takes for this force to stop it.

The brakes have to do work on the car to transfer its kinetic energy into other forms, and slow the car down (see chapter 3, *Work and power*). Most of the energy is transferred to heat as friction between the brakes and brake discs opposes the motion of the wheels.

WORKED EXAMPLE

A 400 kg car is travelling at 13.0 m/s (about 30 mph or 47 km/h) when a child runs into the road ahead. The driver applies the brakes, which exert a force of 2000 N. How far will the car travel before it stops?

Energy is always conserved, so:

change in kinetic energy of car = work done by brakes

initial KE − final KE = force × distance moved

$$\tfrac{1}{2}mu^2 - \tfrac{1}{2}mv^2 = Fs$$

Final velocity, $v = 0$, so:

$$s = \frac{\tfrac{1}{2}mu^2}{F}$$

$$= \frac{\tfrac{1}{2} \times 400 \times 13.0^2}{2000}$$

$$= 16.9 \text{ m}$$

If the driver was travelling at twice the speed (26 m/s), the stopping distance would be much longer:

$$\tfrac{1}{2}mu^2 - \tfrac{1}{2}mv^2 = Fs$$

$$s = \frac{\tfrac{1}{2}mu^2}{F}$$

$$= \frac{\tfrac{1}{2} \times 400 \times 26.0^2}{2000}$$

$$= 67.6 \text{ m}$$

Remember that the distances in the worked example do not include the reaction time of the driver (the time from when the driver sees a hazard to when the brakes are applied). At 13 m/s, reaction time will add 13 m to the stopping distance. At faster speeds, reaction time adds even greater distances (see table 1).

1 Plot a graph of total stopping distance (y-axis) against speed (x-axis) for a 1000 kg vehicle moving at speeds in the range 0 to 40 m/s. The brakes exert a maximum force of 2500 N, and the driver's reaction time is 1 s.

Speed of vehicle (km/h)	Distance travelled while reacting (m)	Braking distance (m)	Total stopping distance (m)
30	6	6	12
45	9	15	24
60	12	24	36
90	18	60	78
120	24	96	120

Table 1 *Typical braking distances for a moving car.*

What is momentum?

Note

Kinetic energy (KE) has the formula KE = $\frac{1}{2}mv^2$. In some ways momentum (*mv*) is similar to KE. Massive objects that move rapidly have large amounts of both KE and momentum. But there are important differences between them.

1 KE is just one form of energy, and can be changed into other forms. Momentum cannot be changed into any other form.

2 Because velocity (*v*) is a vector, momentum (*mv*) is also a vector quantity. It has direction as well as size, and can therefore have a negative value. Kinetic energy involves v^2, so it can never have a negative value, and is not a vector. The direction of a moving object does not affect its kinetic energy.

A moving object with a large amount of **momentum** is hard to stop. A small object that is moving quickly has a large amount of momentum. So too does an object with a large mass that is moving very slowly.

momentum = mass × velocity = *mv*

Mass is normally measured in kg, and velocity has the units m/s, so momentum has the units kgm/s.

A speeding bullet and a slow-moving whale both have a great deal of momentum.

2 Calculate the momentum of the following objects, in kg m/s.

a a 600 kg car travelling at 12 m/s

b a 3 kg bowling ball rolling at 5 m/s

c a 700 g hockey ball, hit with a speed of 15 m/s

d a 75 kg runner, winning a 100 m race in 10.0 s

What happens when something has momentum?

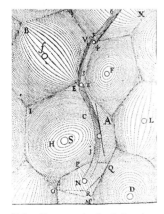

Before Newton, scientists believed swirling currents provided forces that kept the planets in motion.

Once an object has momentum, it keeps the same amount unless it feels a force. This means that, provided no force acts on it, a moving object will keep going in a straight line, at a steady speed, forever. In the same way, a stationary object will remain stationary forever, unless a force acts on it.

This rule was first suggested around 1660 by Isaac Newton, and is now called Newton's First Law of Motion. Up until Newton's time, most scientists believed that to keep an object moving, you had to keep applying a force. This seemed sensible. After all, you have to keep kicking a ball to keep it moving along the ground. Newton argued that the only reason you have to keep kicking the ball is because the force of friction acts on the ball to slow it down. He said that if you could get rid of friction, and any other forces on a moving object, then it would keep going forever, with the same velocity.

Newton's First Law of Motion helped to explain what keeps the Moon and planets moving. If the old ideas about motion were correct, the planets would each need a continual push to keep them orbiting. Some scientists believed that angels using gear wheels provided that push. Others thought there must be a swirling fluid called the 'ether' surrounding the planets and dragging them round in its flow.

Newton argued that each planet keeps moving because there is no force to *stop* it, not because there is a force *keeping* it moving. In space, air resistance and friction cannot affect motion, as they do here on Earth.

Newton's First Law has many applications. Space scientists use it when planning paths of space probes that travel to the furthest planets using very little fuel. Television designers use it to predict the paths of electrons so they produce a picture on a screen. Forensic scientists use it to work out the paths of bullets, and positions of people when the gun was fired.

What is inertia?

Newton's First Law is linked with the idea of **inertia**. All objects are said to have inertia. The more massive an object is, the more inertia it has. Inertia is an object's tendency to keep moving just as it is, or to stay still just as it is.

3 Select examples from below where Newton's First Law appears to apply.
   a the launch of a space rocket
   b a car sliding off at a tangent on an icy bend
   c a book resting on a shelf
   d a car accelerating away from traffic lights
   e a footballer heading the ball towards the goal
4 The space probe Pioneer 10 was launched in 1972, to study the outer planets. After it visited Jupiter, it left our Solar System and it is estimated that it will travel 3000 light years during the next 100 million years. How do you think it can travel so far without refuelling?

How big a force do you need to change an object's momentum?

To change the momentum of an object, a force is needed. The greater the change of momentum, the larger the force required. The size and direction of the force are given by this formula:

net force = rate of change of momentum

$$F = \frac{mv - mu}{t}$$

$$= \frac{m(v - u)}{t}$$

But:

$$\frac{(v - u)}{t} = a$$

So:

$$F = ma$$

where F = net force (N), u = initial velocity (m/s), v = final velocity (m/s), m = mass (kg), t = time (s) and a = acceleration (m/s^2).

This relationship is known as Newton's Second Law of Motion, and shows that the acceleration of an object depends not just on the force you apply to make its motion change, but also on the object's mass.

5 An Austin Montego has a mass of 1018 kg. A Ford Granada has a mass of 1280 kg. Both can accelerate from 0 to 100 km/h in 9.8 s. How do the accelerating forces of the two cars compare?

6 To leap upwards, you must push down with your legs with a force that is larger than your weight.

a Which of the following dancers will move upwards with the greatest acceleration, if Newton's Second Law is correct?

Dancer	Mass (kg)	Weight (N)	Force (N)
A	60	600	660
B	50	500	575
C	40	400	480

b Why do you think it is easier to be a dancer if you are small than if you are large?

What do we mean by conservation of momentum?

In any event, momentum is always conserved. There is always the same amount of momentum after the event as there was before it happened. Remember that momentum is a vector quantity, so it can have a negative value.

When you are looking at an event, like a collision between two objects, decide which direction to take as positive. If an object moves in this direction it will have a positive velocity and a positive momentum. If it moves in the opposite direction, it will have a negative velocity and a negative momentum (see figure 2). Normally it will not matter which direction you choose to take as positive, as long as you are consistent throughout that problem.

Momentum and kinetic energy

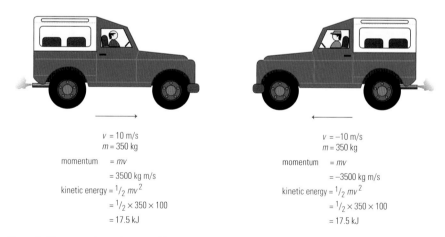

$v = 10$ m/s
$m = 350$ kg

momentum $= mv$
$= 3500$ kg m/s

kinetic energy $= \frac{1}{2} mv^2$
$= \frac{1}{2} \times 350 \times 100$
$= 17.5$ kJ

$v = -10$ m/s
$m = 350$ kg

momentum $= mv$
$= -3500$ kg m/s

kinetic energy $= \frac{1}{2} mv^2$
$= \frac{1}{2} \times 350 \times 100$
$= 17.5$ kJ

Figure 2 These cars have the same kinetic energy. But the car moving to the right has positive momentum, while the other has negative momentum.

WORKED EXAMPLE

When the dodgems below collide, both cars come to a stop. Show that momentum is conserved.

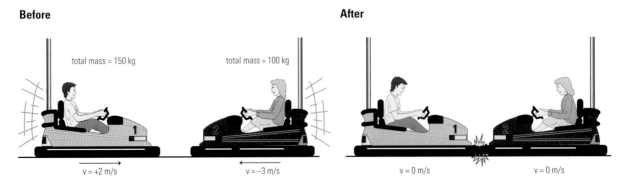

Before

total mass = 150 kg

total mass = 100 kg

v = +2 m/s

v = −3 m/s

After

v = 0 m/s

v = 0 m/s

total momentum before collision = momentum of car 1 + momentum of car 2

= (mass 1 × velocity 1) + (mass 2 × velocity 2)

= (150 × 2) + (100 × −3)

= 300 − 300

= 0 kg m/s

total momentum after collision = (mass 1 × velocity 1) + (mass 2 × velocity 2)

= (150 × 0) + (100 × 0)

= 0 kg m/s

Momentum before and after collision is 0 kg m/s. So momentum has been conserved.

In some situations, a continuous force is exerted on an object rather than a sudden one, as in a collision. The law of conservation of momentum still applies.

For example, a jet engine is propelled forwards as it pushes gas out behind it at high speed. Because the gas is less massive than the engine, it has to be thrown out very quickly to make the engine move more slowly in the other direction.

What is a reaction force?

The rule that momentum is always conserved means that a force can never be felt by one object on its own. Whenever a force acts on an object, something else, somewhere, must be feeling an equal and opposite push, and gaining an equal amount of momentum in the opposite direction.

This idea was summarised by Isaac Newton in his Third Law of Motion. This says that to every action there is an equal and opposite **reaction**.

force produced by squid squirting water

friction

reaction force of water pushing back

Forces are not balanced, and the squid moves forward.

Figure 3 The squid squeezes a high speed jet of water from its body, to push itself in the opposite direction.

Sometimes the action and reaction are obvious. If a gun is fired, the bullet goes one way, and the gun recoils in the other direction. When a squid squirts a jet of water one way, it gets pushed the other way (see figure 3). Sometimes the action and reaction are not obvious. When two masses move away from each other, if one mass is very large, it might not appear to move as the smaller object moves away (see figure 4).

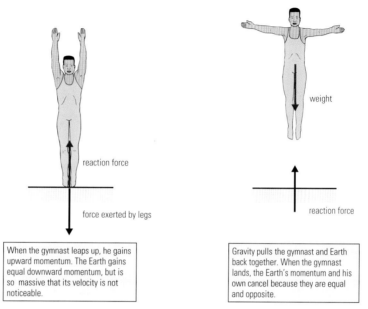

When the gymnast leaps up, he gains upward momentum. The Earth gains equal downward momentum, but is so massive that its velocity is not noticeable.

Gravity pulls the gymnast and Earth back together. When the gymnast lands, the Earth's momentum and his own cancel because they are equal and opposite.

Figure 4

Newton's Third Law applies to stationary objects as well as objects moving together or apart. An object is stationary because the forces on it are in balance. The total force on it acting upwards is as large as the total force acting downwards, and so on.

7 How is momentum conserved in these events?

a a skater sliding on the ice and coming to a stop as he hits the edge of the rink

b a Space Shuttle taking off

c a goalkeeper catching a football in mid air

d a diver using a spring board to spring into the air

8 Show that momentum is conserved as the rifle in the diagram is fired.

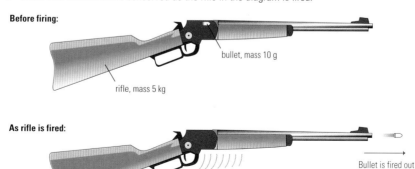

Before firing:

bullet, mass 10 g

rifle, mass 5 kg

As rifle is fired:

Bullet is fired out at 500 m/s.

Rifle recoils at 1 m/s.

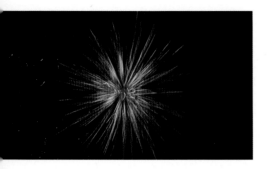

9 Look at the photo. How can you tell from this firework explosion that momentum is conserved?

10 A 2.2 kg squid squirts out 1.6 kg of water, and accelerates to 16 m/s from rest.

  a Calculate the momentum of the squid after ejecting the water.

  b How fast was the water squirted out?

  c Suggest two ways in which a more massive squid might behave differently from a less massive one, in order to travel at the same speed.

Summary of motion, momentum and inertia

- Newton's three Laws of Motion are:

  1 Provided there is no net force on it, an object will remain stationary, or keep moving in a straight line at a steady speed, forever.

  2 Acceleration is directly proportional to the net force applied to an object, or $F = ma$, when force is in N, mass is in kg and acceleration is in m/s^2.

  3 Whenever a force acts on an object, there is an equal and opposite reaction force, usually acting on a different object.

- All objects resist changes in motion. The resistance is sometimes called inertia, and is due to the mass of the object.
- Kinetic energy, KE $= \frac{1}{2} mv^2$.
- When a car brakes, kinetic energy is converted into heat energy. Work done by brakes = change in kinetic energy, or $Fs = \frac{1}{2} mu^2 - \frac{1}{2}mv^2$.
- The braking distance of a car is much longer at higher speeds.
- Momentum $= mv$.
- Momentum is conserved in all events where no outside force is acting.

13.2 Impulse

What is impulse?

Any unbalanced force causes the momentum of an object to change. The larger the force is and the longer it lasts for, the greater the change of momentum will be. The change in momentum is called the **impulse**. Impulse is really a special case of Newton's Second Law of Motion.

$$F = ma$$

$$F = \frac{mv - mu}{t}$$

$$Ft = mv - mu$$

Ft is given the name impulse, so in words, the equation can be written

impulse = change in momentum

A large impulse (change in momentum) can be produced by applying a small force for a long time, or by applying a large force for a short time.

Why is impulse important in sport?

Keeping the club in contact with the ball for longer increases the impulse, and so gives a larger increase in momentum.

Understanding the relationship between force, time and impulse is vital where changes in momentum have to be controlled. For example it is important in any sport where you strike a ball, to 'follow through' with the swing or kick, keeping the ball in contact with your bat, racket or foot for as long as possible. This not only allows better control over the ball's direction, it also gives the ball a greater change in momentum, because the impulse is greater. With increased momentum, the ball travels with greater speed.

WORKED EXAMPLE

A golfer hits a stationary 46 g ball with a force of 50 N. Calculate the ball's speed as it leaves the club, if the ball and club are in contact for:

a 0.001 s (no follow through):

$$Ft = (mv - mu)$$

$$mv = Ft + mu = (50 \times 0.001) + (0.046 \times 0)$$

$$= 0.05$$

$$v = \frac{0.05}{0.046}$$

$$= 1.1 \text{ m/s}$$

b 0.02 s (with follow through):

$$Ft = (mv - mu)$$

$$mv = Ft + mu = (50 \times 0.02) + (0.046 \times 0)$$

$$= 1.0$$

$$v = \frac{1.0}{0.046}$$

$$= 21.7 \text{ m/s}$$

The force was the same each time, but with a follow through the impulse was greater, so the final speed was greater.

Why is impulse important in car safety?

11 Climbing ropes are designed to stretch permanently by about 50% when they are put under a sudden load.

a Why is it a good idea to have climbing ropes which stretch?

b What problems would there be if the rope stretched too much ?

When the van hits the wall, the bonnet crumples. This increases the time it takes to stop, and reduces the force felt by the passengers.

Safety belts in cars are designed to stretch when they are put under a sudden load. The stretching increases the time it takes for the passenger to be brought to rest, so although the momentum change is the same, the force the passenger feels (and the chance of serious injury) is smaller.

WORKED EXAMPLE

A passenger of mass 70 kg is in a car travelling at about 14 m/s. The car has a head-on collision that brings it to a stop. Calculate the force the passenger feels if she is brought to a stop in:

a 0.01 s (with a seat belt that does not stretch):

$$F = \frac{mv - mu}{t} = \frac{(70 \times 0) - (70 \times 14)}{0.01}$$

$$= -98\,000 \text{ N}$$

b 0.2 s (with a seat belt that does stretch):

$$F = \frac{mv - mu}{t} = \frac{(70 \times 0) - (70 \times 14)}{0.2}$$

$$= -4900 \text{ N}$$

(Notice that the force felt by the passenger is negative, because it is acting in the opposite direction to the way she was travelling.)

Modern cars are designed with a rigid cage around the cabin, to protect the driver and passengers. Around this cage are areas that are designed to crumple if there is an impact. In a crash, the crumpling of these regions makes the car slow down over a longer time than if the body was rigid. Increasing the stopping time means that the same change of momentum can be brought about with a smaller force. The people in the car feel a smaller impact.

12 The space probe Pioneer 10 had a mass of 258 kg, and small rocket motors that each provided a thrust of 4.5 N. On its approach to Jupiter, it fired one of the motors twice – once for 8 minutes and 7 seconds, and again for 4 minutes and 16 seconds.

a What change of momentum was produced each time the motor fired?

b The thrusts increased Pioneer's speed, but did not change its direction. What was the change in speed each time?

Summary of impulse

- Impulse = change of momentum
  = $Ft = (mv - mu)$.
- In sport, following through when striking a ball increases the impulse, and therefore the final speed of the ball.

- Crumple zones and seat belts increase the time it takes for a car's passengers to come to a stop in a collision. This reduces the force on the passengers.

13.3 Motion and gravity

How do objects move as they fall?

Note

Large masses fall with the same acceleration as small masses.

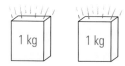

Two identical 1 kg objects fall with the same acceleration.

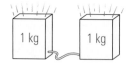

Even if linked with string, they will fall with the same acceleration.

Side by side, they are effectively a single object of twice the mass. But they still fall with the same acceleration.

All objects on Earth are accelerated towards the Earth's centre by the force of gravity. According to Newton's Second Law, the acceleration, a, of a falling object is given by

$$a = \frac{F}{m}$$

where F is the force on the object due to gravity (its weight) and m is its mass. For more massive objects, F is larger. But m is also larger by the same proportion. So the acceleration of a falling object is always the same, whatever its mass. On Earth, the acceleration due to gravity is about 10 m/s^2.

The rule that all objects fall with the same acceleration works well for compact objects that feel little air resistance. But most objects do feel a force due to air resistance, which tends to oppose their motion as they fall. The opposing force increases as the falling object speeds up, and can eventually become as large as the weight of the object. When this happens, there is no net force on the object. The force due to air resistance and the weight cancel each other. Newton's First Law now applies. The object falls at a constant velocity, called its **terminal velocity** (see figure 5).

Larger objects tend to be affected more by air resistance, so they reach their terminal velocity sooner. An object which is strongly affected by air resistance will have a lower terminal velocity than one which is more compact and streamlined.

To reach the others, the higher sky diver should bring in her arms and dive forward so she reduces air resistance on her body, and accelerates until she reaches her new terminal velocity.

Terminal velocity

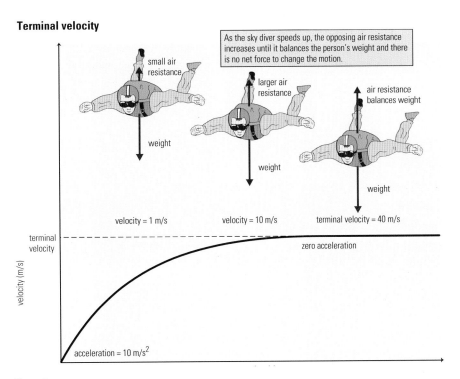

Figure 5

13 Each of the objects below is falling through the air at its terminal velocity. Put the objects in order of velocity, with the fastest one first.

> a hailstone   a snowflake   a feather falling from a bird   a rock falling from a cliff

14 The graph shows the motion of a sky diver as he jumps from a plane and falls for several minutes, before opening the parachute. Describe what is happening at each point on the graph.

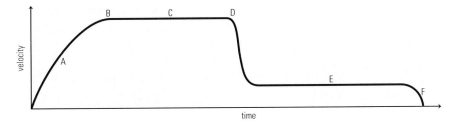

Summary of gravity and motion

- According to Newton's Second Law, if there is no air resistance, all objects fall with the same acceleration regardless of their mass.
- Air resistance depends on the shape of an object, not on its mass.

- When an object falls, air resistance increases with its velocity. When the resistance balances its weight, the object travels at a steady speed called its terminal velocity.

Motion in two dimensions

Learning objectives

By the end of this chapter you should be able to:

- **describe** the path of a projectile as a parabola
- **describe** the circular motion of an object
- **calculate** certain values for an object in circular motion

- **understand** how planets and satellites move in orbits
- **explain** what a geostationary orbit is

What is motion in two dimensions?

The chapters so far have looked at objects moving in straight lines. But usually objects move in a curved path. A dart thrown at a board, a ball kicked into the air, and a satellite orbiting the Earth are all examples of objects moving in curved paths. These objects are moving in two dimensions.

The motion of objects moving in two dimensions is caused by two independent parts: a steady speed in one direction, and a force acting to move the object in a different direction. In some situations, the force acts in the same direction all the time. In others, its direction changes depending on the position of the object. For example, in circular motion an object feels a force towards the centre of the circle, which changes direction as the object moves round.

14.1 Projectiles

What is a projectile?

These photos show projectiles, each moving in a curved path called a parabola.

A **projectile** moves with sideways *and* vertical motion. When an object has sideways as well as vertical motion, remember that the motion in one direction has no effect at all on the motion in the other direction. Suppose an object has a steady sideways velocity. If it accelerates vertically, this will not affect the sideways motion at all. The sideways velocity will stay the same. But the vertical velocity will change.

Imagine someone kicks a stone from the top of an 80 m vertical cliff with a speed of 5 m/s (first making sure that there is nobody beneath!). Figure 1 shows how the stone moves in a curve called a **parabola**. The stone has no sideways acceleration, but it does have a sideways velocity. It has a vertical acceleration due to gravity of -10 m/s^2 (taking downward motion as negative), but it has no initial vertical velocity.

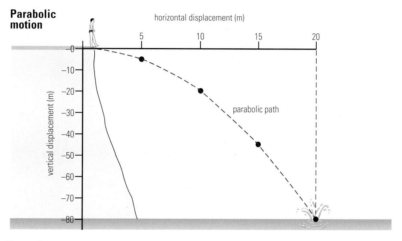

Figure 1

Summary of projectiles

- The motion of a projectile is determined by independent vertical and horizontal components.

- The curved path of a projectile is called a parabola.

14.2 Circular motion

What makes something move in a circle?

Whenever an object moves in a circle, there must be a force pulling the object inwards, towards the centre of the circle. Because it is a 'centre seeking' force, the inward force is called a **centripetal force**. The source of the centripetal force depends on the context. Gravity, friction, the tension in a string or the reaction of a solid surface can all provide a centripetal force to keep an object moving in a circle. If the centripetal force suddenly stops, the object travels in a straight line, and moves away at a tangent to the circle it was following (see figures 2 and 3 on page 98).

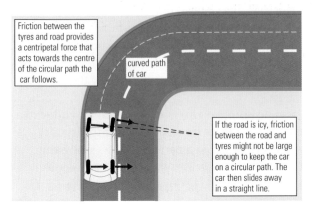

Friction between the tyres and road provides a centripetal force that acts towards the centre of the circular path the car follows.

curved path of car

If the road is icy, friction between the road and tyres might not be large enough to keep the car on a circular path. The car then slides away in a straight line.

Figure 2 The force of friction pulls the car around the bend.

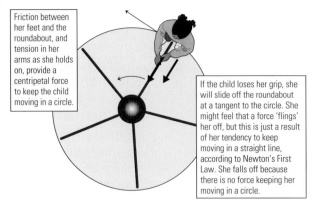

Friction between her feet and the roundabout, and tension in her arms as she holds on, provide a centripetal force to keep the child moving in a circle.

If the child loses her grip, she will slide off the roundabout at a tangent to the circle. She might feel that a force 'flings' her off, but this is just a result of her tendency to keep moving in a straight line, according to Newton's First Law. She falls off because there is no force keeping her moving in a circle.

Figure 3 Friction and muscle tension, keep the child moving in a circle.

In these photos, centripetal forces are provided by the friction between the motorbike tyres and the road, and the tension in the arms and legs of the skaters.

How big does the centripetal force have to be?

The size of the centripetal force, F, needed to keep something moving in a circle depends on the mass of the object, the radius of the circle, r, and the speed at which the object is travelling, v.

$$F = \frac{mv^2}{r}$$

This formula shows that faster objects, and more massive ones, need a larger centripetal force to keep them moving in a circular path than slower and less massive objects, for the same radius of rotation.

The formula also shows that the centripetal force needed to keep an object moving in a circle is smaller if the radius is larger, as long as the velocity and mass stay the same. But, if the time for each rotation (the **period**, T) is the same, an object moving in a large circle moves faster than one moving in a small circle, because it has a longer distance to travel in the same time (see below). So in the formula for centripetal force above, although r is bigger, v is also bigger, and overall F is *not* smaller.

$$\text{speed of object moving in circle} = \frac{\text{distance}}{\text{time}}$$

$$v = \frac{2\pi r}{T}$$

The formula for the speed of an object moving in a circle shows that if the speed, v, is kept constant, the period, T, increases with the radius of rotation. This is important in determining geostationary orbits (see page 100).

According to Newton's Second Law, $F = ma$. But for centripetal force:

$$F = \frac{mv^2}{r}$$

So centripetal acceleration, towards the centre of the circle

$$a = \frac{v^2}{r}$$

1 A child of mass 30 kg spins on a roundabout with a speed of 20 m/s, standing 1.5 m from the centre.
  a What is the value of the centripetal force?
  b If the child feels unsafe, should he move nearer the centre of the roundabout, or further towards the edge?
  c What is the child's acceleration towards the centre of the roundabout?

2 A child swings a conker on a string in a vertical circle. The string breaks when the conker is at the bottom (because the string has to support the weight of the conker, as well as provide the centripetal force).
  a Draw a diagram showing the path the conker will follow once the string has broken.
  b The child tries the trick again with a stronger string. The string breaks at the same position, but at a higher speed. Draw on your diagram, in a different colour, the path that the second conker will follow.

Summary of circular motion

- When an object moves in a circle at a steady speed the direction of motion is constantly changing.
- When an object moves in a circle at a steady speed there must be a force acting towards the centre of the circle, called the centripetal force.
- The size of the centripetal force, F, required to keep an object moving in a circle is given by the formula $F = mv^2/r$.
- The size of the centripetal force needed is greater if the object's mass is greater, when the speed and radius stay the same.

- The size of the centripetal force needed is greater if the speed of the object is greater, when the mass and radius stay the same.
- The size of the centripetal force needed is greater if the radius of the circle is smaller, when speed and mass stay the same.
- If T is the period of rotation, the speed of an object moving in a circle is given by $v = 2\pi r/T$.
- When the period of the rotation stays the same, the speed is greater if the radius is greater.
- The centripetal acceleration of an object moving in a circle is given by $a = v^2/r$.

14.3 Orbits

What keeps planets and satellites in orbit?

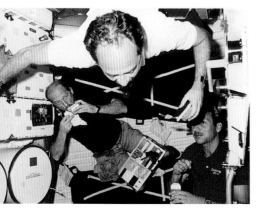

All objects in an orbiting space station can orbit in the same way, regardless of their mass, so they appear to be 'weightless', and float about.

When an object moves in a circular path or **orbit** around another object, there is a gravitational force of attraction, F, between the two objects.

$$F = \frac{GMm}{r^2}$$

M and m are the two masses attracting each other. G is the universal gravitational constant. If M and m are kept the same, you can see that the size of the gravitational force, F, is inversely proportional to the square of the radius, r. That means that F gets smaller as the distance between the two masses increases. This is called an **inverse square law**.

$$F \propto \frac{1}{r^2}$$

For an orbiting object, the gravitational force of attraction *is* the centripetal force keeping it moving in a circle. So:

$$\frac{GMm}{r^2} = \frac{mv^2}{r}$$

Rearranging and cancelling m and r: $v^2 = \dfrac{GM}{r}$

Notice that the mass of the orbiting object, m, does *not* appear in this final formula, and therefore does not affect how the object orbits. So the speed of a satellite orbiting the Earth, for example, will always depend only on the radius of its orbit and not on its mass (since the universal gravitational constant, G, and the mass of the Earth, M, are always the same).

What is a geostationary orbit?

This shows the Russian Mir space station docking with an American Space Shuttle while in orbit in 1995.

If a satellite travels round the Earth at the same rate as the Earth turns on its axis, it will always be above the same point on the Earth's surface. The satellite is then in a **geostationary** orbit. Geostationary satellites are very useful, because transmitting and receiving satellite dishes on Earth can stay pointed in one direction, fixed on the satellite 24 hours a day.

Satellite television and international telephone systems rely on geostationary satellites. Global weather conditions can be monitored continuously using geostationary satellites, and sailors and pilots use them to pinpoint their positions on the Earth's surface to within 50 m.

There are problems with geostationary satellites. For example, the radius for the geostationary orbit around the Earth is very large. A satellite must be taken up to a height of 35 900 000 m before its orbit will be in time with the Earth's spin: that is one tenth of the distance to the Moon. The speed at which the satellite must orbit is also very high, at around 2618 m/s.

3 Why is it that only three geostationary satellites are required to communicate over the whole inhabited surface of the Earth? Use a diagram to help explain your answer.

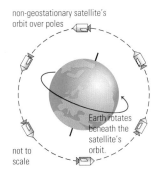

non-geostationary satellite's orbit over poles

Earth rotates beneath the satellite's orbit.

not to scale

Figure 4

All geostationary satellites have to be the same distance above the Earth, travelling at the same speed, and they all have to be above the equator. In fact, only three geostationary satellites are required to provide transmission to every inhabited point on the Earth's surface, but many more are required to handle the vast amounts of information to be communicated.

Each satellite needs some distance between it and the next, so that signals meant for one are not picked up by the other. So there are only a certain number of 'slots' available, and there is already concern that countries who wish to launch geostationary satellites in the future might not be able to do so, because the slots will all be taken up.

Satellites do not have to be geostationary, and there are many that are not. Because the Earth turns beneath them at a different rate, they gradually pass over all points on the Earth's surface along the path of their orbit. Data, such as images of weather systems or land masses, collected by these satellites and transmitted back to the ground station when they next pass overhead. Many non-geostationary satellites take only about 90 minutes to orbit. These are the ones you can see on a clear night, as fast moving dots of light moving from north to south (see figure 4).

Height above ground (km)	Period (mins)	Time above horizon (mins)
600	96.8	12.9
700	98.9	14.1
800	101.0	15.4
900	103.2	16.5
1000	105.3	17.7
1200	109.6	19.9
1400	114.0	22.1
1600	118.4	24.3

4 The table shows some data for non-geostatioary satellites in circular orbits.

   a Describe in words any patterns you see in the data.

   b Use the data to plot two graphs: **i** period against time visible, **ii** time visible against height.

   c One night, you spot a satellite which takes 15 minutes to cross overhead, from one horizon to the other. Use your graphs to work out: **i** how high it is, **ii** what its period is.

   d Suggest some uses the satellite might have.

   e Why is it not sensible to extrapolate your graphs to lower heights and shorter periods than those in the table?

Summary of orbits

- Space craft orbit the Earth because of gravity, not because they have escaped from it.

- Space craft in geostationary orbits are useful for communications, navigation and weather monitoring.

Investigation

The path of a projectile is affected by its speed and the angle at which it is launched. Because of air resistance, its mass, shape and size are important too. At what angle should

a a shuttlecock

b a table tennis ball

be hit for it to travel as far as possible?

Learning objectives

By the end of this chapter you should be able to:

- **describe** what an electron is
- **explain** how an electron affects other charges around it

- **explain** what is meant by static electricity
- **discuss** some effects caused by static electricity
- **describe** some of the hazards of static electricity

15.1 Electric charge

What is electricity?

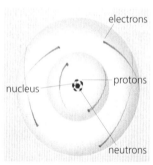

Figure 1

All atoms are made up of three main kinds of particles, called electrons, protons and neutrons. Electrons are the tiniest of these, and have a negative charge. Protons and neutrons have about the same mass, but protons are positively charged, while neutrons have no charge (see figure 1).

In most objects there are as many electrons as protons. So normally an object has no overall charge, because the positive charge on all the protons is matched by the negative charge on the electrons. If there are more electrons than protons the object carries an overall negative charge. If there are fewer electrons than protons, the object carries an overall positive charge.

Every proton and electron produces an **electric field**. So around any object in which the charges are not balanced, there is an electric field. When a charged particle moves into the field, it feels a force towards or away from the other particle (see figure 2). The strength of the force depends on:
- how close the particles are: the closer they are, the larger the force
- how much electrical charge they carry: the more charge, the larger the force

Because the static charge on each hair is similar, the hairs repel each other and stick up in all directions.

Like charges repel each other.

Unlike charges attract each other.

Figure 2 Field lines show the shape of an electric field.

When an unbalanced charge collects on the surface of an object, the charge is called **static electricity**. ('Static' means 'not moving'.) When electrons move, or flow, from one place to another, they produce an **electric current**.

How does static electricity come about?

Contraptions like this Wimshurst Machine were used to produce and store electric charge, in the 18th century.

When you charge an object with static electricity, you are giving or taking away negatively charged electrons, so that the charge on the object overall is unbalanced. For example, when you rub a glass or acetate rod with a cloth, electrons from the rod get rubbed onto the cloth (see figure 3). So the cloth becomes negatively charged overall, and the rod is left with an overall positive charge. When you rub a polythene rod with a cloth, electrons from the cloth get transferred to the rod, so the polythene carries a negative charge overall, and the cloth carries a positive charge.

If you suspended charged polythene and acetate rods so they could move freely, and brought the two close together, they would attract each other, since unlike charges attract (see figure 2). Both the polythene and the acetate rod would attract small bits of paper or dust, because they give each bit an opposite charge by **induction** (see figure 3).

Materials like glass, acetate and polythene can only become charged with static electricity because they are **insulators**. Electrons do not move easily through insulating materials, so when extra electrons are added, they stay on the surface instead of flowing away, and the surface stays negatively charged. Similarly, if electrons are removed, electrons from other parts of the material do not flow in to replace them, so the surface stays positively charged. A material through which electrons flow easily is called a **conductor**. Conductors, such as metals, cannot be charged with static electricity by rubbing.

How can you measure static electricity?

You can show how much charge is on an object, and whether it is positive or negative, using a **gold leaf electroscope** (see figures 3 and 4).

Figure 3

Charging an electroscope by induction

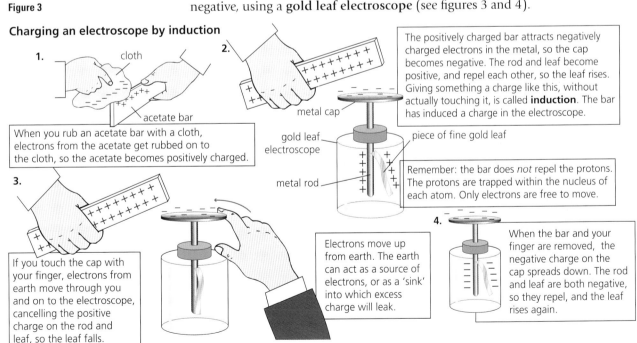

1. cloth / acetate bar

When you rub an acetate bar with a cloth, electrons from the acetate get rubbed on to the cloth, so the acetate becomes positively charged.

2. metal cap

The positively charged bar attracts negatively charged electrons in the metal, so the cap becomes negative. The rod and leaf become positive, and repel each other, so the leaf rises. Giving something a charge like this, without actually touching it, is called **induction**. The bar has induced a charge in the electroscope.

gold leaf electroscope / piece of fine gold leaf / metal rod

Remember: the bar does *not* repel the protons. The protons are trapped within the nucleus of each atom. Only electrons are free to move.

3.

If you touch the cap with your finger, electrons from earth move through you and on to the electroscope, cancelling the positive charge on the rod and leaf, so the leaf falls.

Electrons move up from earth. The earth can act as a source of electrons, or as a 'sink' into which excess charge will leak.

4.

When the bar and your finger are removed, the negative charge on the cap spreads down. The rod and leaf are both negative, so they repel, and the leaf rises again.

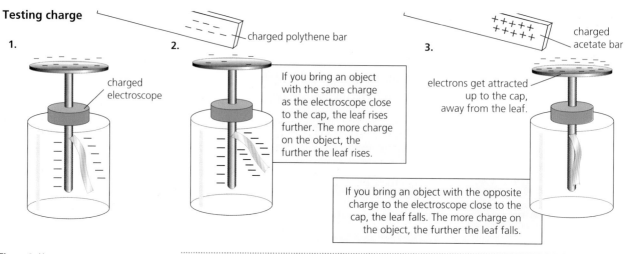

Testing charge

1.

charged electroscope

2.

charged polythene bar

If you bring an object with the same charge as the electroscope close to the cap, the leaf rises further. The more charge on the object, the further the leaf rises.

3.

charged acetate bar

electrons get attracted up to the cap, away from the leaf.

If you bring an object with the opposite charge to the electroscope close to the cap, the leaf falls. The more charge on the object, the further the leaf falls.

Figure 4 You can use an electroscope to test if an object is positively or negatively charged.

1 You could say that 'charging' an object is like 'putting something into it'. Why is this *not* a good description when an object is given a positive charge?

2 When you bring a freely suspended charged acetate strip close to a charged perspex strip, you find they push away from each other.

a What sort of charge do you suspect the perspex has?

b What do you suspect would happen if you brought the charged perspex strip close to a charged polythene strip? Explain your answer.

c If you found that the perspex repelled *both* the acetate *and* the polythene, what might you conclude?

Does static charge stay put for ever?

The photo on page 102 shows a Van der Graaf generator, with a wig on top to show you that it is charged. The surface of the sphere holds a positive charge, so if an object connected to earth touches it, electrons from earth flow in and cancel the charge on the sphere. This is called **discharging**. If the charge on the sphere is large enough, it can attract electrons from a nearby object without actually touching it. The electrons move suddenly through the air as a spark. Whenever static electricity builds up there is a chance it might cause a spark, which is why static can be so dangerous.

Because opposite charges attract, any stray charges in the air are attracted towards the charged sphere slowly discharging the generator. This 'leaking' discharge happens more quickly if the air is damp.

Summary of electric charge

- There are two types of electrical charge, called positive and negative charge.
- Identical charges repel each other. Opposite charges attract each other.
- Usually, only the negatively charged particles move. These are called electrons.

- An excess of electrons makes an object negatively charged overall. A lack of electrons makes it positively charged.
- Insulating materials can be made to lose or gain electrons by rubbing them with suitable materials.
- Earth acts as a source or a sink for excess charge.

15.2 Static effects

What use is static electricity?

- **Scrubbing air**. Smoke from coal-burning power stations and factories contains particles of ash, which are electrically charged. If the smoke is passed between two electrically charged plates, the ash particles are attracted to one or other of the plates. The gases that pass out into the atmosphere are much cleaner, and cause less pollution.
- **Photocopiers**. Static electricity is used to produce copies of images in photocopiers, and in ink-jet and bubble-jet computer printers.
- **Paint spraying**. The object to be painted is given an electric charge. As the paint droplets leave the spray gun, they gain an opposite charge, so they are attracted to the object.

Can static electricity be destructive?

Connecting an object to earth prevents static building up by providing electrons to cancel the charge, or by letting electrons leak away slowly.

- **Flour mills.** In a flour mill, the air can become filled with tiny flour particles. As the particles move past each other in air currents, they become charged with static electricity. Small sparks can occur which could ignite the fine flour, and cause explosions. Because of this danger, there are strict safety regulations for factories dealing with fine powders, to prevent air currents.
- **Petrol pipes.** When a tanker unloads fuel, friction causes the fuel to gain an opposite charge to the pipes (and to the tanker). If this build up of charge caused a spark it could be disastrous, so an earth wire is connected to the tanker before unloading.
- **Lightning.** The movement of water droplets by air currents in clouds can cause a large build up of charge. Opposite charges build up at the bottom and at the top of tall storm clouds. When the cloud suddenly discharges, the rapid flow of charge causes a huge spark called lightning. To avoid damage by lightning, most tall buildings have lightning conductors.

---

3 A moving car gains an electric charge as the tyres rub on the ground. As you get out, you often feel an electric shock. In what sort of weather are you most likely to feel a shock? Why?

4 On very long journeys, aircraft sometimes refuel in the air, from another aircraft. An electrical connection is always made between the two aircraft. Explain why this is important.

Lightning conductors help to discharge thunder clouds gently before lightning can strike. When lightning does strike, conductors guide the charge directly to earth through a thick metal wire.

Summary of electric effects

- Static electricity can be useful in 'scrubbing' waste gases from factories, in photocopiers and computer printers, and in spray painting.

- A build-up of electrical charge can be dangerous, because there is a risk of sudden discharge in a spark, which could cause a fire or explosion.

Learning objectives

By the end of this chapter you should be able to:

- **describe** what is meant by electric current
- **recognise** how small the particles are which make up an electric current
- **measure** current and potential difference

- **calculate** unknown values in a circuit, using known values of current and potential difference
- **apply** ideas about current and potential difference to a wide range of situations

16.1 Moving charge

What is an electric current?

Electricity is made up of electrical charge. Static electricity is a build-up of charge that stays in one place, until the object is discharged. Current electricity is a flow of tiny charged particles in a conductor. In most conductors, the particles are electrons.

All materials contain electrons, but in many materials they are all 'locked' into the material's atoms and cannot move about. These materials cannot carry an electric current, and are called electrical **insulators**. Materials in which there are large numbers of electrons that are free to move around from atom to atom are called **conductors**.

When there is no current in a conductor, the free electrons move randomly between atoms, with no overall movement. When you connect it in an electrical circuit with a power source like a battery, there is a current in the conductor. Now the electrons drift in one direction, while still moving in a random way as well (see figure 1). The **drift speed** is very slow – often only a few millimetres each second. A current can only flow in a conductor if it is connected in a complete circuit. If the circuit is broken, the current stops.

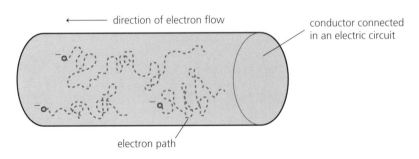

← —— direction of electron flow

conductor connected in an electric circuit

Figure 1 Electrons in a conductor move randomly from atom to atom, but when there is a current they drift in one direction as well.

electron path

Electrons are very tiny indeed. About 1 100 000 000 000 000 000 000 000 000 000 (1.1×10^{30}) electrons would have a mass of 1 kg. You would need to place 3 550 000 000 000 000 (3.55×10^{15}) electrons side by side to cover a metre. (The same number of frozen peas would cover 20 000 000 000 km – 500 000 times around the Earth!)

Each electron carries a tiny electrical charge, measured in units called **coulombs** (C). About 6 250 000 000 000 000 000 (6.25×10^{18}) electrons together give a charge of just 1 coulomb.

How is current measured?

Note

When measuring current, using the total charge as a measure of the number of electrons is similar to using volume as a measure of the number of water molecules. It is easier to measure the volume the molecules take up (in cm^3 or m^3) rather than the actual number of water molecules.

The size of an electric current depends on the number of electrons that are moving and how fast they are moving. But instead of measuring the actual number of electrons we use the total charge carried by the electrons round the circuit each second.

Electric current is measured in **amperes**, or amps (A). One amp is the number of coulombs of charge that flow past a point in a circuit in one second (1 A = 1 C/s).

$$\text{current} = \frac{\text{amount of charge passing}}{\text{time taken}}$$

$$I = \frac{Q}{t} \quad \text{or} \quad Q = I \times t \quad \text{or} \quad t = \frac{Q}{I}$$

where I = current (A), Q = charge (C) and t = time (s).

You use an **ammeter** to measure current in an electrical circuit. If the current is very small, you might use a milliammeter, which measures current in milliamps (1 mA = 0.001 A). Even smaller currents are measured with a microammeter (1 μA = 0.000 001 A).

What happens to current in a circuit?

Figure 2

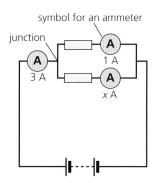

symbol for an ammeter

junction

The unknown current here is 2 A, flowing away from the junction.

In a circuit, no electric current ever gets lost or disappears. Current is always conserved. This means that the total current which arrives at a junction in a circuit must be the same as the total current leaving it. This is a useful rule for predicting the size of unknown currents, and in which direction they are flowing. When a current flows into a junction, it is given a positive sign in these calculations. When a current flows out of a junction, it is given a negative sign (see figure 2). This rule is known as Kirchhoff's First Law.

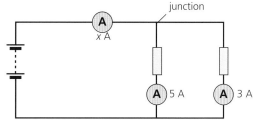

junction

The unknown current here is 8 A, flowing towards the junction.

How does current flow?

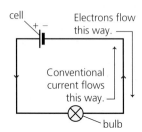

Figure 3

People investigated electricity long before anyone had even thought about electrons, and they had to make a decision about which way an electric current flows. It was decided that current must flow out of the 'positive' terminal of a cell, and into the 'negative' terminal. This is called **conventional current** direction. Unfortunately, it was discovered much later that the electrons actually flow the opposite way, from the negative terminal to the positive terminal, because they carry a negative charge (see figure 3). When you read about current, always assume that it means conventional current unless it specifically tells you to think about the electron flow.

1 The current in a torch bulb is 0.1 A.
   a How many coulombs of charge flow through the bulb each second?
   b How long will it take for one coulomb to pass through the bulb?
   c How many coulombs will pass through the bulb in one hour?
2 Work out the missing ammeter readings in the circuits shown on the left.

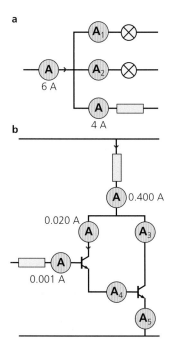

When some conductors, such as some solutions or molten materials, are connected in a circuit it is a flow of charged particles called **ions** that makes up the electric current rather than electrons.

An ion is an atom or molecule that has an unbalanced amount of positive and negative charge. If the ion has more electrons than protons, it is called a negative ion. If it has fewer electrons than protons, it is a positive ion.

When some substances are dissolved or melted, they split into positive and negative ions. If you put the solution or liquid into an electrical circuit, the positive ions move towards the **cathode**, while the negative ions move towards the **anode** (see figure 4), so a current flows. Passing a current through a liquid in this way is called **electrolysis**. The process can be used to separate the elements in a compound, as shown in figure 4.

Electrolysis

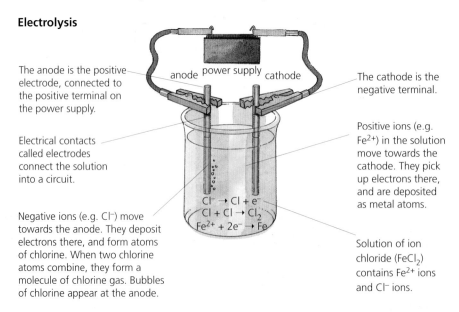

The anode is the positive electrode, connected to the positive terminal on the power supply.

Electrical contacts called electrodes connect the solution into a circuit.

The cathode is the negative terminal.

Positive ions (e.g. Fe^{2+}) in the solution move towards the cathode. They pick up electrons there, and are deposited as metal atoms.

Negative ions (e.g. Cl^-) move towards the anode. They deposit electrons there, and form atoms of chlorine. When two chlorine atoms combine, they form a molecule of chlorine gas. Bubbles of chlorine appear at the anode.

$$Cl^- \rightarrow Cl + e^-$$
$$Cl + Cl \rightarrow Cl_2$$
$$Fe^{2+} + 2e^- \rightarrow Fe$$

Solution of ion chloride ($FeCl_2$) contains Fe^{2+} ions and Cl^- ions.

Figure 4 Current is a flow of charge. It does not matter if it is positive or negative charge. So positive ions moving through a solution can carry a current.

Once all the ions in the liquid have moved to the electrodes, the current eventually stops. However, if one of the electrodes dissolves into the liquid, ions from that electrode can replace those arriving at the other electrode. This means the current can continue to flow for as long as the electrode lasts. So if the anode is made of a metal, ions from it go into the solution, move through the liquid, and become deposited on the cathode as metal atoms. A layer of the metal builds up on the cathode. This principle is used to **electroplate** objects with a layer of another metal, such as chromium or silver. The object to be plated acts as the cathode, and the source of the metal coating acts as the anode (see figure 5). The thickness of the metal coating is controlled by how long the current flows in the liquid, and how large the current is.

There are many other uses of electrolysis including the separation of water into oxygen and hydrogen, the extraction of aluminium from its ore, and the extraction of chlorine from sea water.

Electroplating

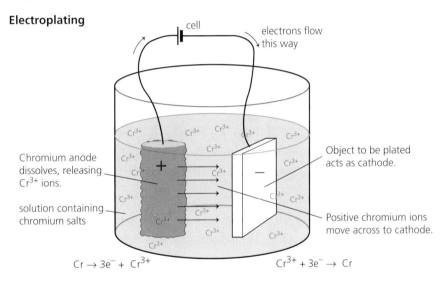

Figure 5 The object to be electroplated is used as the cathode, to which ions from the anode are attracted.

$$Cr \rightarrow 3e^- + Cr^{3+}$$

$$Cr^{3+} + 3e^- \rightarrow Cr$$

Electroplating has been used to coat these bumpers with a thin, even layer of chromium metal.

3 Some copper sulphate solution was electrolysed using copper electrodes.

Time (mins)	Mass of anode (g)	Mass of cathode (g)	Charge passed between electrodes (C)
0	20.00	10.01	0
10	19.91	10.10	10 000
20	19.81	10.18	20 000
30	19.69	10.29	30 000
40	19.60	10.41	40 000

a i Why did the cathode gain weight? **ii** Where did this extra weight come from?
iii Are copper ions positive or negative? (Hint: remember that opposites attract.)
b What is the link between the amount of copper deposited and the number of coulombs that pass?
c Estimate the masses of the electrodes after 50 minutes.
d Explain why the solution cannot keep carrying a current indefinitely.

Summary of moving charge

- An electric current is a flow of particles, usually electrons, each carrying a tiny electric charge.
- For an electric current to flow you need a complete circuit.
- Charge is measured in units called coulombs (C).
- Electrons flow in a circuit from the negative terminal towards the positive terminal on a cell. Conventional current flows from the positive to the negative terminal of a cell.

- Current is always conserved.
- Electric current is measured in amperes (A) where 1 A = 1 C/s. Current = charge/time, or $I = Q/t$.
- Current is measured using an ammeter.
- During electrolysis, a current is passed through a liquid containing positive and negative ions. The ions are attracted towards the electrode with the opposite charge, which causes the liquid to be split up.

16.2 Potential difference

What makes a current flow?

Measuring PD

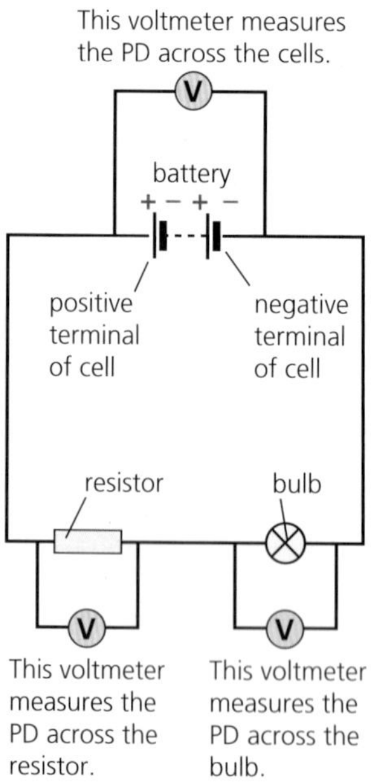

This voltmeter measures the PD across the cells.

battery
+ – + –

positive terminal of cell

negative terminal of cell

resistor

bulb

This voltmeter measures the PD across the resistor.

This voltmeter measures the PD across the bulb.

Figure 6

To make electrons flow, you need to give them energy, from a source such as a cell. As the current flows round the circuit, the electrons' energy is transferred to other forms, such as light, sound or heat, in components such as bulbs, buzzers or resistors.

To work out how much energy has been given to the electrons by the cell, you need to compare the amount of energy they have before the cell, with the amount of energy they have after it in the circuit. (Similarly, to work out how much energy has been transferred into other forms in a component, you need to compare the amount of energy the electrons have before and after the component in the circuit.) The difference between the two amounts of energy is a measure of the 'push' the electrons are given by the cell to move around the circuit. Because electrical energy is a form of potential energy, the difference is called **potential difference (PD)**. It is potential difference that makes a current flow through the wires and components in a circuit.

$$\text{potential difference} = \frac{\text{energy}}{\text{charge}} \qquad V = \frac{E}{Q}$$

If energy is measured in joules, and charge is measured in coulombs, then potential difference is measured in volts (V). One volt is a difference of one joule of energy per coulomb of charge (1 V = 1 J/C). So if there is a PD of 1 V cross a cell, it means the cell gives 1 J of extra energy to the electrons in each coulomb of charge passing through. If there is a PD of 1 V across a bulb in a circuit, it means each coulomb of charge passing through it loses 1 J of energy, which is transferred into light and heat.

To measure the PD across a component, you use a **voltmeter**. You need to compare the energy at two places in a circuit, so the voltmeter must be connected in two positions, in parallel with the component (see figure 6).

4 A cell has a PD of 1.5 V across it. How much electrical energy does the cells provide to
  a 1 coulomb of charge
  b 5 coulombs of charge?
5 A rechargeable battery is labelled '9 V 100 mAh'.
  a Explain what is meant by '9 V'.
  b What do you think '110 mAh' means ? (Hint: look at section 16.1.)
  c Use your answers to **a** and **b** to calculate the total energy stored in the cell.

Potential difference is very different from current. Current is the number of coulombs of charge that flow each second. Potential difference is the amount of energy each of those coulombs gets from a cell to make it flow. If you think of coulombs of charge as buckets, the current is the number of buckets going round the circuit each second. The potential difference is the amount of energy that goes into each bucket.

It is possible to have a large current and small PD (there are lots of buckets going round, but they are all almost empty). It is also possible to have a small current and a large PD (there are only a few buckets, but they are all full).

Water flows from high places, where is has lots of potential energy, to lower places where it has less potential energy. As it flows, its potential energy is transferred to other forms, like kinetic energy. In the same way, electrical charge flows from places of high potential to places of lower potential. On the way, its energy is transferred to other forms.

If you think of coulombs of charge as drops of water, a large PD and small current is like rain drops falling in a light shower. Each drop has lots of potential energy as it falls from the cloud, but the number of drops falling each second is quite small. A small PD and large current is like running a tap. The water drops do not have so much potential energy, because they do not fall from such a height, but lots of drops flow each second.

What happens to energy in a circuit?

Energy is never lost or destroyed. It is always conserved. If you apply this rule to an electrical circuit, you can work out the potential difference across a component, by using voltmeter readings from other components (see figure 7).

Figure 7

Series circuit $V_3 = V_1 + V_2$
$= 1.5 + 3.0 = 4.5$ V

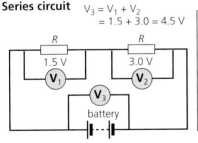

The reading on V_3 is the sum of the readings on V_1 and V_2, because all the extra energy put into the circuit by the battery is transferred to heat in the resistors.

Parallel circuit

$V_3 = V_2 = V_1$
So $V_1 = 4.5$ V and $V_2 = 4.5$ V

All three voltmeters show the same reading because the ends of each component are connected, so the PD across each one is the same.

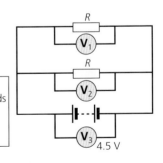

6 Work out the missing voltmeter readings in the following diagrams.

a

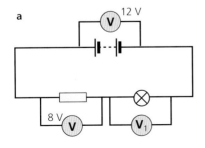

b

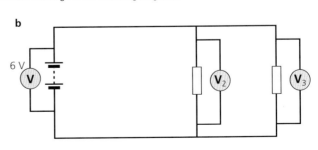

How do you give electrons energy to move?

When light shines on a photoelectric cell, it produces an EMF which powers this car park machine. The EMF depends on the wavelength (colour). The current depends on the intensity .

When electrons are given energy to move around a circuit, they feel a push called an **electromotive force (EMF)**. The size of an EMF depends on how many joules of energy are given to each coulomb of charge. If a coulomb of charge gains one joule of energy, the EMF is 1 V. EMFs can be generated in many ways, by transferring energy from almost any other form, such as chemical potential energy, heat, light, sound, kinetic energy, and even magnetic energy (see chapter 20, *Magnets and electromagnetism*).

The first device to reliably produce an EMF, and therefore an electric current, was invented in 1799 by Alessandro Volta, an Italian Count. He found that if he placed paper soaked in salt solution between two thin discs of zinc and silver, he could produce a small electric current (see figure 8). Volta's arrangement became known as an **electrochemical cell**, but it could not produce a very large EMF. Connecting several cells together in a pile increased the effect, and this became known as a **battery**.

The cell works because the two different metals react with the salt in the soaked paper at different rates. If the cell is connected in an electric circuit, electrons come out of the cell from the end where the metal is corroding. This end is called the negative terminal of the cell. The other end, which receives the electrons as they move round the circuit, is the positive terminal. The most reactive metal reacts quickly and corrodes, leaving the other metal intact. Different combinations of metals give different amounts of energy to the electrons, and so produce different EMFs. The cell stops working when the more reactive metal is eaten away, or the salt solution dries up.

The cells we use today are based on Volta's original idea. Most produce an EMF of 1.5 V. Figure 6 shows the circuit symbol for a battery: the dotted line indicates that there are two or more cells connected together.

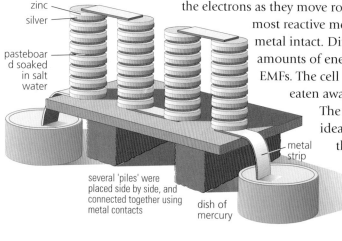

zinc
silver

pasteboard soaked in salt water

several 'piles' were placed side by side, and connected together using metal contacts

metal strip

dish of mercury

Figure 8 Volta's first electric cell was made from piles of metal discs, separated by paper soaked in salt solution.

Summary of potential difference

- Energy is transferred to other forms as an electric current flows round a circuit.

- The amount of energy transferred as charge passes through a component is measured in volts (V), or joules per coulomb, and is called the potential difference across that component. PD = energy/charge = E/Q.

- To measure PD, a voltmeter must be connected in parallel with the component being investigated.

- The PD across components connected in parallel is the same for each one.

- The sum of the PDs across components connected in series is equal to the PD across all the components. This is true because energy is always conserved.

- To produce a current in a circuit, there must be a source of energy to produce an electromotive force, or EMF.

- An EMF can be produced using other sources of energy such as magnetism, heat, light, sound, motion or chemical potential energy.

Resistance

Learning objectives

By the end of this chapter you should be able to:

- **describe** how resistance is measured
- **calculate** unknown values using known values of resistance, PD and current
- **apply** ideas about resistance to a wide range of situations
- **describe** how resistance varies for certain components
- **appreciate** and predict the effects of factors that affect the resistance of materials

17.1 Resisting the flow

What does the size of an electric current depend on?

There can only be an electric current in a component or wire if there is a potential difference across it. The larger the PD, the larger the current will be. In a similar way, when water flows through a pipe, the larger the pressure difference between its ends, the more water flows through each second.

However, the size of the PD is not the only factor that affects the size of a current. In any circuit, there is always a **resistance**, which restricts the current. Circuits that only allow a small current for a given PD have a high resistance. Circuits with a low resistance allow current to flow easily.

You can work out the resistance of a component using this formula:

$$R = \frac{V}{I} \quad \text{or} \quad V = IR \quad \text{or} \quad I = \frac{V}{R}$$

If the current, I, is measured in amps (A), and the potential difference, V, is in volts (V), the resistance, R, has units called **ohms** (Ω).

A conductor with a large resistance transfers more of the electrical energy it carries into heat than one with a small resistance. So in an electric fire, you need an element with a high resistance, to give out heat. To reduce energy wastage in power cables, you need wires with low resistance.

1 Copy the table below, and calculate the missing values for each device, using the formula $V = IR$.

Device	V (V)	I (A)	R (Ω)
i Car window heater	12	0.5	?
ii Torch bulb	?	0.2	12.5
iii Toaster	240	?	96.0

Is a component's resistance always the same?

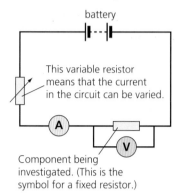

battery

This variable resistor means that the current in the circuit can be varied.

A

V

Component being investigated. (This is the symbol for a fixed resistor.)

For some components, the resistance is the same value for a wide range of PDs. i.e. *V/I* gives the same value whatever the value of *V*. This rule was noted by Georg Ohm in 1827, and is called Ohm's Law. If a component obeys Ohm's Law, it is an ohmic conductor, and has a fixed resistance.

To test if a component is ohmic, you need to collect data for a range of PDs, and to plot a graph of PD against current (see figure 1). If the graph is a straight line, the conductor is ohmic. If the graph shows a curve, the conductor is not ohmic (see figure 2).

Figure 1 This circuit can be used to see if a conductor obeys Ohm's Law.

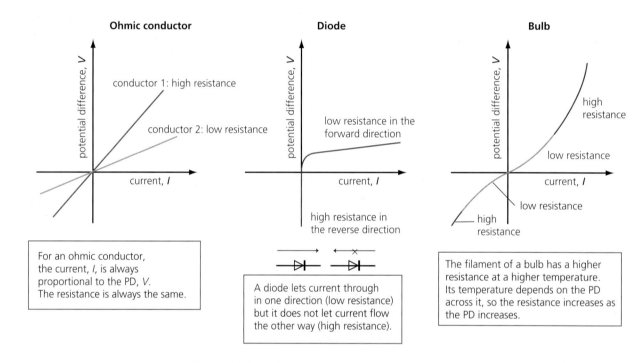

Ohmic conductor

conductor 1: high resistance

conductor 2: low resistance

For an ohmic conductor, the current, *I*, is always proportional to the PD, *V*. The resistance is always the same.

Diode

low resistance in the forward direction

high resistance in the reverse direction

A diode lets current through in one direction (low resistance) but it does not let current flow the other way (high resistance).

Bulb

high resistance

low resistance

low resistance

high resistance

The filament of a bulb has a higher resistance at a higher temperature. Its temperature depends on the PD across it, so the resistance increases as the PD increases.

Figure 2 Diodes and bulbs are not ohmic conductors. Their resistances vary with the PD.

2 a Plot the data for each component in the table on a single pair of axes.

b Which components are ohmic conductors (if any)? How did you decide?

c Suggest what sort of component produced each set of data.

Potential difference (V)	6.0	4.0	2.0	1.0	0	−1.0	−2.0	−4.0	−6.0
Current (mA)									
component A	1060	658	263	62	0	0.0	0.0	0.0	0.0
component B	12.1	7.9	4.2	1.8	0	−1.9	−3.8	−8.2	−11.9
component C	898	599	404	206	0	−198	−389	−605	−902

Summary of resisting the flow

- Resistance is the ratio of the potential difference across a component and the current in it: $R = V/I$. This is sometimes written as $V = IR$ or $I = V/R$.
- For some components the resistance is constant for all values of V. These components obey Ohm's law, and are called ohmic conductors.

- Resistance is measured in units called ohms (Ω).
- The resistance of a bulb increases as it becomes warmer. It does not have a fixed resistance.
- A diode only allows current in one direction. It has a low resistance in the forward direction, but a very high resistance in the reverse direction.

17.2 **Factors affecting resistance**

Almost every material resists the flow of electrical current to some extent. The only exceptions are superconductors, and even they have only been able to carry current without resistance over very short distances (about 0.01 mm) and at very low temperatures. The factors that affect resistance are:
- the conductor's size and shape
- the type of material used
- the temperature

How do size and shape affect resistance?

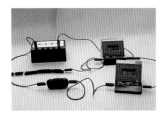

These resistors contain the same volume of putty. But the short, fat resistor has a lower resistance than the long, thin conductor.

Electrical resistance happens because atoms in materials vibrate, and interfere with the movement of the electrons. Imagine trying to walk between two lines of people who are close together, when they are all jumping about. The longer the lines of people are, the harder it is. But the more lines of people there are, the more gaps there are, and the better chance you have of squeezing through.

It is similar for electrons in electrical conductors. The longer a conductor is, the more difficult it is for electrons to get all the way along, so the more resistance it has. Doubling the length of the conductor doubles the resistance. The greater the cross-sectional area of the conductor, the easier it is for electrons to move along, so the lower the resistance. Doubling the cross-sectional area halves the resistance. These relationships are expressed more precisely as follows. The resistance of a conductor is:
- directly proportional to its length.
- inversely proportional to its cross-sectional area.

3 The thickness of nichrome wire used in heating elements is often indicated by a 'standard wire gauge' or SWG number.

Thickness of wire (SWG)	22	24	26	28
Resistance of 1 m of wire (Ω)	2.7	4.4	6.6	9.6
Diameter (mm)	0.711	0.559	0.457	0.376

a What happens to the resistance of the wire as the diameter increases? Explain why this happens.

b Suggest two ways of making a resistor of 13.2 Ω if you had a whole spool of each wire listed.

c Suggest ways of making a resistor of 2.2 Ω, **i** without using SWG 24 wire, **ii** using SWG 24 wire.

How do different materials affect resistance?

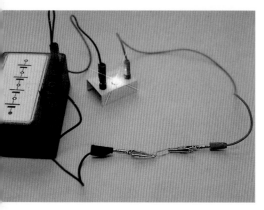

This simple circuit can be used to test whether a material is a conductor.

Different materials have different resistances. Materials can be placed in one of three main groups, depending on how well they conduct electricity.
- Conductors (e.g. all metals) allow electric current to flow easily.
- Insulators (e.g. plastics) block the flow of electric current.
- Semiconductors (e.g. silicon or germanium) are roughly half way between these two extremes.

In metals, each atom has at least one free electron, which can move around the material and make up an electric current. All metals are excellent conductors. In insulators, all the electrons are held inside the atoms or are used to bond the atoms together. There are none left over to make an electric current. Only if the material gets very hot are any electrons released.

Carbon is unusual. Because carbon atoms can bond together in several ways, it can sometimes be a conductor (as graphite) and sometimes be an insulator (as diamond). Water is a very good insulator, provided there are no ions in it (de-ionised water). If a few ions are introduced, by adding a small amount of acid for example, then water conducts well.

How does temperature affect resistance?

A light bulb filament has a high resistance so that much of the electrical energy passing through it is transferred to heat, and it glows white.

When a conductor is warmed, the atoms in it vibrate more rapidly, and interfere with the movement of electrons more than when the conductor is cold. For conductors, the higher the temperature, the higher the resistance.

....

4 A light bulb filament must be short to fit inside the glass, but it must also have a high resistance so it gets hot enough to glow. Think of two ways in which this is achieved.

....

In semiconductors at room temperature, there are a relatively small number of electrons that are free to move, but a small rise in temperature releases more, and so they become better conductors. This effect is useful in **thermistors**. The higher the temperature, the lower the resistance of the thermistor (see figure 3).

In insulators, too, some electrons can be released as the material gets hot, so the resistance reduces as the temperature rises.

free electron   atom

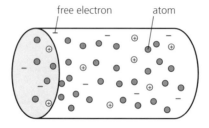

semiconductor material at low temperature

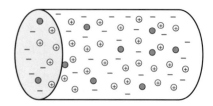

semiconductor material at high temperature

Figure 3

Does anything else affect resistance?

The electrical resistance of some materials depends on the brightness of the light falling on it. For example, the resistance of a piece of cadmium sulphide can be a few million ohms in the dark. In bright sunlight, the resistance drops to just a few thousand ohms. Cadmium sulphide can be used to make a **light-dependent resistor (LDR)**. Figure 4 shows how the resistance of an LDR varies with light intensity.

Light-dependent resistor

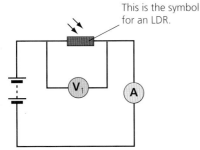

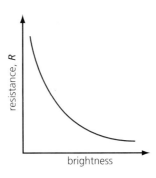

Figure 4

5　a　Which line on the graph below shows the measurements made at a higher temperature?

　　b　Sketch a graph to show how the resistance of the thermistor changes with increasing temperature.

　　c　Explain why the resistance changes with temperature, in terms of free electrons.

Thermistor

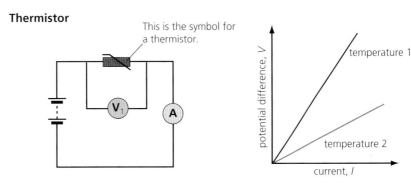

Summary of factors affecting resistance

- The longer a resistor is, the higher is its resistance.
- The greater the cross-sectional area of a resistor, the lower is its resistance.
- Different materials have different resistances.
- For semiconductor materials, resistance decreases significantly at higher temperatures. Such materials can be used to make thermistors.

- For conductors, resistance increases slightly at higher temperatures.
- For insulators, resistance decreases slightly at higher temperatures.
- For some materials, resistance decreases as the light intensity increases. Such materials can be used to make light-dependent resistors (LDRs).

Circuits *and* power 18

Learning objectives

By the end of this chapter you should be able to:

- **draw** series and parallel circuits
- **calculate** the overall effect of several cells connected in series or in parallel
- **calculate** the overall resistance of several resistors connected in series or in parallel
- **calculate** the output from a potential divider
- **understand** what is meant by electrical power
- **calculate** power using values for current and potential difference
- **apply** these ideas to a variety of problems

18.1 Series and parallel circuits

What's the difference between cells in series and in parallel?

cells in series

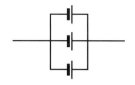

cells in parallel

Figure 1 Cells can be connected in series or in parallel.

If several cells are connected side by side in a circuit, they are **in parallel**. If they are connected end to end they are **in series** (see figure 1).

When cells are connected in parallel, they can drive a larger current around the circuit than one cell can on its own. But the potential difference across all the cells together is the *same* as across each cell on its own (assuming all the cells are pointing the same way).

When cells are connected in series, there is a larger potential difference across all the cells together than across one cell on its own (assuming they all point the same way). But the maximum current they can drive is the same as the current with one cell on its own.

....

1 Look at these diagrams. Are the cells in series or parallel? How can you tell?

a   b

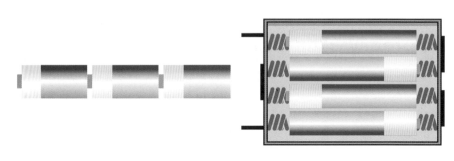

....

Does it make a difference if bulbs are in series or in parallel?

The more bulbs you connect in series, the dimmer each bulb will be. But, if they are all the same sort of bulb, the energy is shared equally between them and they will all be equally bright. The first bulb does *not* 'use up' all the energy, leaving the others less bright. In a series circuit, the current is always the same all the way round.

When you connect bulbs in parallel, each bulb will be *almost* as bright as one bulb on its own. The cell provides a larger current, which divides at junctions in the circuit to supply each bulb with almost as much current as if it were on its own in the circuit.

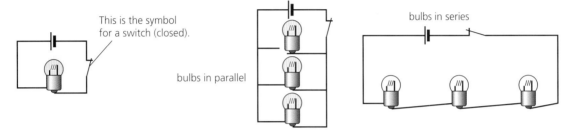

This is the symbol for a switch (closed).

bulbs in parallel

bulbs in series

Figure 2 The bulbs are brighter when connected in parallel.

If you add a large number of bulbs in parallel, eventually the bulbs will not shine as brightly as a single bulb. Whenever a current flows through a cell, some energy is wasted inside the cell as heat. The more current that flows, the more energy is wasted. As you go on adding more and more bulbs in parallel, the cell drives a larger and larger current, which means more and more energy is wasted. So the bulbs become dimmer as you add more.

A good way to test whether bulbs are connected in series or parallel is to remove one bulb. If they all go off, they are in series. If the others stay on (and perhaps go slightly brighter) they are in parallel.

These photos show lights connected in series or in parallel.

2 A single bulb connected to a cell shines with 'normal' brightness. Draw diagrams to show the circuits described below, and describe how brightly each bulb would shine.

  a one cell with two bulbs in series
  b one cell with two bulb in parallel
  c two cells in series with on bulb
  d two cells and two bulb all in parallel

3 Are the bulbs in each photo above connected in series or parallel? How do you know?

Does it make a difference if resistors are in series or in parallel?

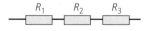

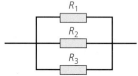

resistors in parallel

Figure 3

When resistors are connected in series, as in figure 3, the total resistance is equal to the sum of the individual resistances. So the total resistance is always larger than the largest individual resistance.

$$R_{TOTAL} = R_1 + R_2 + R_3$$

When resistors are connected in parallel, the total resistance is always smaller than the smallest individual resistance.

$$\frac{1}{R_{TOTAL}} = \frac{1}{R_1} + \frac{1}{R_2} + \frac{1}{R_3}$$

4 Calculate the total resistance in these circuits.

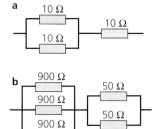

WORKED EXAMPLE

To work out the total resistance of a complicated circuit like the one below, deal with each section on its own, and gradually simplify the circuit.

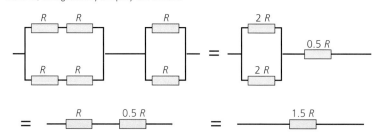

What is a potential divider?

If two resistors are connected in series, the potential difference across the second one depends on the value of both of the resistors. The larger first the resistor is, the smaller is the potential difference across the second, and vice versa. It is their relative size which is important, not just their own value.

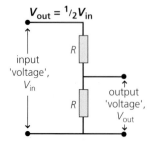

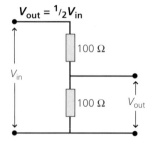

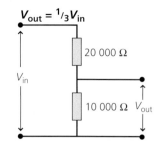

Figure 4 The output voltage of a potential divider depends on the relative resistances of the top and bottom resistors.

When two resistors are connected in series like this they form a **potential divider**. The resistors *divide* the total potential difference between them. You can work out the output 'voltage' from a potential divider using this formula:

$$V_{out} = V_{in} \times \frac{R_{bottom}}{R_{TOTAL}}$$

How can you get a potential difference of zero?

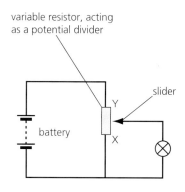

variable resistor, acting as a potential divider

slider

Y

battery

X

When the slider is set at X there is no current flowing in the bulb. When the slider is set at Y, the bulb shines with maximum brightness.

Figure 5

In a series circuit, a variable resistor can never make the potential difference or the current in a circuit absolutely zero. It can only reduce them. Even at its lowest setting it has some resistance, and therefore has a potential difference across it. Even if you could set it as high as a million ohms, it would still let some current through.

A variable resistor can be used as a potential divider to give a full range of potential differences, and currents, from the highest value all the way down to zero. Part of the resistor acts as the 'top' resistor of the potential divider, and part of it acts as the 'bottom' resistor (see figure 5). As you turn the slider, the top resistor effectively gets longer, and has a larger resistance, while the bottom part gets shorter until it has no length and therefore has no resistance. The output voltage across the bulb is zero at that point. Potential dividers are often used for volume controls on music systems because you can turn the volume right down to silence, rather than just reducing it.

Potential dividers that include a sensor as one of the resistors can be used as input sub-systems to control other processing circuits, as chapter 21 *Electronics* describes in more detail.

5 Work out the output 'voltages' in the circuits below.

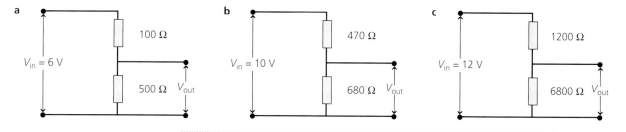

a $V_{in} = 6$ V   100 Ω   500 Ω V_{out}

b $V_{in} = 10$ V   470 Ω   680 Ω V_{out}

c $V_{in} = 12$ V   1200 Ω   6800 Ω V_{out}

Summary of series and parallel circuits

- In a series circuit, components are connected end to end, one after the other. The current through each part of the circuit is the same.

- In a parallel circuit, components are connected side by side. The current through each branch of a parallel circuit can be different.

- The overall voltage produced by several cells in series is the sum of the voltages of the individual cells, but they drive the same current as a single cell.

- Several cells connected in parallel produce the same voltage as one cell on its own, but they can drive more current.

- The total resistance of resistors in parallel can be calculated using the formula
  $1/R_{TOTAL} = 1/R_1 + 1/R_2 + 1/R_3$.

- The total resistance of resistors in series can be calculated using the formula $R_{TOTAL} = R_1 + R_2 + R_3$.

- The output from a potential divider depends on the ratio of the two resistances in it, and on the supply voltage.

$$V_{out} = V_{in} \times \frac{R_{bottom}}{R_{TOTAL}}$$

18.2 Power

What is power?

By definition, 1 volt is 1 joule per coulomb, and 1 amp is 1 coulomb per second.

$$1 V = 1 \frac{J}{C} \qquad 1 A = 1 \frac{C}{s}$$

so

$$1 V \times 1 A = 1 \frac{J}{C} \times 1 \frac{C}{s}$$
$$= 1 \text{ J/s}$$

One joule per second (J/s) is always called a watt (W).

The electric motors that operate this ski lift have to generate a great deal of power to lift people up the mountain.

Electrical energy can be generated from other forms of energy and transmitted over long distances, but it is not much use on its own. To be of any use, the electrical energy has to be converted into other forms such as heat, sound or light by a suitable transducer such as a light bulb or a loudspeaker. The rate at which electrical energy is converted into other forms is called the **power**, and it is calculated using this formula:

power = potential difference × current

$$P = V \times I \quad \text{or} \quad V = \frac{P}{I} \quad \text{and} \quad I = \frac{P}{V}$$

If potential difference is measured in volts (V), and current is measured in amps (A), the power is measured in watts (W).

There are other ways of writing the power formula that involve $V = IR$.

If you substitute $V = IR$ into $P = VI$, you get: $P = I^2R$

If you substitute $I = \dfrac{V}{R}$ into $P = VI$, you get: $P = \dfrac{V^2}{R}$

6 A light emitting diode (LED) has a potential difference of 2 V across it, and a current of 0.006 A through it. Use the formula $P = VI$ to work out how rapidly electrical energy is changed into other forms.

7 You are designing a hot air hand drier with a power rating of 4 kW, to be run from the 240 V mains. Use the formula $P = V^2/R$ to work out what resistance the heating element should have.

8 The current flowing in an overhead cable, of resistance 1 W, is 300 A.
   a Use the formula $P = I^2R$ to work out the rate at which electrical energy is converted to heat in the wire.
   b If the current doubled, how much energy would be wasted each second?

9 Mains electricity in the USA uses 120 V AC, whereas 240 V AC is used in the UK.
   a Calculate the current passing through a 960 W heater **i** in the UK, **ii** in the USA.
   b Describe the problems that might occur if the lead to the heater was a long one.
   c Explain why the problem will be worse in one country than the other.

Summary of power

- Power is the rate at which energy is transferred from one form to another. An appliance with a power rating of 1 watt converts 1 joule of electrical energy to other forms every second.

- Power can be calculated using the relationships $P = VI$, $P = V^2/R$, and $P = I^2R$.
- Power is measured in watts (W) or kilowatts (kW). 1 kW = 1000 W.

Investigation

How accurate are the ratings which are marked on light bulbs? Plan and carry out an investigation to find out.

Learning objectives

By the end of this chapter you should be able to:

- **discuss** in detail how domestic electricity is made as safe as possible
- **distinguish** alternating current from direct current
- **calculate** the value of the fuse that is required for an appliance
- **calculate** the cost of running some appliances in your home

- **wire** a three pin plug competently
- **recognise** how much your everyday life depends upon using electrical appliances
- **describe** how a beam of electrons is produced by thermionic emission
- **describe** ways of controlling an electron beam
- **recall** how X-rays are produced

19.1 Electricity in the home

What is our domestic electricity supply like?

Because of the way electricity is produced in power stations, and the way it is transmitted, the potential difference of 'mains' electricity varies in size and sign. In the UK, it varies between almost 340 V and –340 V, moving between the two values 50 times each second. In other countries, either the range or the speed of the change, or both, is different (see figure 1). This varying potential difference drives electric current backwards and forwards in the wires, producing an **alternating current (AC)**.

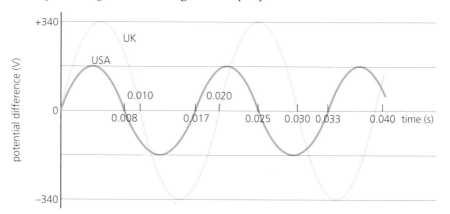

Figure 1 The AC supply in different countries varies in different ways.

In the UK, the varying PD delivers the same power as a steady 240 V supply would deliver, so it is usually called a 240 V AC supply.

1 When the electricity bill arrives one morning, your next door neighbour complains 'Electricity needs two wires – one to bring it into the house, and one to take it away. If all the electricity gets taken away, why should I pay for it?' Explain why you *do* need to pay for electricity.

All appliances need at least two wires to make them work, because it takes two wires to connect them into a complete circuit. One wire is called the **live** wire, and the other is the **neutral** wire. The neutral wire is *always* at, or close to, 0 V, and the live wire varies from 340 V to –340 V *relative* to the neutral wire. When it rises to 340 V, the current is pushed one way, and when it falls to –340 V, the current is pushed the other way.

The neutral wire does not change its value at all. It is *not* like a see-saw, with *both* the live and neutral 'ends' going up and down alternately. Don't think of the live wire as *bringing* you electricity and the neutral wire as *taking* it away. Because the current is alternating, it will flow out of one wire at one moment, and 0.01 s later it will change direction and flow out of the other wire.

How can you make electrical devices safer?

Every action your body makes relies on electricity. Small electrical signals in your nerves communicate between your brain and every part of your body. These signals are so small, that a current of less than 1 mA flowing through you from an outside source disrupts the messages, and is enough to kill you. Your heart is especially vulnerable.

Electricity can also cause fires and burns. If an electric current is large enough, it can make the wires in which it flows get very hot. (Copper wires have such a low resistance that they normally stay fairly cool.) If the plastic insulation around the wire melts, the live and neutral wires might touch and allow a much larger current to flow. If a **short circuit** like this occurs then the wires could become even hotter, and start a fire.

To ensure that current in electrical appliances never gets too high, to make them as safe as possible, manufacturers use a number of safety features.

Insulation

The plastic insulation on these wires provides insulation, but also helps to identify each wire by its colour.

Plastic and rubber are good insulators. They do not conduct electricity, so they can be used to prevent current 'leaking' from wires and conductors. Cables are coated in plastic or rubber, and many electrical items such as kettles, televisions and computers have plastic cases. Modern plugs, sockets and switches are all plastic. But even plastic cases may not be enough to make sockets and switches safe in bathrooms, because if they get wet the water will act as a conductor. For this reason, mains sockets are not allowed in bathrooms, and light switches must use a cord.

Fuses

A fuse is a thin piece of wire that melts if too much current flows through it. Its job is to prevent the current getting too large, and perhaps damaging the wiring in a device, or even causing a fire. The current is cut off as soon as it gets above a certain 'rated' value, because the circuit is broken once the fuse has melted. Fuse wire is available in different thicknesses – the thickness you use depends on how much current you want to allow before it melts.

You can buy fuses designed to 'blow' at different current ratings.

'Quick blow' fuses are particularly thin so they melt rapidly, while 'slow blow' or 'anti-surge' fuses only melt if the current stays above the rated limit value for a while. Fuses are often fitted inside special cartridges for convenience.

Because a fuse must let through a normal current for an appliance, and only melt if the current gets too high, it is important to select the correct value of fuse for an appliance. For most household devices, there are only two types of fuse to choose from – 3 A and 13 A. To select the correct fuse, calculate the current that would normally flow, and select the fuse that will blow at the nearest value above that.

WORKED EXAMPLE

A table lamp uses a 60 W bulb. What fuse is needed?

First, calculate the current:

$$I = \frac{P}{V} = \frac{60}{240} = 0.25 \text{ A}$$

A 3 A fuse has the nearest value above 0.25 A, so that is the one to choose.

2 Which of the appliances in the table will need a 13 A fuse, and which will need a 3 A fuse?

	Appliance	Power (W)
a	Kettle	2400
b	Hair drier	1600
c	Television	60
d	Electric drill	600
e	Toaster	1400

Miniature circuit breakers (MCBs)

An MCB acts like a fuse that can be reset. MCBs are designed to respond to two sorts of problems:
• a short circuit where a very fast response is needed
• a small overload where a slower response is acceptable

These two separate goals are achieved by a thermal-magnetic MCB (see figure 2). If there is a rapid surge of current, caused by a short circuit, a sudden, strong magnetic field is produced in the magnetic coil, which pulls the armature down. This lever releases the trip catch, and breaks the circuit. All this happens in about 0.01 s. If for some time the current is just slightly higher than the rated limit value for the MCB, the bimetallic strip gets warm and bends, releasing the trip catch and breaking the circuit. If the current is twice the rated value, this could take around 20 s to happen. Once the problem has been solved, the MCB can be reset by pressing a button to re-position the trip catch.

Figure 2 MCBs are more expensive than fuses, but they can be reset once the problem in the circuit is solved. This consumer unit (fuse box) has MCBs for different circuits, with different current ratings.

Miniature circuit breaker (MCB)

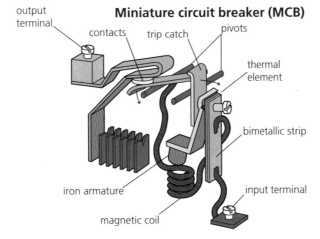

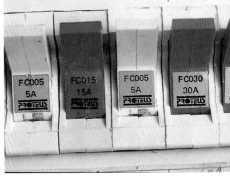

Residual current devices (RCDs)

If a problem occurs in an electrical appliance, and someone receives an electric shock, some current flows through the person's body to the ground instead of through the live and neutral wires. A residual current device (RCD) detects the change in the current and breaks the circuit.

Residual current device

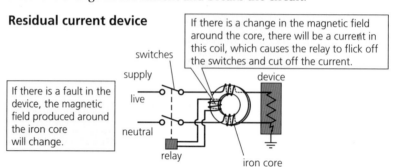

If there is a change in the magnetic field around the core, there will be a current in this coil, which causes the relay to flick off the switches and cut off the current.

If there is a fault in the device, the magnetic field produced around the iron core will change.

switches
supply
live
neutral
device
relay
iron core

Figure 3 An RCD breaks the circuit if somebody gets a shock from an appliance.

In figure 3, current flowing in each of the top and bottom coils on the iron core produces a magnetic field (see chapter 20, *Magnets and electromagnetism*). Because the currents in the live and neutral wires are normally equal but in opposite directions, the magnetic fields they produce cancel. If a fault occurs, and the currents are not equal, the magnetic fields do not cancel, and the 'left over' magnetism is used to activate the relay and break the circuit. The difference needs to be about 30 mA to activate the cut off.

RCDs cannot detect a current overload, or detect a simple short circuit between the live and neutral wires, so they are usually used in addition to fuses and MCBs. You plug an RCD into a socket, and then plug your appliance into the RCD. Many people use RCDs when they use power tools such as hedge trimmers.

Earth wires

Appliances with metal casings often have a special wire connecting the case to a metal stake driven into the ground. This is called an **earth connection**.

If the live wire becomes loose inside the appliance, and touches the casing, a very large current flows through the live wire, through the casing, through the earth wire, and into the ground. The current is so high that the fuse melts ('blows'), disconnecting the appliance from the mains, and making it safe. If the earth connection was not there, and you touched the metal casing, the current would flow from the live wire, through the casing, through *you*, and into the ground. Since only a few mA can be lethal, you could receive a deadly electric shock before the current was large enough to blow the fuse.

Not all appliances have an earth wire. If the object has no metal parts on the outside through which a user could receive a shock, it is not thought necessary to have an earth wire. Hair dryers, televisions and power tools are 'double insulated' like this, so they only have a live and a neutral wire.

In the UK, electrical plugs are fitted with an earth pin. If an appliance has an earth wire, it is connected to the earth pin in the plug. Inside the plug socket, the earth pin connects to an earth wire that runs away into the ground. The

The green and yellow earth wire on the back of this fridge carries current away into the ground, and helps make the device safe if a fault occurs.

earth pin on a UK three-pin-plug is longer than the other two pins, to ensure that it makes contact first. When the socket is not being used, the holes are often closed over to prevent objects entering accidentally, which could cause electrocution. The long earth pin is used to open the holes so that the other two pins can enter.

When you wire a UK three-pin-plug, you should use the following checks.

1 Make sure you connect the wires to the correct terminals (see figure 4).
2 Make sure the screws are tight and there are no stray strands of wire that might touch another terminal.
3 Make sure the cable clamp is tight, and the cable cannot be pulled out.

The plug sockets in a house are wired up in parallel, as shown in figure 4. Light circuits are wired up separately, since they need to carry far less current than the plug circuits, but they too are wired in parallel.

House wiring

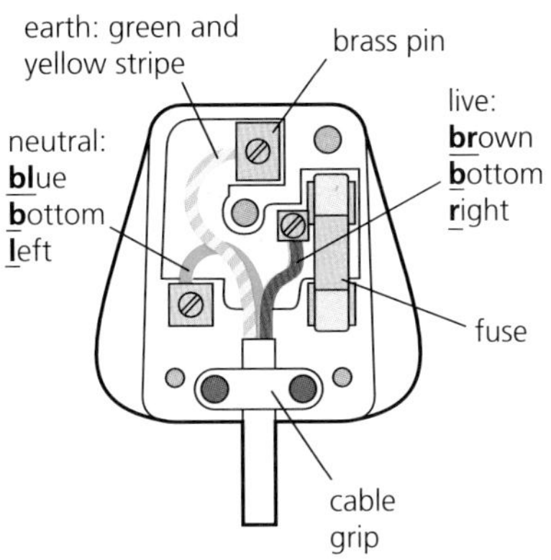

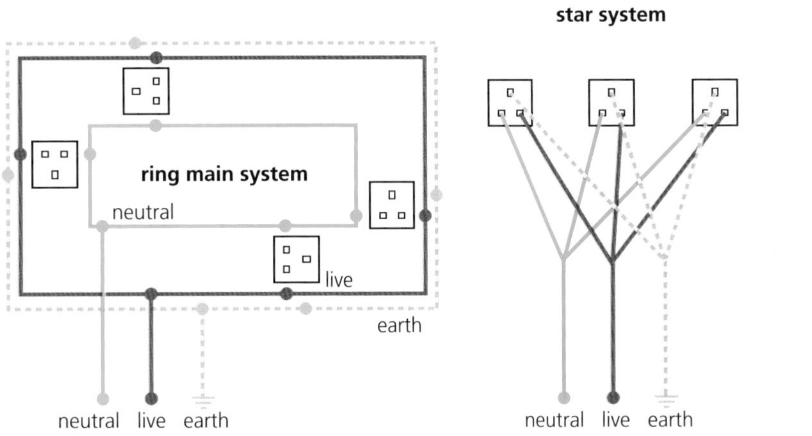

Sockets in a house are normally wired in a ring main or star system, which both use parallel circuits. The wires in a ring main system have to carry more current than in a star system, but it is easier to add more sockets if required.

Figure 4 You must connect the right wires to the right terminals when you wire a three-pin-plug.

3 Why do you think sockets and lighting circuits are wired in parallel, rather than in series?

How is electricity measured?

An electricity meter records the amount of electrical energy used in a house. Then, every three months, the electricity supplier takes a reading so it knows how much to charge the householder. Although the usual way to measure energy is to use joules, this unit is just too small for use in a home – it would be like measuring the distance to the Moon in millimetres! A more convenient unit for measuring domestic electrical energy is the kilowatt hour (kWh). This is the amount of energy that a 1 kW appliance transfers if it runs for one hour. On electricity bills, it is usually simply called 'a unit'.

The electricity meter records the number of kWhs used.

WORKED EXAMPLE

Work out the amount of electrical energy used by a 120 W television switched on for four hours one evening.

In joules: energy used = power in watts × time in seconds
$$= 120 \times (4 \times 60 \times 60) = 1\ 728\ 000 \text{ J}$$

In kWh: energy used = power in kilowatts × time in hours
$$= 0.12 \times 4 = 0.48 \text{ kWh}$$

If the electricity supplier charges the customer 7p per kWh, the cost of watching television for one evening = 0.48 × 7 = 3.36p.

4   How many joules are there in 1 kWh?

5   If electrical energy costs 7p per unit (kWh), calculate the cost of each of the tasks in the table.

Task	Power (kW)	Time
a Boiling a kettle	2.4	5 minutes
b Having a shower	6.0	10 minutes
c Video recording a TV programme	0.2	2 hours
d Drying your hair	1.6	6 minutes
e Lighting a room	0.1	4 hours

Summary of electricity in the home

- Electricity in the home can be very dangerous. Safety measures to protect users include:
  1 insulation
  2 earth wires
  3 fuses, MCBs and RCDs
- Electrical energy is measured in joules on a small scale, but for household use it is measured in kilowatt hours (kWh). 1 kWh = 3600 000 joules.

- Sockets and lights in homes are wired in parallel.
- When wiring a plug, you should ensure that:
  1 you connect the wires to the correct terminals
  2 the screws are tight and there are no stray strands of wire or bare sections
  3 the cable clamp is tight, and the cable cannot be pulled out of the plug

19.2 Electron beams

How can you make an electron beam?

All metals contain electrons which are free to move inside the material. They behave very much like particles in a gas or liquid, moving in a random way due to collisions with each other and with the atoms in the metal.

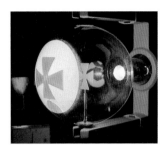

In a Maltese cross tube, electrons are accelerated through a vacuum and hit a fluorescent screen.

If a liquid is warmed, particles can evaporate from it. In the same way, if the electrons are given enough energy, they can leave the metal. This is actually happening in every metal even at room temperature, but more electrons are released if the wire is made hotter. The process is called **thermionic emission** ('therm' means 'relating to heat', and 'ionic' means 'relating to charges'). If the metal is in air, the electrons might be picked up by stray positive ions, or attracted back to the metal. But if the wire is placed in a vacuum, and it is made electrically negative compared to a nearby positive plate, the electrons can be pulled away from the hot wire and accelerated to a high speed (see figure 5). This is the principle on which an electron gun works.

Electron gun

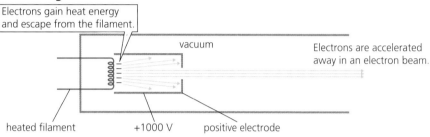

Figure 5

You can demonstrate the behaviour of the electrons from an electron gun using a Maltese cross tube. This is a glass tube, containing a vacuum, with an electron gun at one end and a cross-shaped electrode in the middle, which can be made electrically positive or negative, or left uncharged. The other end of the tube has a fluorescent screen so that when electrons strike it, they make it glow. The larger the accelerating 'voltage' between the cathode and the cross-shaped electrode, the more kinetic energy the electrons have as they hit the screen, and the brighter it glows.

kinetic energy = charge on electron × accelerating voltage

$$KE = eV$$

The Maltese cross tube can be used to show:
- that electrons carry a negative charge
- that electrons tend to travel in straight lines
- that an electron beam can be deflected by a magnetic field, which makes it follow a circular path (see figure 6)

6 a Calculate the kinetic energy of an electron in a TV tube, if it is accelerated by a PD of 3000 V. (Charge on an electron = 1.6×10^{-19} C.)
b State what happens to this kinetic energy when the electron hits the screen.

How can you control an electron beam?

If two electrodes are placed either side of the electron beam, it can be pulled left or right, depending on the electrodes' charges. These electrodes are called x-plates. The electrons are attracted towards the positive plate, and repelled by the negative plate. Another pair of electrodes placed above and below the beam deflects the electrons up and down, in the same way. These are called y-plates. In each case, the deflection is proportional to the 'voltage' across the plates, and the deflected beam follows a **parabolic** path (see chapter 14, *Motion in two dimensions*).

Figure 6 An electron beam is a flow of electrons, like a current, so it feels a force in a magnetic field which makes it move, just like a current-carrying wire (see chapter 20, *Magnets and electromagnetism*). The beam is also deflected by an electric field.

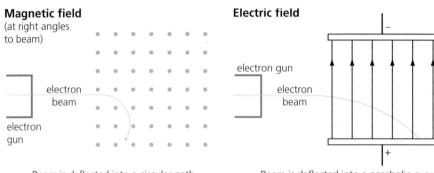

Magnetic field
(at right angles to beam)

electron beam

electron gun

Beam is deflected into a circular path.

Electric field

electron gun

electron beam

Beam is deflected into a parabolic curve.

A **cathode ray oscilloscope** (CRO) is an instrument used to measure and compare rapidly changing electrical signals. A CRO contains a vacuum tube much like a Maltese cross tube, with x-plates and y-plates to control the electron beam (see figure 7).

A varying voltage is applied to the x-plates to gradually pull the beam more and more to the right (as seen on the screen), and then flick it back to the far left side. When this is done quickly and repeatedly, the movement of the beam is seen as a continuous line. The speed of the beam is controlled by the **timebase** controls and it can be varied so that the beam passes across each division on the screen in a few milliseconds, or a few microseconds. In this way even very rapidly changing signals can be displayed clearly. The electric signal that you want to look at is applied (via an amplifier) to the y-plates. These control the vertical movement of the beam. By changing the gain of the amplifier (the **y-gain**), even small signals can be displayed (see figure 8).

7 A student says to her teacher 'When you showed us the Maltese cross tube, the end had a green glow, but the CRO you showed us had a white spot on the screen. Is that because the tubes use different sorts of electrons?' How would you answer the student if you were the teacher?

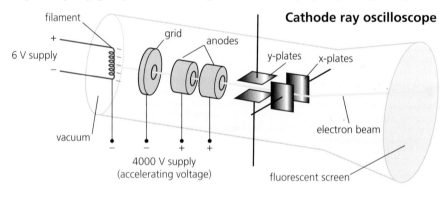

Cathode ray oscilloscope

filament

6 V supply

grid

anodes

y-plates   x-plates

vacuum

4000 V supply
(accelerating voltage)

electron beam

fluorescent screen

Figure 7 The x-plates in a CRO control the horizontal movement of the electron beam. The y-plates control its vertical movement.

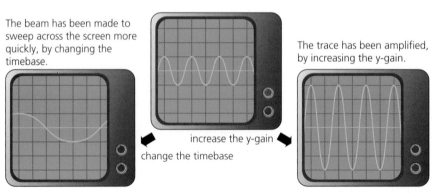

The beam has been made to sweep across the screen more quickly, by changing the timebase.

The trace has been amplified, by increasing the y-gain.

increase the y-gain

change the timebase

Figure 8 You can examine an input signal in great detail using a CRO. The signal could be produced by any kind of source, from a sound wave or radio wave, to an electrical source.

What use are electron beams?

TV raster

television screen

Path of scanning electron beam is called a raster.

beam off   beam on

625 lines

Beam off, as it flicks back to top of screen.

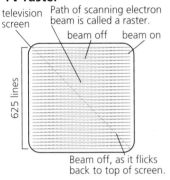

Figure 9

Televisions

A television works in a similar way to a CRO, but the deflection of the electron beam is controlled by magnetic fields rather than electric fields. Larger deflections can be produced in a shorter space than with electric fields, so the whole television can be much smaller than it otherwise would be.

To obtain a full picture, the electron beam must be deflected up and down as well as side to side. To achieve this, the beam is pulled slowly downwards, and scanned from side to side at the same time. It is then flicked up to the top of the screen ready for the next scan. The overall pattern on the screen is called a **raster**. On a monochrome (black and white) television or monitor, the picture is displayed by varying the speed of the electrons, so that as they scan across, the screen's brightness varies, producing white, grey and black tones.

Colour televisions use three electron beams – one for each of the three primary colours: green, red and blue. The screen is covered in three types of phosphor dots which glow when the electrons strike them. All three beams are scanned at the same time, but each beam is aimed so that it will only hit one type of phosphor dot. A metal plate with holes, called a shadow mask, is placed near the phosphor screen, to help stop the beams from hitting the wrong phosphor dots. (You should never place a magnet near the front of a television, because it can bend the delicate shadow mask, and ruin the television for good.) By making the three primary coloured phosphor dots light up at different brightnesses, any colour can be produced on the screen.

X-rays

Figure 10 When a metal target is bombarded by an electron beam, it emits X-rays of a range of frequencies. Different metals produce 'peaks' of intense X-rays at particular frequencies, characteristic of that metal. You can read more about X-rays in chapter 25, *Electromagnetic spectrum*.

X-ray tube

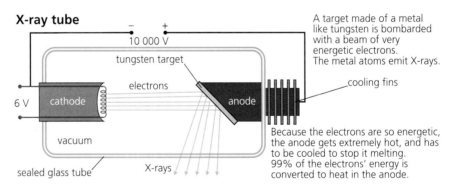

A target made of a metal like tungsten is bombarded with a beam of very energetic electrons. The metal atoms emit X-rays.

10 000 V

tungsten target

electrons

6 V   cathode   anode

cooling fins

vacuum

sealed glass tube   X-rays

Because the electrons are so energetic, the anode gets extremely hot, and has to be cooled to stop it melting. 99% of the electrons' energy is converted to heat in the anode.

Summary of electron beams

- Electrons can be released by thermionic emission.
- Electrons can be accelerated and deflected using electric fields. Kinetic energy of electron = charge on electron × accelerating PD, or KE = *eV*.
- Electron beams are deflected by magnetic fields.

- X-rays can be produced when high speed electrons strike a target.
- To make a television picture, electron beams scan across and down the screen, and then flick back up. The pattern is called a raster.

Learning objectives

By the end of this section you should be able to:

- **discuss** the importance of magnetic fields
- **describe** the shape of magnetic fields produced by a range of magnets and wires
- **describe** how magnetism and the current in a wire interact to make the wire feel a force
- **name** some devices that use magnetism, and explain how they work
- **discuss** how generators and dynamos work

- **describe** the factors that affect the output from a dynamo and an alternator
- **discuss** how transformers work, and how they are made efficient
- **calculate** the output from a transformer
- **describe** how and why high 'voltages' and alternating current are used to transport electricity over long distances.

20.1 Magnetism and motion

Why are magnets useful?

The first magnets were magnetic rocks called lodestones.

The first people to use magnets were probably ancient Chinese sailors, who used magnetic rocks as crude compasses to help them navigate. When they hung one of these rocks from a thread or placed it on wood floating in water, so that it was free to turn, it lined up with the Earth's magnetic field, and indicated which way was north.

Rocks that helped travellers navigate in this way were called 'lodestones' ('lode' means 'way' or 'journey'). The end which pointed towards the north became known as the north pole of the lodestone. The other end was called the south pole. These terms are still used for magnets today.

The Earth's magnetic field traps particles coming from the Sun and moves them towards the poles, where they make the sky glow in an aurora.

This scanner uses an intense magnetic field to make protons in hydrogen atoms 'line up' and produce a picture of the body's tissues.

Sunspots are strong magnetic fields on the Sun. Particles released from them affect the Earth's climate.

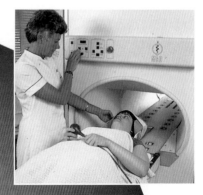

What is a magnetic field?

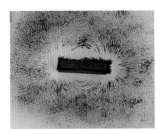

If a magnet is symmetrically shaped, its field is symmetrical.

A magnet has a **magnetic field** around it, which affects anything that is magnetic. You can see the shape of a magnetic field using iron filings sprinkled on paper above the magnet, because each iron filing lines up with the field just as a compass needle lines up with the Earth's magnetic field. The pattern the iron filings produce shows many **magnetic field lines**, that never cross each other. These field lines have a direction which has been agreed by scientists. The field lines always *come out* of the north pole and *go into* the south pole of a magnet.

If two magnets are brought close together, they might attract each other, but they might also repel each other because of the way their fields interact. The rule is that opposite poles attract each other, and like poles repel each other (see figure 1).

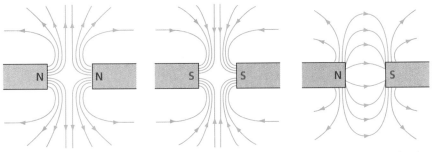

Figure 1   Like poles repel each other.   Like poles repel each other.   Unlike poles attract each other.

Is a magnet always a magnet?

Magnets can be divided into two types – permanent magnets and temporary or 'induced' magnets. Once magnetised, a permanent magnet stays magnetised, although heating or hitting it repeatedly will reduce its strength. An induced magnet is only a magnet while something else is magnetising it. If this source of magnetism is taken away, the induced magnet loses its magnetism.

You can test whether a magnet is induced or permanent, by bringing a permanent magnet close to it. If the magnets always attract each other, no matter which way you turn them, the mystery magnet is an induced magnet (see figure 2). Permanent magnets are capable of repelling each other if you bring the like poles together.

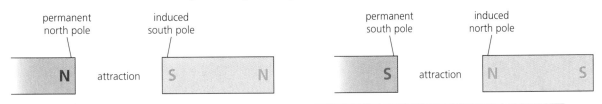

The pole of a permanent magnet always induces the opposite pole in an unmagnetised piece of magnetic material (e.g. an iron bar). So an induced magnet is *always* attracted to a permanent magnet.

Figure 2

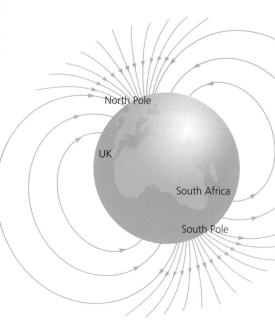

Magnetism is used for all kinds of jobs.
For example, it is used:

- in electric motors
- to contain secret code numbers on credit cards
- to store data on computer disks
- to store music on cassette tapes
- to hold fridge and cupboard doors shut
- to measure flow rates in the petrochemical industry

1 Describe three things that you should avoid doing to computer disks, credit cards and cassette tapes to make sure the stored data is not corrupted.

2 The diagram shows how the Earth's magnetic field is shaped. In the UK, a well balanced magnet comes to rest with its north pole pointing downwards at about 67° to the horizontal.

   a Explain why the Earth's magnetic field would cause this to happen.

   b How could you use a well balanced magnet to show that you were near the Equator?

   c How do you think a well balanced magnet would come to rest in South Africa?

What makes magnets magnetised?

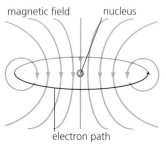

Figure 3 An electron moving in a circular orbit makes a field like this.

All magnetism is caused by the movement of electrically charged particles such as protons or electrons. The faster they move, the stronger is the magnetic field the particles make. The shape of the magnetic field depends on how the particles are actually moving. For example, an electron orbiting the nucleus of an atom will create a magnetic field as shown in figure 3.

Because most atoms have several electrons, all moving in different ways, the magnetic fields made by the electrons cancel each other out, leaving no overall field. Even if each atom has a magnetic field, there will probably be equal numbers of atoms 'facing' in each direction, so again the fields will all cancel out, leaving the material unmagnetised overall (see figure 4). Only if each atom has a magnetic field, and there are more atoms facing one way than any other will the material be magnetised.

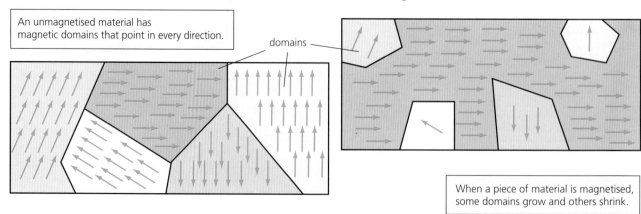

An unmagnetised material has magnetic domains that point in every direction.

domains

When a piece of material is magnetised, some domains grow and others shrink.

Figure 4

How can you make a magnet?

You can make an unmagnetised piece of steel into a permanent magnet by repeatedly moving another magnet over it, always in the same direction. This makes the atoms in the steel 'face' in the same direction. The atoms in steel will retain the pattern and make a permanent magnet, but if you use pure iron, it will lose its magnet straight away. Pure iron only ever makes a temporary magnet.

Even non-magnetic materials such as aluminium and copper can produce magnetic fields, if enough electrons can be persuaded to move in the same way. In all metals, there are many free electrons, which can make an electric current if a potential difference is applied across a sample. Each electron produces its own field and if there are enough electrons moving through a sample, together they produce a detectable field. The direction of the magnetic field depends on the direction of the current. You can remember it using the Right Hand Thumb Rule (see figure 5).

Right hand thumb rule

Figure 5 If your thumb points in the direction of the current, your curved fingers show the direction of the field.

What use is the magnetic field from a current?

The Joint European Torus project on nuclear fusion uses huge solenoids like this, formed into a ring. The magnetic field inside contains material at around 100 000 000 °C!

The magnetic field produced by a current has many uses. By making the wire into a coil with a large number of turns, you can make the magnetic field much stronger. It can be strong enough to pull a piece of iron into the coil. These coils are called **solenoids** and they are used to activate many systems, such as electric door locks on cars, and the buffers on pin ball machines.

A ferrite rod inside this live wire detector becomes an induced magnet in a magnetic field. A circuit senses the change and beeps to alert the electrician.

Electricians find live wires hidden in plastered walls by detecting the magnetic field made by the current in the wire.

If a solenoid is coiled around an iron core, the core becomes magnetised whenever there is a current in the coil. The field created by an **electromagnet** like this is stronger than the field from a solenoid on its own.

The strength of the field depends on:

- the number of turns of wire
- the size of the current flowing
- how magnetic the material in the core is

This electromagnet is strong enough to lift huge lumps of scrap.

3 If a person got a tiny piece of steel stuck in her eye, magnetism could be used to remove it. Suggest a design for a device that can produce an intensely strong field in a very small area.

4 Why is iron used for the core of an electromagnet rather than steel?

What use are electromagnets?

A **relay** is an electric switching device that uses an electromagnet. It uses an electric signal in a 'switching' circuit to trigger current to flow in a separate outside circuit (see figure 6). Relays are important in all kinds of electrical engineering including telecommunications, computers and car electrics.

Buzzers and bells work like the relay, with a pivoted armature and an electromagnet. But in a buzzer or bell, the contacts are part of the 'switching' circuit *to* the electromagnet (see figure 7).

Loudspeakers use electromagnetism to convert rapidly changing electrical signals from an amplifier into sound (see figure 8).

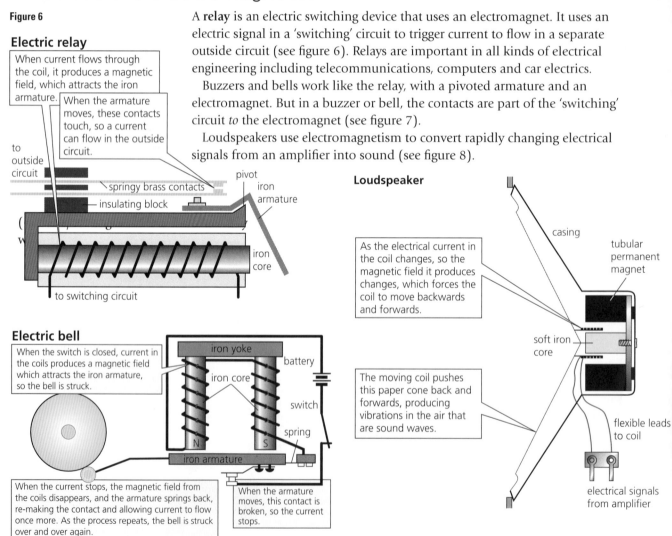

Figure 6

Electric relay

When current flows through the coil, it produces a magnetic field, which attracts the iron armature.

When the armature moves, these contacts touch, so a current can flow in the outside circuit.

to outside circuit

springy brass contacts

insulating block

pivot
iron armature

iron core

to switching circuit

Electric bell

When the switch is closed, current in the coils produces a magnetic field which attracts the iron armature, so the bell is struck.

iron yoke

battery

iron core

switch

spring

N   S

iron armature

When the current stops, the magnetic field from the coils disappears, and the armature springs back, re-making the contact and allowing current to flow once more. As the process repeats, the bell is struck over and over again.

When the armature moves, this contact is broken, so the current stops.

Figure 7

Loudspeaker

As the electrical current in the coil changes, so the magnetic field it produces changes, which forces the coil to move backwards and forwards.

The moving coil pushes this paper cone back and forwards, producing vibrations in the air that are sound waves.

casing

tubular permanent magnet

soft iron core

flexible leads to coil

electrical signals from amplifier

Figure 8

5 Design a way for a third floor resident to unlock the front door of a block of flats using electromagnetism. Make sure the door locks again when the door is closed and the switch is released.

6 The doorbell in your home has just stopped working. List some possible faults with the bell.

What happens when a current flows in a magnetic field?

If two permanent magnets are brought close together, they repel or attract each other because their fields interact. A wire carrying an electric current produces a magnetic field, which can also interact with the field from a permanent magnet, so that the wire and the magnet each feel a force.

You can work out the direction of the force by looking at the magnetic field lines produced by the wire and the magnet. When a wire carrying a current is placed in a magnetic field, the field lines move so that they do not overlap, as shown in figure 9. The direction of the wire's movement depends on the direction of the current, *and* the direction of the outside field. When the field and the current are at right angles to each other, the direction of motion is at right angles to them both (see figure 10).

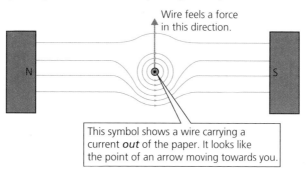

This symbol shows a wire carrying a current *out* of the paper. It looks like the point of an arrow moving towards you.

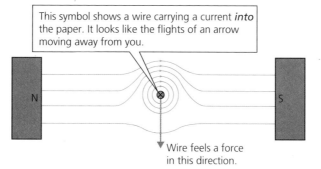

This symbol shows a wire carrying a current *into* the paper. It looks like the flights of an arrow moving away from you.

Figure 9 The outside magnetic field is sometimes called a 'catapult field', because the field lines appear to act like stretched elastic, springing the wire up or down.

The size of the force on the current-carrying wire is increased by:
- increasing the strength of the magnetic field
- increasing the size of the current
- increasing the length of the wire in the field (assuming it is not bent back on itself)
- having several coils of wire (each coil feels the same push as a single wire, but the combined effect of all the coils is that a larger force is produced.)

Figure 10 Fleming's Left Hand Rule helps you to remember how the direction of the force on a current-carrying wire depends on the directions of the current and the outside field.

Fleming's left hand rule

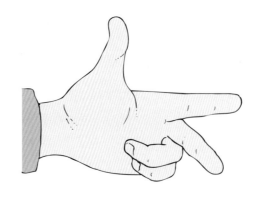

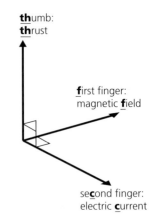

thumb:
thrust

first finger:
magnetic **f**ield

se**c**ond finger:
electric **c**urrent

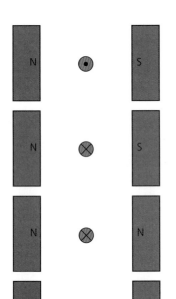

7 Copy the diagrams on the left and draw field lines to explain how each wire moves, if at all.

8 When a wire in a magnetic field feels a force, the source of the outside field also feels a force, in the opposite direction. So the size of the force on a wire can be measured by holding the wire in the field produced by magnets on a balance.

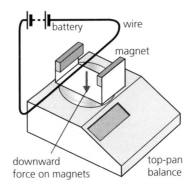

Length of wire (cm)	Current (A)	Force (N)
2.0	2.0	0.08
2.0	4.0	0.16
3.0	2.0	0.12
3.0	4.0	0.24
4.0	2.0	0.16
4.0	4.0	0.32

The table below shows data gathered using the apparatus shown.

a Write two conclusions from the data.

b If you had conducted this experiment, what more might you do to test your conclusions?

What use is the force on a current in a field?

An electric **motor** contains a rectangular coil, pivoted on an axle, in a magnetic field (see figure 11). When there is a current in the coil, a **couple** of forces makes it turn (see chapter 11, *Turning forces*). The coil turns until the current no longer causes a turning force. To keep the coil turning, the current needs to be reversed at this stage, so that instead of being forced 'up', the wire on one side is forced 'down', and vice-versa. Provided the coil has enough momentum to carry it past each crucial point when there is no turning force, it can keep turning continually. Alternating current automatically changes direction at the right moment. If you use direct current, you need a **commutator** to reverse the current in the coil every half turn.

9 The motor in the diagram below was not very successful. What could be done to make it turn with a larger force?

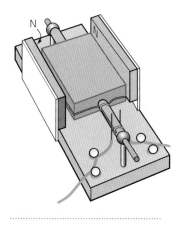

Figure 11 Electric motors are used to spin the drums in washing machines, to rotate the blades in electric lawn mowers, and in all kinds of other devices.

Electric motor

wooden block

magnet

coil of wire

split pin

commutator

to direct current supply

coil

When current flows in the coil, A and B feel forces making the coil turn.

In this position, there is no current in the coil, but its momentum keeps it moving.

After half a complete turn, the current in A and B is reversed, so they feel forces keeping the coil turning the same way.

Summary of magnetism and motion

- There are two types of magnetic poles: north poles and south poles.
- Like magnetic poles repel and unlike poles attract.
- Some materials, such as steel, retain magnetism and form permanent magnets. Some materials, such as iron, can only be made into temporary or induced magnets.
- A current-carrying wire produces a circular magnetic field whose direction can be predicted using the Right Hand Thumb Rule.
- A simple electromagnet can be made by coiling wire around a suitable core such as iron.

- The strength of the field produced by an electromagnet depends on the size of the current, the type of core, and the size of the coil.
- Relays, buzzers, bells, loudspeakers and motors make use of electromagnetism.
- A current-carrying wire feels a force in a magnetic field. The direction of the force can be predicted using Fleming's Left Hand Rule.
- The strength of the force depends upon the strength of the magnetic field, the size of the current, and the length of wire in the field.
- This force is used to make electric motors spin.

20.2 Making electricity using electromagnetism

How can you make a current using magnets?

Michael Faraday (1791–1867) discovered the effect of **electromagnetic induction**. He knew that a magnetic field and an electric current could together produce motion. He predicted that it should be possible to use motion and a magnetic field to produce an electric current (see figure 12).

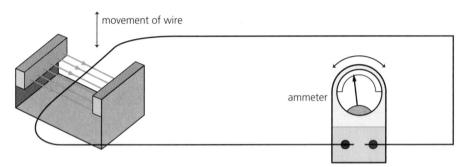

movement of wire

ammeter

To induce a current, the wire must move. However strong the magnetic field is, if the wire does not move, no EMF will be induced so there will be no current. The direction of the induced current reverses as the direction of movement of the wire reverses.

Figure 12 When you move a wire in a magnetic field, a current is induced.

As the wire moves through, or cuts, the field, the electrons in the wire feel a push called an **electromotive force (EMF)**. If there is a complete electric circuit, this EMF makes the electrons move and produce a current. Making a current flow like this is called electromagnetic induction. The direction of the current depends on the direction of the magnetic field and the direction of movement.

How do generators work?

Generators use electromagnetic induction to produce a continuous supply of electricity. Wire is wound into a coil, which is spun in a magnetic field. As it spins, each side of the coil cuts through the field repeatedly, so a larger EMF is produced. The size of the EMF can be increased by:
- spinning the coil faster, so the wires move faster through the field
- using a coil and magnets with a larger area
- using more turns on the coil
- using a stronger magnetic field

There are two main types of generator. **Alternators** produce alternating current (AC). **Dynamos** produce direct current (DC) (see figure 14). As the coil in a generator turns, the amount of magnetic field passing through the coil changes. It is this *changing* amount of magnetism which produces electricity in the coil (see figure 13).

Figure 13

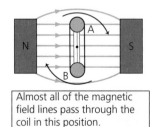

Almost all of the magnetic field lines pass through the coil in this position.

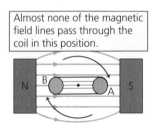

Almost none of the magnetic field lines pass through the coil in this position.

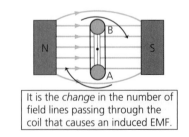

It is the *change* in the number of field lines passing through the coil that causes an induced EMF.

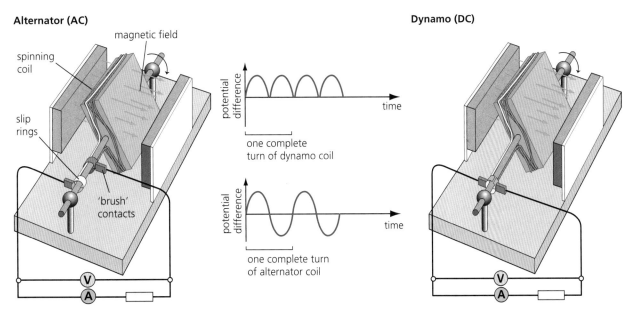

Alternator (AC)

magnetic field

spinning coil

slip rings

'brush' contacts

potential difference

time

one complete turn of dynamo coil

potential difference

time

one complete turn of alternator coil

Dynamo (DC)

Figure 14 Spinning a coil of wire in a magnetic field produces a continuous, varying EMF much larger than that from a single wire.

10 The alternator on a car needs to generate more electric current than one on a motorbike, even though it turns at approximately the same rate. Suggest how the designs of the two alternators are different so this is achieved.

What is a transformer?

Figure 15 Transformers only work if the current is alternating (AC). No electricity is transformed if the current is steady (DC).

Spinning a coil in a permanent magnetic field is not the only way to make the coil feel a changing amount of magnetism. If you use an electromagnet instead of permanent magnets, changing the current in the electromagnet has the same effect as turning the coil in a steady field. As the current in the electromagnet increases and decreases, the size of the magnetic field it produces increases and decreases. The coil, which is still, feels an increasing and decreasing amount of magnetism, just as if it were spinning. So changing the current in the electromagnet coil produces a changing EMF in another coil. This is the principle of a **transformer** (see figure 15).

Transformer

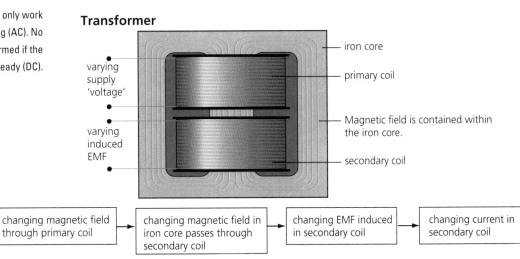

varying supply 'voltage'

varying induced EMF

iron core

primary coil

Magnetic field is contained within the iron core.

secondary coil

| changing current in primary coil | → | changing magnetic field through primary coil | → | changing magnetic field in iron core passes through secondary coil | → | changing EMF induced in secondary coil | → | changing current in secondary coil |

The efficiency of a transformer can be increased by wrapping the coils around an iron core. The core is usually made from thin plates of iron, insulated from each other, but clamped tightly together. This helps to stop electric currents flowing inside the core, and so stops it getting too hot and wasting energy.

There would be little point in using a transformer if the EMF produced in the secondary coil was the same as the voltage across the primary coil. Transformers are useful because the voltage in one coil can be *different* from the voltage in the other, depending on the number of turns of wire on the two coils.

$$\frac{\text{volts across primary coil}}{\text{volts across secondary coil}} = \frac{\text{number of turns in primary coil}}{\text{number of turns in secondary coil}}$$

$$\frac{V_p}{V_s} = \frac{N_p}{N_s}$$

In a 'step up' transformer, the secondary coil has more turns than the primary coil. This makes the voltage in the secondary coil higher than in the primary coil. In a 'step down' transformer the primary coil has more turns. This makes the voltage in the secondary coil lower than in the primary coil.

In neither type of transformer can you create electrical energy or power from nowhere. So although the voltage is 'stepped up' by a step up transformer, the *current* in the secondary coil is lower than in the primary coil. In a step down transformer, the current is higher in the secondary coil than in the primary.

$$\text{power produced in secondary coil} < \text{power provided in primary coil}$$

$$V_s I_s < V_p I_p$$

$$\frac{I_s}{I_p} < \frac{N_p}{N_s}$$

The useful power produced in the secondary coil is always less than the power provided by the primary coil, because energy is always wasted in the system, in the form of heat. That is why, in the relationship above, the ratio of the number of turns, on the right, is always greater than the ratio of the currents in the two coils, on the left.

WORKED EXAMPLE

A laptop computer uses a step down transformer to convert the 240 V AC mains supply into 15 V AC. If the primary coil has a thousand turns, how many turns does the secondary coil need?

$$\frac{V_p}{V_s} = \frac{N_p}{N_s} \qquad \frac{240}{12} = \frac{1000}{N_s}$$

$$N_s = \frac{1000}{20} = 50 \text{ turns}$$

11 UK business people travelling in the USA have problems with their laptop computers because they are designed to run on the UK supply of 240 V AC, and parts of the USA use 120 V AC.

a Design a transformer for UK business people to use in the USA.

b Design a transformer for business people from the USA to use when visiting the UK.

What use are transformers?

Some of the largest transformers are those used in the National Grid, which transport electricity to homes, schools and work places all over the country. These transformers are designed to handle very high currents as well as high voltages. A typical power station generates electricity at about 25 000 V, but this is stepped up to 275 000 V, or even to 400 000 V to be transported. The voltage is stepped up so that the current is as low as possible, to reduce the energy wasted as heat in the cables.

rate of energy loss (power) = I^2R

The resistance of the cables is represented by R. Because the power loss depends on the current *squared* (I^2), it is really important to keep the current as low as possible, by stepping up the voltage. Once the electricity has been transported, the high voltages are stepped down in stages, using transformers, to provide a 240 V supply for use in homes (see figure 16).

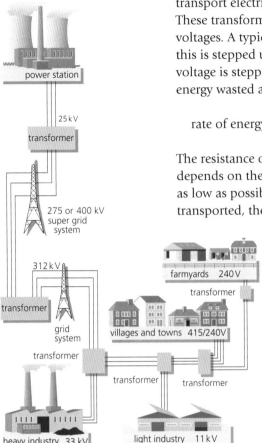

12 The box in the photo houses a transformer used to step-down high 'voltages' from the National Grid, for use in nearby homes. The pipes on the sides are filled with oil – they do not contain the coils.

a If high 'voltages' are used in the National Grid because they are more efficient, why are low ones used in people's homes?

b Why do you think there are oil filled pipes sticking out of the side of the transformer?

Figure 16

Summary of making electricity using electromagnetism

- When a wire cuts a magnetic field an EMF is produced by electromagnetic induction.
- If the wire is formed into a coil, and rotated, a varying EMF can be generated. This principle is used in alternators and dynamos.
- The size of the EMF produced depends upon
1 the number of turns of wire
2 how fast the coil is rotated
3 the strength of the magnetic field
4 the size of the coils and the magnets
- A changing current in the primary coil of a transformer produces a changing magnetic field,

which is passed to the secondary coil by the core. An EMF is induced in the secondary coil.
- Alternating voltages can be stepped up or down using transformers, depending on the number of turns in the coils. $V_s/V_p = N_s/N_p$.
- When the voltage is stepped down, the current in the secondary coil is larger than in the first, and vice versa. Energy is always wasted as heat, so $I_s/I_p < N_p/N_s$.
- High alternating voltages are used to transport power across the National Grid to minimise the current, so reducing power loss.

Electronics

Learning objectives

By the end of this chapter you should be able to:

- **describe** the basic elements of any electronic system
- **describe** the features of a range of electronic sensors
- **distinguish** between analogue and digital signals
- **describe** a range of digital process sub-systems
- **describe** a range of analogue process sub-systems

- **describe** the features of a range of electronic output devices
- **recognise** the need for feedback in some electronic systems
- **design** electronic systems to solve simple problems

21.1 Using electronics

Why is electronics important?

The first transistor was quite large, but it was the basis of all modern electronics. Now billions of transistors fit on a single chip.

A REPLICA OF THE FIRST TRANSISTOR INVENTED AT BELL LABORATORIES, MURRAY HILL, NEW JERSEY, ON DECEMBER 23, 1947.

Probably the most significant technological development in the twentieth century is electronics. Electronics has affected the way people live in their homes, how people are entertained, how people learn at school, how people work, and how people are treated in hospitals.

Electronics is built upon the properties of semiconductors, and the transistors and chips that are made from them. The basic theory behind semiconductor chips was developed around 1930, but it was not until 1948 that the first transistor was made. Since then people have made smaller and smaller transistors, so that today it is possible to place several billion of them on a single computer memory chip. Techniques are currently being developed to increase this number by one thousand times, which will bring further savings in energy and an increase in processing speed.

What is the difference between digital and analogue?

Electronics can be divided into two main areas – those systems dealing with analogue signals, and those dealing with digital signals. An analogue signal in an electronic circuit can have any voltage value, positive or negative, and the size of the signal is used to represent some physical variable such as light, sound or heat. For example, a loud sound would produce a proportionally larger signal than a quiet sound (see figure 1).

In contrast, digital systems use signals that are classified either as 'high' (e.g. above 2.5 V) or 'low' (e.g. between 0 and 2.5 V). Any signal or number can be represented by a combination of highs and lows. The counting system that uses sequences of 'highs' and 'lows' is called **binary** (see figure 1).

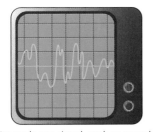 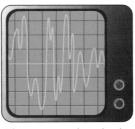 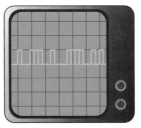

010011100100011110010 1

An analogue signal, such as sound, would give a trace like this on a CRO.

The same sound at a louder volume would look like this.

A digital signal would give a trace like this on a CRO.

A digital signal can be represented by a number in binary, like this.

Figure 1

Because there are only two possible values for digital signals, even if they become distorted the sequence of 'highs' and 'lows' is still recognisable. This means that digital signals are more reliable than analogue signals for transmitting data, and information can be sent more rapidly.

CDs use digital codes, and provide much better sound quality than cassette tapes and vinyl records, which use analogue codes. The main telephone networks in the UK and USA already use digital systems, and soon television stations will broadcast using digital signals too. With digital television, the sound is clearer, and hundreds more channels are available.

What is an electronic system?

Electronic system

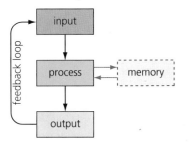

Figure 2

All electronic control systems have the basic structure shown in figure 2. As technology advances, the contents of the sub-systems will change, but this basic structure will stay the same.

The role of the input sub-system is to detect a change in some variable such as temperature or light level. It then converts that input into an electrical signal that the process sub-system can handle. The process sub-system reacts to this signal, perhaps by referring to a memory where other data and instructions are stored, or perhaps by amplifying the signal. The signal from the process sub-system is fed into the output sub-system, which produces the response required (heat, light or sound, for example). The feedback loop ensures that the system can respond to the new conditions created by the output.

What kinds of devices are used in input sub-systems?

Most input sub-systems involve a potential divider, which consists of two resistors in series, with the output taken from between them (see chapter 18, *Circuits and power*). The output voltage depends on the relative resistances of the two resistors.

$$V_{\text{out}} = V_{\text{in}} \times \frac{R_{\text{bottom}}}{R_{\text{TOTAL}}}$$

A thermistor is a sensor whose resistance depends on its temperature. For 'negative temperature coefficient' (NTC) thermistors the higher the temperature is, the lower the resistance becomes. The resistance of a light dependent resistor (LDR) responds to light intensity. It is about 300 Ω in bright light, and about 300 kΩ in the dark.

Potential dividers that include sensors like these can be used to control the input signal to a process sub-system. For example, a potential divider with a LDR could be used to trigger the process and output systems to turn on a security light as darkness falls. The value of the other resistor in the potential divider has to be set bearing in mind the level of brightness or temperature you want to trigger the next part of the circuit (see figure 3).

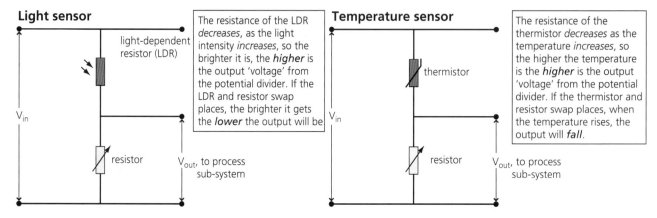

Light sensor

light-dependent resistor (LDR)

V_{in}

resistor

V_{out}, to process sub-system

The resistance of the LDR *decreases*, as the light intensity *increases*, so the brighter it is, the *higher* is the output 'voltage' from the potential divider. If the LDR and resistor swap places, the brighter it gets the *lower* the output will be

Temperature sensor

thermistor

V_{in}

resistor

V_{out}, to process sub-system

The resistance of the thermistor *decreases* as the temperature *increases*, so the higher the temperature is the *higher* is the output 'voltage' from the potential divider. If the thermistor and resistor swap places, when the temperature rises, the output will *fall*.

Figure 3 The output voltages of these potential dividers depend on the resistances of the thermistor and LDR.

In many circuits, a switch is used as one of the 'resistors' in a potential divider (see figure 4). You could think of a switch as a variable resistor with just two resistance values – zero and infinity. So the signal to the process sub-system is either a maximum or a minimum, depending on whether the switch is pressed, or not. The keys on a computer keyboard, and on a push-button telephone, all operate switches in potential divider circuits.

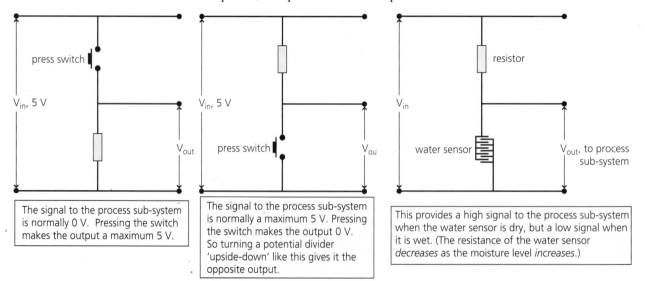

press switch

V_{in}, 5 V

V_{out}

The signal to the process sub-system is normally 0 V. Pressing the switch makes the output a maximum 5 V.

V_{in}, 5 V

press switch

V_{ou}

The signal to the process sub-system is normally a maximum 5 V. Pressing the switch makes the output 0 V. So turning a potential divider 'upside-down' like this gives it the opposite output.

resistor

V_{in}

water sensor

V_{out}, to process sub-system

This provides a high signal to the process sub-system when the water sensor is dry, but a low signal when it is wet. (The resistance of the water sensor *decreases* as the moisture level *increases*.)

Figure 4

Figure 5 This circuit could be used as part of a moisture monitoring system.

What kinds of devices are used in process sub-systems?

Logic gates

The behaviour of a process sub-system device depends upon the inputs it receives. The circuit symbols for devices called **logic gates** are shown below. The **truth tables** alongside each symbol show the outputs produced for each combination of inputs.

NOT gate

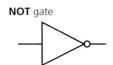

Input	Output
low	high
high	low

OR gate

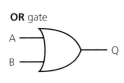

Input A	Input B	Output Q
low	low	low
low	high	high
high	low	high
high	high	high

NOR gate

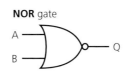

Input A	Input B	Output Q
low	low	high
low	high	low
high	low	low
high	high	low

AND gate

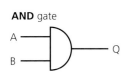

Input A	Input B	Output Q
low	low	low
low	high	low
high	low	low
high	high	high

NAND gate

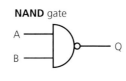

Input A	Input B	Output Q
low	low	high
low	high	high
high	low	high
high	high	low

Bistables

A **bistable** can permanently give a 'high' or a 'low' output. It can be made to 'flip' from one state to the other by changing the inputs. The output of a bistable depends on the order that the inputs change state, so a truth table is not a suitable way to represent the behaviour. A timing diagram displays it better. Figure 6 shows timing diagrams for bistables made up of NOR gates and NAND gates.

Figure 6

Bistables

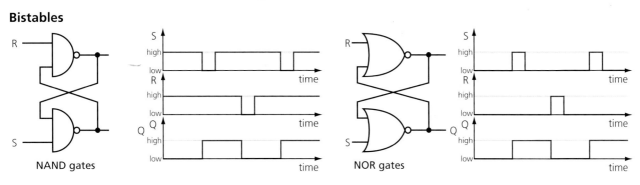

A bistable is also known as a 'latch', because the output can be 'locked' into one state or the other, high or low, until it is reset. This makes the device ideal for alarm systems and computer memories. The latch could be 'locked' in by the high temperature caused by a fire, or by the pressure of an intruder stepping on a sensitive pad. The output of the bistable then stays high, causing an alarm to sound, until it is reset using the other input. In computer memories, there are vast numbers of latches, each used to lock into and remember a single signal. In a 16-bit computer, with 2 megabytes of RAM, there are over 32 million bistable latches.

Monostables

A **monostable** has just one stable state, but it can be triggered to 'flip' to the other state for a short time, when the input reaches a certain level (see figure 7). A monostable often uses a resistor and a capacitor. The length of time for which a monostable remains in the unstable state depends upon the values of these components.

A **capacitor** consists of two metal plates which are very close together, but insulated from each other. They can be used to store small amounts of charge, so they are useful in time delay circuits as part of a monostable. The larger the capacitor, the more charge it stores, and the larger the time delay can be. The charge-storing ability of a capacitor is measured in farads (F) or microfarads (μF).

charge stored (C) = capacitance (F) × voltage across capacitor (V)

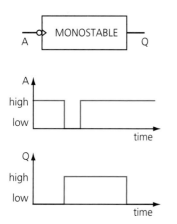

Figure 7 A monostable can be triggered to reach an unstable state for a short while, but then it reverts to its stable state.

Capacitor

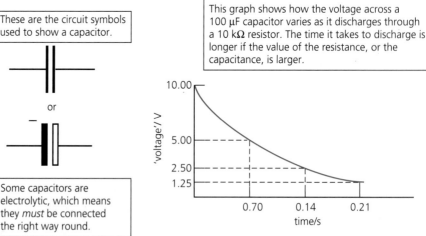

These are the circuit symbols used to show a capacitor.

or

Some capacitors are electrolytic, which means they *must* be connected the right way round.

This graph shows how the voltage across a 100 μF capacitor varies as it discharges through a 10 kΩ resistor. The time it takes to discharge is longer if the value of the resistance, or the capacitance, is larger.

Figure 8 This graph shows how the voltage across a 100 μF capacitor varies with time as it discharges through a resistor.

A monostable could be used in a car alarm circuit, to switch the alarm on if the car is disturbed, but turn it off after a set time to prevent the battery running flat. Monostables are also used in photographic developing equipment, to ensure that the developing process switches off after a set time. The time delay can be adjusted by the photographer to achieve just the right exposure, and recreated again and again to produce identical prints.

Analogue process devices

All the process devices covered so far have involved digital inputs and outputs. The devices in figure 9 process analogue input signals.

Figure 9

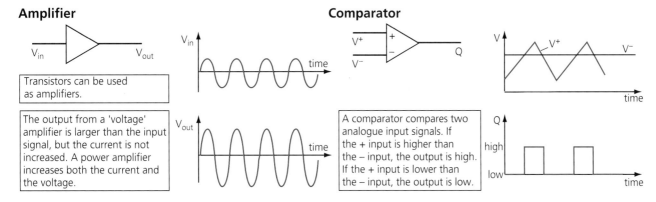

Amplifier

Transistors can be used as amplifiers.

The output from a 'voltage' amplifier is larger than the input signal, but the current is not increased. A power amplifier increases both the current and the voltage.

Comparator

A comparator compares two analogue input signals. If the + input is higher than the − input, the output is high. If the + input is lower than the − input, the output is low.

Figure 9

What kinds of devices are used in output sub-systems?

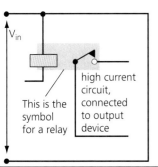

A small current in the relay switches on a much larger current in a separate circuit, which allows the output device to function.

Figure 10

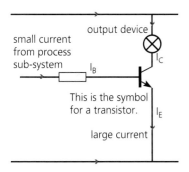

Figure 11 A transistor uses a small current to control a large one.

You need a **buffer** as part of the output sub-system in almost all circuits, because the chips that provide the signal for the output sub-system cannot cope with very much current. A circuit is needed which can take the small current that the chip *can* deliver, and use it to control a much larger current. Figures 10 and 11 show two ways to do this.

In figure 10, a small current in the relay, produced in response to suitable inputs by the process sub-systems, causes the high current circuit to be completed. (See chapter 20, *Magnets and electromagnetism*, for more details on relays.) So a large current flows through the output device, producing the required response (see table 1).

In figure 11, the required output response is for the bulb to be lit. When the appropriate input signals have been detected and processed, a small 'base' current (I_B) flows through the transistor, which allows a large 'collector' current (I_C) to flow through the right hand side of the circuit, lighting up the bulb. The 'emitted' current (I_E) is the sum of the base and collector currents, according to Kirchhoff's law (see chapter 16, *Current electricity*).

$$I_E = I_B + I_C$$

A transistor acts as a current amplifier. The **current gain** of a transistor is a measure of how much the collector current is larger than the base current.

$$\text{current gain} = \frac{I_C}{I_B}$$

So a transistor can be used to switch on a large current in a circuit when triggered by a tiny base current from a process sub-system.

1 **a** In figure 11, if $I_C = 0.50$A and $I_B = 0.01$A: **i** Calculate I_E **ii** Calculate the gain of the transistor
   b Explain why a transistor is required in this circuit.

Output device	Circuit symbol	Effect	Features
Motor		Produces rotational motion	Requires a higher current when starting or going slowly than when running freely. Speed of rotation is usually so high that it must be geared down before the motion is much use.
Bulb		Produces light	Filament glows white hot when there is a current in it. Bulbs have a lower resistance when cool, and have a short lifespan if the current is switched on and off regularly.
Light emitting diode (LED)	protective resistor / Current passes diode this way only. / LED	Produces light	LEDs, like all diodes, allow current in one direction only, from anode to cathode. More compact and durable than bulbs, require less current and waste less energy as heat. Require a protective resistor in series with them, to reduce the PD, but require such a small current that they can be connected to a chip without a buffer circuit.
Buzzer or bell		Produces sound	Buzzers require a current of several mA to produce sound. Do not need a resistor in series with them, and they can run from a range of PDs.
Loudspeaker		Reproduces specific sounds, like speech or music	Most have low resistance and need relatively high current. Current must change rapidly for sound to be produced.

Table 1 *Some output devices.*

How would you design a system for a hot air hand drier?

2 A gardener wants a system to warn her if her greenhouse gets too cold.

a Design a system that makes a light turn on if the temperature falls below a certain value.

b Modify the design to make the light flash instead of just coming on steadily.

When designing any circuit, you should follow these three main steps:

1 Make a clear statement about what you want the system to do.
2 Decide which tasks are 'input', 'processing' and 'output'.
3 Select circuits which do each of these tasks, and link them together.

Of course, you then need to test your system, and make adjustments. For example, you might try out different capacitor values to get the right timing, or try different circuits that could do the job better than the ones you used.

Step 1 What do you want the hand drier to do?
When someone presses the switch, a heater and motor should come on for 30 s.

Step 2 What parts of this function are 'input', 'process' and 'output'?
When someone presses the switch …
You need an input circuit that produces a signal when a switch is pressed.

3 The residents of some flats are fed up with people leaving the stairway lights on, wasting electricity.

a Design a system to allow a person at the bottom of the stairs to switch a light on, which automatically switches off after a delay (allowing the person time to climb the stairs).

b Expand the system to include more switches, so that if the person does not reach the required floor before the light goes off, he or she can press another switch to reactivate the circuit.

… for 30 s.

Your process sub-system needs to include a monostable timing device.

…a heater and motor should come on …

You need a heater and a motor in your output circuits. Both transducers need to come on at the same time, and you will need to include a buffer circuit so as not to overload the monostable.

Step 3 How will you set up circuits to carry out each task?

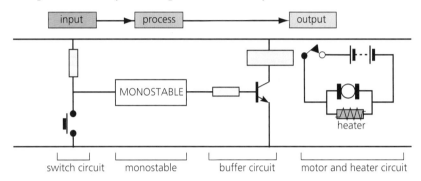

Figure 12 This circuit could be used to operate a hot air hand drier.

Summary of using electronics

- Electronic systems include input, processing and output sub-systems. They often include a feedback loop.
- Analogue signals can have any value, positive or negative. Digital signals have only two possible values, called high and low, or 0 and 1.
- Switches, LDRs and thermistors can be used in input sensors.
- Buzzers, Lamps, LEDs and motors can be used as output devices.
- Capacitors can be used to store charge and are useful in delay systems.
- Transistors can be used as amplifiers or switches.

- Relays and transistors use a small current to control a large current. In a transistor, $I_E = I_B + I_C$. Current gain = I_C/I_B.
- Diodes allow current to flow in one direction only.
- Logic gates deal with digital input signals, and include NOT, AND, NAND, OR and NOR gates.
- A bistable is a digital device with two stable states.
- A monostable is a digital device. It has a single stable state. If it is moved to the other state it returns to the stable state after an interval.
- Electronic circuits can be used in a wide variety of control systems.

Investigation

Thermistors are used in many electronic circuits. Carry out an investigation to find out how their resistance varies with temperature. Over which range of temperatures are they most sensitive?

Oscillations 22

Learning objectives

By the end of this chapter you should be able to:

- **recall** that energy is carried in waves
- **recognise** two kinds of waves
- **describe** the properties of waves
- **calculate** values using the wave formula

- **explain** how waves affect each other
- **describe** how energy in oscillations can be useful or cause damage

22.1 Swings, twangs and waves

What are oscillators?

Swingers, bouncers and shakers are all oscillators.

Figure 1 One child is oscillating with a bigger amplitude than the other.

The objects in the photos are all moving from side to side, or up and down. These movements are called vibrations or **oscillations**. The objects all need energy to start them oscillating. They stop vibrating when all the energy has been transferred to the surroundings.

To get the swing going, each child in figure 1 has to transfer energy from the food he has eaten to movement in the swing. The time it takes for the child to complete one swing is called the **period** of the oscillation. The number of swings he completes in one second gives the **frequency**, which is measured in **hertz (Hz)**. The distance from the middle of the swing to the end is the **amplitude** of the oscillation.

1 **a** In figure 1, which child travels the furthest distance on each swing?
   b What difference does the length of the chains make to the amplitude of the swing?
   c Which child can swing the fastest?
   d What difference does the chain length make to the frequency of the swing?

2 A pendulum swings 20 times in 10 s. The highest points of the swings to each side are 7 cm apart.
   a Draw a labelled diagram to represent the swinging pendulum.
   b Work out **i** the frequency, **ii** the period, **iii** the amplitude of the pendulum's oscillation.

Figure 2 When you 'twang' a ruler, you can see it vibrate up and down. The way it vibrates depends on its length and thickness, what material it is made of, and how hard you twang it.

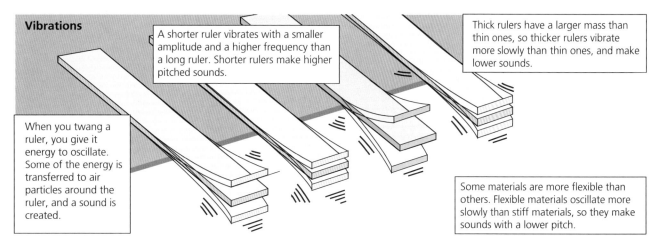

Vibrations

A shorter ruler vibrates with a smaller amplitude and a higher frequency than a long ruler. Shorter rulers make higher pitched sounds.

Thick rulers have a larger mass than thin ones, so thicker rulers vibrate more slowly than thin ones, and make lower sounds.

When you twang a ruler, you give it energy to oscillate. Some of the energy is transferred to air particles around the ruler, and a sound is created.

Some materials are more flexible than others. Flexible materials oscillate more slowly than stiff materials, so they make sounds with a lower pitch.

3 **a** Some musical instruments use vibrating strings to make sounds. What kinds of strings do you think make higher notes?
   b What will happen to the sound if the string becomes too slack (too flexible)?

Sometimes the sea is very calm. At other times, waves up to 15 metres high cover its surface. The highest parts of the wave are called peaks or **crests** and the lowest parts are called **troughs**. The distance from one crest to the next, or from one trough to the next, is called the **wavelength** of the wave. The height of the wave above normal water level is called the amplitude (see figure 3).

Estimate the amplitude of this wave.

Figure 3 The oscillations of the bar in the ripple tank make wave patterns on the water surface.

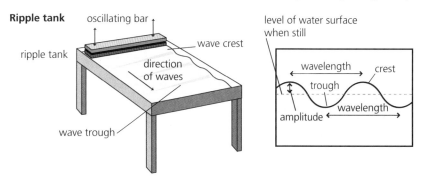

A ripple tank is a shallow tank containing water. When a bar moves up and down, it makes waves on the surface of the water. You can make the bar vibrate at different frequencies, which changes the wavelength of the wave produced (see figure 4).

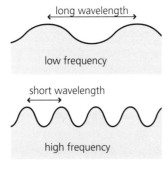

long wavelength

low frequency

short wavelength

high frequency

Figure 4 When you change the frequency of a wave, the wavelength changes.

4 How does increasing the frequency affect the wavelength?

5 Which of the waves in the diagram below has the:

  i highest frequency   **ii** longest wavelength

  iii smallest amplitude   **iv** shortest wavelength?

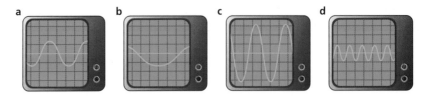

a   b   c   d

What kinds of waves are there?

The waves in this swimming pool are transverse waves. The swimmers bob up and down as the waves go by.

The oscillating bar in a ripple tank makes waves which move along the tank. But the water does *not* move along with the waves. To prove this, you can put a small piece of cork on the water. The cork rises and falls as the waves go past but it does not move along the tank. The energy in the wave moves along, but each water particle oscillates up and down in one place, like the piece of cork.

When the oscillations are at *right angles* to the direction of the wave like this, it is called a **transverse wave** (see figure 5). Light, X-rays and radio waves are examples of transverse waves. In figure 6, the coils in the Slinky oscillate backwards and forwards as the wave travels along the spring. The oscillations are in the *same direction* as the wave. This kind of wave is called a **longitudinal wave**.

Transverse waves

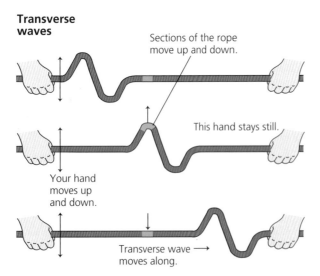

Sections of the rope move up and down.

This hand stays still.

Your hand moves up and down.

Transverse wave → moves along.

Figure 5 You can demonstrate transverse waves using a rope.

Longitudinal waves

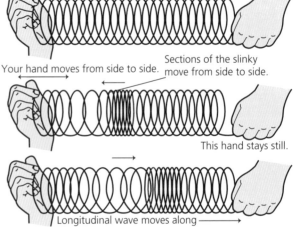

Your hand moves from side to side.

Sections of the slinky move from side to side.

This hand stays still.

Longitudinal wave moves along ——→

Figure 6 Oscillations in a longitudinal wave are lengthways.

Summary of swings, twangs and waves

- An oscillation is a vibration or repeated movement backwards and forwards, or from side to side. Energy is required to start an oscillation.
- The frequency is the number of complete oscillations per second. The units of frequency are hertz (Hz). 1 Hz = 1 oscillation per second.
- The period is the time taken for one complete oscillation, in seconds (s).
- The amplitude is the maximum displacement of the oscillation from the rest position.

- Waves are oscillations that transfer energy from place to place. But the particles of the material through which the wave moves do not move along with the energy.
- Particles in transverse waves oscillate at right angles to the direction the energy travels.
- Particles in longitudinal waves oscillate in the same direction as the energy travels.
- The wavelength of a wave is the distance between two consecutive crests, or two consecutive troughs.

22.2 Wave behaviour

How fast do waves travel?

Light waves travel very fast. It only takes 8 minutes 27 seconds for light from the Sun to travel 150 million km to reach us on Earth. That means light waves travel at 300 000 km/s. Sound waves are much slower. They can only travel 330 m in one second, in air. That is why you can see a flash of lightning before you hear the crash of thunder in an electric storm.

You can calculate the speed of any wave if you know its frequency and wavelength using this formula:

$$\text{wave speed (m/s)} = \text{frequency (Hz)} \times \text{wavelength (m)}$$
$$v = f\lambda$$

Wavelength (m)	Frequency (Hz)
1	3
0.2	2
5	0.3
3	9

WORKED EXAMPLE

The bar on a ripple tank vibrates with a frequency of 3 Hz. That means three waves are made every second. Each wave has a wavelength of 10 cm. What is the speed of the waves?

$v = f\lambda$
$\quad = 3 \times 10$
$\quad = 30$ m/s

6 Calculate the speed of each wave in the table.

7 Simone is watching waves on the beach. One wave reaches her every 6 s and the crests are 4 m apart. How quickly are the waves travelling towards Simone?

What makes waves change direction?

Waves travel in straight lines unless something stops or diverts them. Waves can be reflected, refracted or diffracted.

Reflection

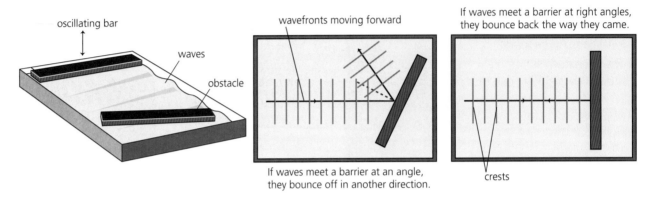

oscillating bar

waves

obstacle

wavefronts moving forward

If waves meet a barrier at an angle, they bounce off in another direction.

If waves meet a barrier at right angles, they bounce back the way they came.

crests

Figure 7 When waves meet a barrier, they bounce off it.

If water waves meet a barrier, they bounce back (see figure 7). This is called **reflection**. Light waves are reflected off shiny surfaces such as mirrors in a regular way, so you can see a clear image (see chapter 24, *Light*). Sound waves are also reflected off hard surfaces. This causes echoes (see chapter 23, *Sound*).

Refraction

Waves slow down as they move into a shallower area. The wavelength decreases and the frequency increases. When they return to deeper water, the waves continue at their original speed.

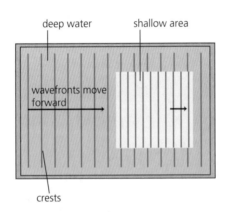

deep water　　shallow area

wavefronts move forward

crests

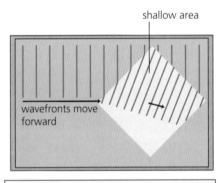

shallow area

wavefronts move forward

When waves hit a shallower area at an angle, they change direction as part of each wave is slowed down.

Figure 8

If water waves move over a shallower area, they are slowed down. If only part of a wave goes over a shallow area then only part will be slowed down. Some of the wave lags behind and the wave changes direction overall. A change in direction due to a change in speed is called **refraction** (see figure 8).

8 Draw a diagram to show how light from a torch enables you to read at night.

9 If you look at someone through a glass of water their image is distorted. Explain why this happens.

10 a At night, layers of air near the ground are colder than those higher up. Using figure 9 to help, draw a diagram to show what would happen to the sound waves from an explosion at night.

b Explain why sounds are easier to hear at night than in the day.

Light is refracted when it passes through a lens, or a prism, or water (see chapter 24, *Light*). Dense glass, and water, slow down the light waves and change their direction. Sound waves can also be refracted (see figure 9).

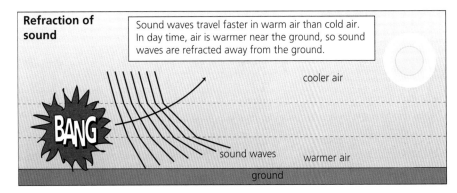

Figure 9 In the daytime, sounds are refracted away from the ground.

Diffraction

Wave fronts can change shape as they pass through a gap or go round an obstacle. The wave carries on in the same direction but the edges of the wave are slowed down, and curve backwards. This change of shape is called **diffraction**. The amount of diffraction depends on the wavelength of the wave and the width of the gap or obstacle (see figures 10 and 11).

Figure 10 Diffraction is most noticeable when the obstacle is about the same size as the wavelength.

Diffraction around obstacles

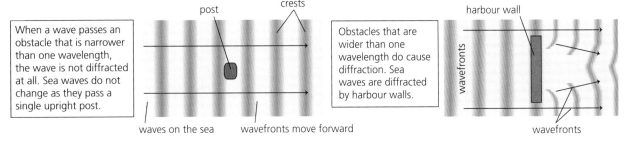

Diffraction by gaps

The narrower the gap, the greater the diffraction.

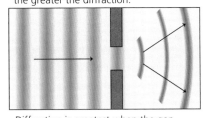

Diffraction is greatest when the gap is roughly the same size as the wavelength.

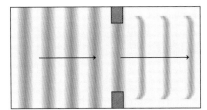

When the gap is wider than the wavelength, diffraction is minimal.

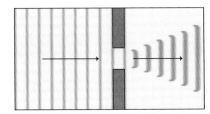

Short wavelengths are diffracted less than long wavelengths.

Figure 11 Waves are diffracted when they pass through gaps.

11 Sound waves can have a wavelength of 0.5 m. Light waves have very small wavelengths (about 6×10^{-7} m). Explain why you can *hear* your friends talking in the next room when the door is open, even when you cannot *see* them.

How do waves affect each other?

The child needs to supply energy to make the rocking horse oscillate.

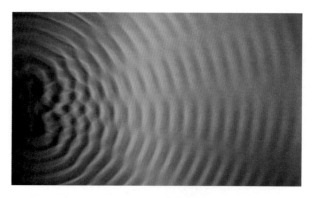

The dark areas in this interference pattern show where waves are adding up. The light areas show where waves are cancelling out.

It takes a little while for the child in the photo to learn just when to push forward and when to lean back to make the horse rock well. If the child matches her own oscillations with those of the rocking horse, then the horse will rock even higher. If the child gets it wrong, and the oscillations do not match up, the rocking horse will not go as high. When oscillations match up like this it is called **resonance**.

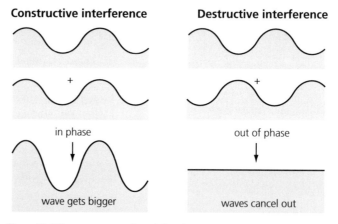

Figure 12 When waves meet there is interference.

When waves on the sea hit a cliff, they are reflected back. Sometimes you will see two crests meet – one from an incoming wave and one from a reflected wave. The waves are said to be **in phase**. The crests combine to make an even bigger wave. This is another example of resonance. It is called **constructive interference**. If a crest meets a trough they cancel each other out. This is **destructive interference** (see figure 12).

....

12 Wave machines in swimming pools work a bit like ripple tanks. Explain why the side of the pool opposite the wave machine has a sloping edge instead of a vertical wall.

13 How is resonance useful to a spring board diver?

....

What do earthquake vibrations show about the Earth?

Using equipment like this, seismologists can monitor earth tremors, and try to predict when large earthquakes will happen.

....

14 Which seismic waves are longitudinal waves and which are transverse waves?

15 Which seismic waves reach a seismograph first? Why?

16 Explain why a single recording station cannot locate the epicentre of an earthquake.

....

Note

....

In 1909, a seismologist called Mohorovicic found that seismic waves travel faster through deep rocks than at the surface. This showed that the Earth has an outer **crust**, above a more dense **mantle**, about 30 km down.

....

> The point on the surface directly above the focus of an earthquake is called the epicentre. To locate it, three recording stations measure how far away the epicentre is. Each draws a circle with this radius on a computer map. The epicentre is where the three circles touch.

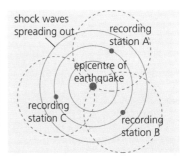

Figure 13

The energy contained in vibrations like earthquakes and stormy seas can be extremely destructive.

Earthquakes occur when rocks in the Earth's crust suddenly move past each other at a **fault**. The place where the quake starts is called the **focus**. Vibrations radiate out from the focus and pass through the deep layers of the Earth. The vibrations cause **seismic waves**. Primary (P) waves make rock particles vibrate backwards and forwards, in the same direction as the wavefront. Secondary (S) waves make rock particles vibrate at right angles to the direction of the wave.

A seismograph is used to detect seismic waves. P waves travel quicker than S waves, so by comparing the time taken for S and P waves to reach an earthquake recording station, seismologists (people who study earthquakes) can work out how far away the earthquake started. By comparing results from three recording stations, they can locate the starting point precisely (see figure 13).

Seismologists have discovered that as S and P waves travel through the centre of the Earth, away from the focus, they are refracted. We know that waves are refracted when they cross a boundary between one medium and another (see page 156). So the refraction of S and P waves shows that the Earth must have layers of different kinds of material.

P waves can travel through solids and liquids. S waves only travel through solids. Seismologists have found that S waves cannot pass through the centre of the Earth, so the Earth's core probably contains liquid. They have also found that P waves speed up deep within the liquid centre, which suggests there could be a smaller solid inner core, probably made of iron and nickel (see figure 14).

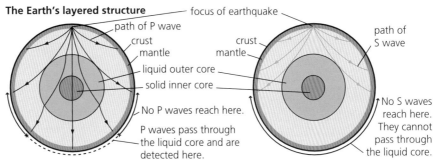

Figure 14

How can we use oscillations?

Controlled swinging vibrations allow builders to break through hard materials such as concrete and brick.

In hammer-action drills, the bit vibrates rapidly back and forward as well as spinning round.

Kidney stones can be broken up by high frequency ultrasound waves. The broken pieces are tiny enough to be passed out in the person's urine.

17 Make a list of problems that vibrations cause, and another list of uses of vibrations. Try to think of more examples than you have read about in this chapter.

18 Ultrasound can be used to clean objects. The dirty object is suspended in water or oil and ultrasound vibrations are passed through it. How do you think this removes the dirt?

Summary of wave behaviour

- The velocity of a wave can be calculated from velocity (m/s) = frequency (Hz) × wavelength (m), or $v = f\lambda$.

- Waves can be reflected (bounced off), diffracted (their direction changed) and refracted (bent).

- When waves interfere constructively, they add to form a larger wave.

- When waves interfere destructively, they cancel each other out.

- The energy in oscillations such as earthquakes or stormy seas can be highly destructive.

- Seismic waves from earthquakes can provide evidence for the internal structure of the Earth.

- Controlled oscillations can be useful in all kinds of applications, from construction sites, to medicine.

Sound

Learning objectives

By the end of this chapter you should be able to:

- **explain** that sounds are vibrations
- **describe** how different sounds are made
- **understand** that sound is a longitudinal wave
- **explain** how sounds travel

- **explain** how echoes are made
- **use** terms such as frequency and wavelength in relation to sound waves
- **describe** how sound waves affect each other.

23.1 Sound waves

What causes sound?

Vibrating objects make sounds.

The photographs all show objects that are vibrating. Vibrating objects make sounds. If you tap a tuning fork it vibrates. You can hear the sound it makes when you hold the tuning fork to your ear.

If you touch the end of a tuning fork on water, the vibrations make the water splash out.

How are different sounds made?

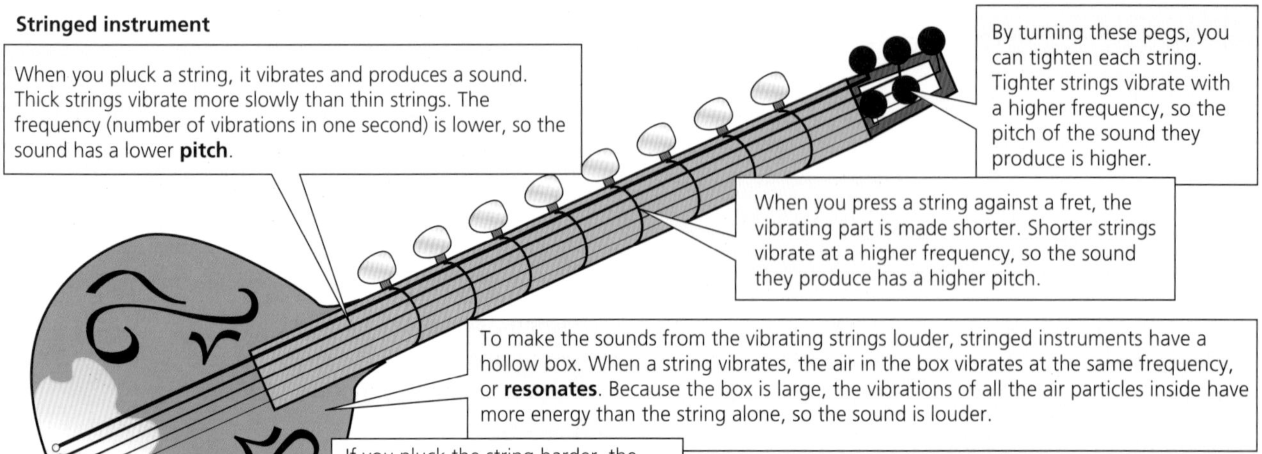

Stringed instrument

When you pluck a string, it vibrates and produces a sound. Thick strings vibrate more slowly than thin strings. The frequency (number of vibrations in one second) is lower, so the sound has a lower **pitch**.

By turning these pegs, you can tighten each string. Tighter strings vibrate with a higher frequency, so the pitch of the sound they produce is higher.

When you press a string against a fret, the vibrating part is made shorter. Shorter strings vibrate at a higher frequency, so the sound they produce has a higher pitch.

To make the sounds from the vibrating strings louder, stringed instruments have a hollow box. When a string vibrates, the air in the box vibrates at the same frequency, or **resonates**. Because the box is large, the vibrations of all the air particles inside have more energy than the string alone, so the sound is louder.

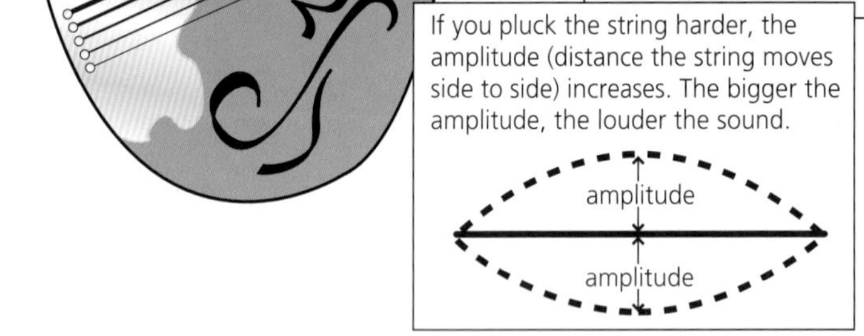

If you pluck the string harder, the amplitude (distance the string moves side to side) increases. The bigger the amplitude, the louder the sound.

amplitude

amplitude

Wind instrument

The air column in the recorder resonates at certain frequencies to give a clear note. The length of the air column and therefore the frequency at which it resonates, can be changed by covering or uncovering the holes drilled in the recorder. In this way, the musician alters the pitch of the note produced.

When someone blows into the mouthpiece of a recorder, the air movement causes slight pressure changes to occur hundreds of times a second. These pressure changes produce a sound wave in the air.

Figure 1 Vibrating strings make sounds. By changing the thickness, length and tautness of the strings you can make different sounds.

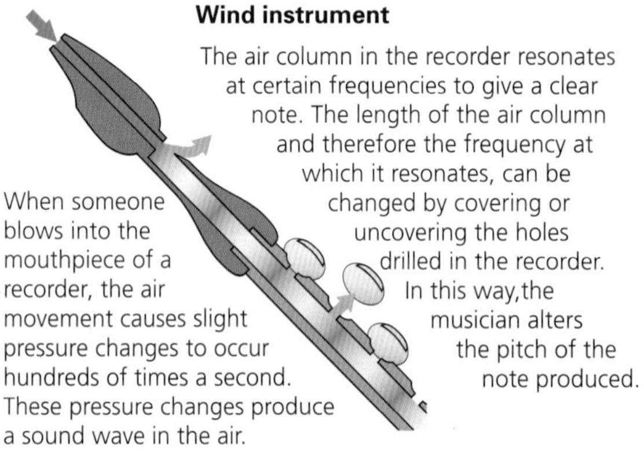

Figure 2 When the air column in a wind instrument vibrates musical notes are made.

1 **a** Two strings are of equal length and thickness. If the first is tighter than the second, which produces the highest sound when plucked?

b Two strings are of equal length and tightness. If the first is thicker than the second, which vibrates with the highest frequency?

2 How does amplitude affect the loudness of a sound?

3 Why do most stringed instruments have hollow boxes? List five instruments with hollow boxes.

Can sound travel through all materials?

Figure 3 Skilled Cherokee Indians could judge where to find a herd of buffalo, the size of the herd, and in which direction it was moving, by listening to vibrations from the hooves travelling through the ground.

4 Why didn't Cherokee Indians just listen to sounds travelling through the air to find buffalo?

5 Explain why sounds seem louder when you put your head under the water in a bath.

Sound can pass through anything that is made of particles. When you tap the end of a desk you transfer energy to molecules in the wood. These molecules vibrate, and bump into molecules next to them. They vibrate too, and so the sound wave gets passed through the desk.

Particles in a solid are packed close together so vibrations pass easily from particle to particle. Sounds travel quickly through solids. Particles in a liquid are packed quite closely together, so sound vibrations pass through liquids easily. Whales sing messages to each other through many kilometres of water. Particles in a gas are much further apart, so it is not so easy for vibrations to spread. Sounds reach our ears through vibrating particles in the air.

If there are no particles to vibrate, a sound wave cannot travel through. There are no air particles in space, so astronauts cannot talk to each other on the Moon unless they use radio waves to carry messages. Radio waves can travel through a vacuum because they do not need particles.

Sounds can be absorbed by a material, or reflected. Reflected sounds can be heard as an echo. If you stand in a tunnel and shout your name, you will hear your name twice. The first time is your own shout. The second time is the echo, reflecting from the walls.

What are sound waves?

Sound waves

When you bang a cymbal you give it energy and it vibrates. Some of its energy, is transferred to the surrounding air particles, which makes them vibrate too.

These particles pass energy to those next to them, and so on, as the sound wave travels through the air.

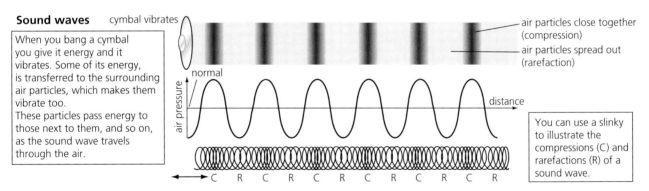

cymbal vibrates

air particles close together (compression)

air particles spread out (rarefaction)

You can use a slinky to illustrate the compressions (C) and rarefactions (R) of a sound wave.

Figure 4 Sound travels through air when vibrations in an object make particles in the air vibrate.

6 Draw a wave of amplitude 1 cm and wavelength 2 cm, as you might see it on a CRO screen. This wave represents a sound. Now re-draw it to represent a sound that is:

a higher pitched but the same loudness

b the same pitch but louder

c quieter and lower

(Hint: look at figure 5 on the next page to help you.)

Energy is carried along by sound waves, but the vibrating particles just oscillate backwards and forwards around the same spot. They do not move along with the wave. In air, the oscillations cause pressure changes. In some places the air particles get squashed up together. These are called **compressions**. In other places the particles move further apart. These are called **rarefactions**. The particles are vibrating in the same direction as the energy flow, so this is a longitudinal wave pattern (see figure 4). Sound passes through solids and liquids in the same way.

The distance between two consecutive compressions, or two rarefactions, is one wavelength. Low pitched sounds have long wavelengths. They have longer distances between compressions than higher pitched sounds.

You cannot see sound waves but you can use a cathode ray oscilloscope (CRO) to represent them on a screen (see chapter 19, *Using electricity*). It is not easy to show longitudinal waves on a screen so they are represented by transverse waves (see figure 5, over the page).

Looking at sound waves

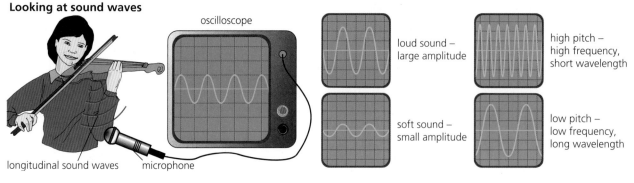

oscilloscope

loud sound – large amplitude

high pitch – high frequency, short wavelength

soft sound – small amplitude

low pitch – low frequency, long wavelength

longitudinal sound waves   microphone

Figure 5

Does sound always travel at the same speed?

Sounds travel at different speeds through different materials (see table 1). The more dense the material is, the faster the sound can travel through it.

Material	Speed of sound (m/s)	Density (g/cm^3)
Natural rubber	1617	0.91
Iron	5000	7.87
Cork	500	0.25
Fresh water	1400	1
Air	330	0.001

Table 1 *The speeds of sound in different materials.*

You can find wave speed using this equation (see chapter 22, *Oscillations*):

$$v = f\lambda$$

Although the frequency and wavelength of sound waves can be different, when sound is travelling through one material, its speed is always about the same. So the speed of all sounds in air is around 330 m/s.

7 Explain the different speeds of sound in solids, liquids and gases, in terms of particles.

8 Look at table 1. Why do you think sound travels much more slowly through cork than through iron?

9 a Calculate the missing values for sound waves travelling in air, in the table below.

Pitch	Frequency (Hz)	Wavelength (m)	Wave speed (m/s)
high	1948	0.17	?
medium	1183	?	331
low	?	0.49	331
very low	50	6.62	?

b What pattern do you notice between frequency and pitch?

c What pattern do you notice between frequency and wavelength for different sounds?

How far can sound travel?

10 When there us a dance party at the community centre near Becky's home, she says she hears the low pitched sounds, but not the lyrics of the music. How would you explain to Becky why she can only hear low notes in the music, from her home.

Sound waves transfer energy to surrounding particles. The further the sound travels the more the energy spreads out. Eventually the sound is so spread out that you cannot detect it. Louder sounds have more energy than quiet ones, so you can hear loud sounds further away than quiet sounds. Loudness is measured in units called decibels (dB). On the decibel scale, an increase of 10 dB doubles the energy in the sound. Normal speech is about 50 dB, but a blue whale can make sounds of more than 180 dB, so the whale song has more than 8000 times as much energy as speech. Whale songs are so loud they can be heard over 850 km away.

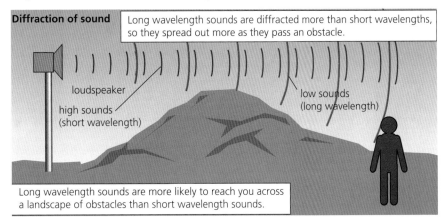

Diffraction of sound Long wavelength sounds are diffracted more than short wavelengths, so they spread out more as they pass an obstacle.

loudspeaker
high sounds (short wavelength)
low sounds (long wavelength)

Long wavelength sounds are more likely to reach you across a landscape of obstacles than short wavelength sounds.

Figure 6 When sounds meet obstacles they can be reflected as an echo, or absorbed, or diffracted as shown here. Low sounds seem to travel further than high sounds, because they are diffracted around obstacles.

Summary of sound waves

- Sound waves are made when objects vibrate.
- Sound travels as a longitudinal wave.
- The larger the amplitude of the vibrations, the louder the sound. To make louder sounds you need more energy.
- The higher the frequency of vibration, the higher the pitch of the sound. Higher frequency sound waves have shorter wavelengths.

- Instruments with shorter, tighter and thinner strings make higher sounds.
- The human ear can detect frequencies between 20 Hz and 20 000 Hz.
- Sound cannot travel where there are no particles.
- Sound travels through the air as a series of compressions and rarefactions.
- In air, sound waves travel at about 330 m/s.

Investigation

Choose and carry out one of the following methods of measuring the speed of sound in air. Repeat your measurements several times.

1 Measure how long it takes for an echo to return to you from a wall about 50 m away.

2 Measure how long it takes for a sound made by a person 300 m away to reach you.

3 Connect two microphones to an electronic timer so that a sound arriving at the first starts the timer, and stops the timer when it reaches the second microphone.

Are any of your results very different from the others? Explain why they are different. How could you improve the accuracy of your results?

Which of the above methods is most accurate? Why?

23.2 Hearing sounds

How do people hear sounds?

From ear to brain

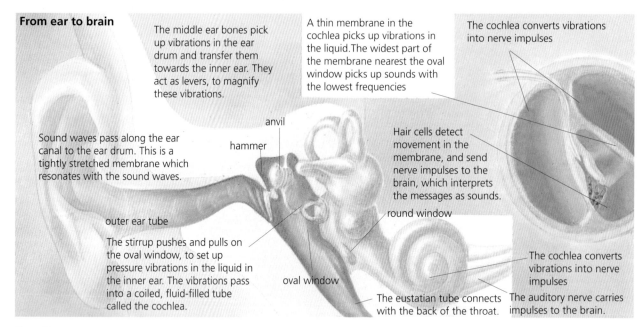

The middle ear bones pick up vibrations in the ear drum and transfer them towards the inner ear. They act as levers, to magnify these vibrations.

A thin membrane in the cochlea picks up vibrations in the liquid. The widest part of the membrane nearest the oval window picks up sounds with the lowest frequencies

The cochlea converts vibrations into nerve impulses

anvil

hammer

Sound waves pass along the ear canal to the ear drum. This is a tightly stretched membrane which resonates with the sound waves.

Hair cells detect movement in the membrane, and send nerve impulses to the brain, which interprets the messages as sounds.

round window

outer ear tube

The stirrup pushes and pulls on the oval window, to set up pressure vibrations in the liquid in the inner ear. The vibrations pass into a coiled, fluid-filled tube called the cochlea.

oval window

The cochlea converts vibrations into nerve impulses

The eustatian tube connects with the back of the throat.

The auditory nerve carries impulses to the brain.

Figure 7

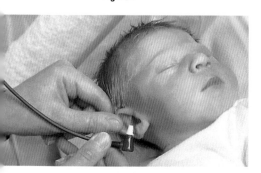

This baby is having her hearing range tested.

Your ear collects sound wave vibrations in the air, and passes them through your ear drum and middle ear, to your **cochlea**. Sound is transferred to electrical energy which travels down your **auditory nerve** to your brain. Your brain interprets the nerve signals as sounds (see figure 7).

Young children can normally hear sounds as low as 20 Hz and as high as 20 000 Hz. Humans are most sensitive to sounds at 1000 Hz. Babies cry at this frequency, perhaps to get the soonest response from their parents.

Your hearing range gets smaller as you get older. Many 60 year olds cannot hear sounds above 12 000 Hz. A build up of wax, damage due to loud noises or infection can also cause hearing loss, so the sufferer hears some sounds but not others.

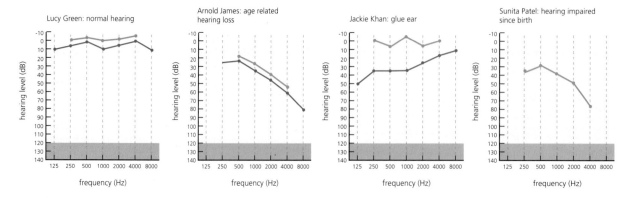

Figure 8 In these graphs, hearing level is the loudness of a sound in dB that can *just* be heard.

11 Explain how you hear the sound of the school bell.

12 **a** In figure 8, which frequencies does Arnold have difficulty hearing?

   b How could Arnold's hearing be improved?

13 Jackie has a condition called glue ear, which means sound waves cannot pass easily through her middle ear. How does Jackie hear?

14 **a** Can Sunita hear high or low frequency sounds better?

   b In speech vowel sounds have a low pitch and consonants have a high pitch. Explain why it can be difficult for people with normal hearing to understand Sunita when she speaks.

15 Towards the end of Beethoven's composing career he became deaf. He 'listened' to his piano using a stick. How do you think this worked?

How can we make sounds louder?

Amplifying sounds

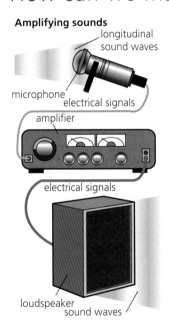

Figure 9

Sounds often need to be amplified.

It is not easy to hear musicians from the back of a crowded venue. Electrical equipment is often needed to **amplify** the sounds so they are loud enough to be heard by the whole audience. To amplify sounds, the energy in the sound wave is transferred to electrical signals by a microphone (see figure 9). The signals are boosted in an amplifier. The boosted electrical signals are turned back into sound waves which have a bigger amplitude, by a loudspeaker (see chapter 20, *Magnets and electromagnetism*).

16 Hearing aids work by amplifying sound. Explain why this could be a problem in a noisy street.

How can you control excess sound?

Unwanted or excess sound is called **noise**. Noise can distract people from their work and make them less efficient. Noise which goes on for a long time can cause high levels of stress, which might lead to physical illness (see figure 10). Some sounds are easier to get used to than others. For example, we can ignore the low rumble of traffic, but sudden or intermittent sounds such as a dog barking are more disturbing.

Figure 10 These graphs show how prescriptions for different medicines varied over a number of years for people living near a new airport.

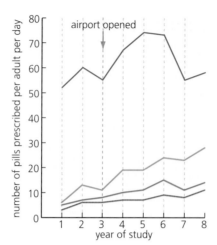

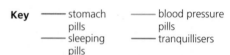

17 a Do the graphs in figure 10 indicate that the opening the airport had an effect on local people's health?
b What other information would you want to have before making a conclusion about the effect of the airport?

18 In one year, night flights were reduced. Which year do you think this could have been? What evidence do you have for your answer?

Key —— stomach pills   —— blood pressure pills
—— sleeping pills   —— tranquillisers

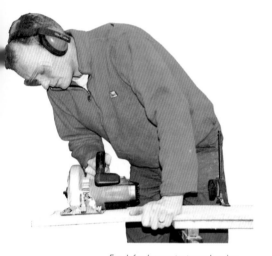

Ear defenders protect your hearing when you are working in noisy conditions.

Some rooms are very noisy. Hard surfaces such as walls reflect sound waves, rather than absorbing them. The sounds bounce around the room, and take a long time to die away. This can be a nuisance. The problem can be solved by covering the walls and floor with a soft materials which absorb sound instead of reflecting it. Carpets and polystyrene tiles are good sound absorbers.

Many people work with loud machinery. The Noise at Work Regulations state that people must wear ear defenders if the sound is 90 dB or above, and employers must minimise noise as much as possible. Noisy machines can be placed on foam or kept in sound proof boxes. Double glazed windows reduce the amount of factory noise which escapes into the surrounding area.

Why do sounds sound different?

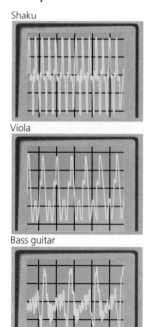

Synthesisers can be used to produce all kinds of sounds, from imitations of other musical instruments, to bizarre sound effects. To understand how it does this you need to know a bit about why different sounds sound different.

Different sounds have different waveforms. Louder sounds have a larger amplitude, and higher pitched sounds have a higher frequency. But even if two notes have exactly the same loudness and pitch, they sound different when produced by different instruments. For example, a shaku, viola and guitar all playing the same note produce a different waveform, tone and sound (see figure 11).

Electronic synthesisers contain thousands of digitally sampled sounds, stored on microprocessors. When you press a key, it triggers a sound to be replayed whose waveform exactly matches that of a 'real' sound. So synthesisers can imitate any sound, like a piano, or a sitar, or even a dog barking.

Figure 11 Each musical instrument has a characteristic waveform.

Summary of hearing sounds

- Sound waves reaching the inner ear produce electrical signals carried to the brain by the auditory nerve, where they are interpreted as sound.
- Young humans can hear sounds in the range 20 Hz to 20 000 Hz.

- Hearing loss can be caused by loud noises, infection and old age.
- Loudness is measured in decibels (dB).
- Unwanted sound, or noise, can be reduced using materials that absorb sound waves rather than reflecting them.

23.3 Using sound

How can you use echoes to take measurements?

Sonar

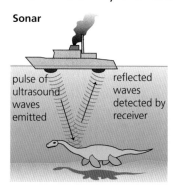

pulse of ultrasound waves emitted

reflected waves detected by receiver

Figure 12 Ultrasound waves are too high for people to hear, but they are ideal for sonar because they are not diffracted by objects on the sea bed.

Sound waves can be used to map out the dark sea bed in the deep ocean, or locate hidden objects like wrecks or mines (see figure 12). Sound waves are sent into the water. When they hit solid objects they are reflected back as an echo. The returning waves are detected by a receiver. The time it takes for the sound waves to make their return journey is used to judge how far away the reflecting object is. The amplitude of the returning wave can indicate the size of the reflecting object. Skilled operators interpret the signals on a screen. Measuring the position and size of an object in this way is called echolocation or **sonar**. Sonar is short for **So**und **Na**vigation and **R**anging.

Audible sounds have long wavelengths, which would be diffracted round small objects on the sea bed and not be reflected back to the ship (see chapter 22, *Oscillations*). So instead, high frequency **ultrasound** waves are used for sonar. Ultrasound waves with a frequency of 150 000 Hz have a wavelength of only 0.01 m (1 cm).

The time it takes for the sound to return to the ship depends on the speed of sound in sea water and the distance it has travelled (see chapter 12, *Looking at motion*). So:

distance = speed × time

As the sound wave has to travel from the ship to the object and back again you need to divide the total distance travelled by two, to get the depth of the reflecting object.

$$\text{depth (m)} = \frac{\text{speed of sound in salt water (m/s)} \times \text{time (s)}}{2}$$

$$d = \frac{vt}{2}$$

19 A fishing trawler uses sonar to detect shoals of fish directly under the boat. If the echo returns to the ship in 2.5 s, how low must the crew cast their nets?

WORKED EXAMPLE

Sonar was used to find a wrecked ship on the sea bed. An echo took 3.00 s to return to the receiver on the searching ship. The speed of sound in sea water is 1445 m/s. How far away was the wreck?

$$d = \frac{vt}{2} = \frac{1445 \times 3.00}{2} = 2167.5 \text{ m}$$

How else can ultrasound echoes be used?

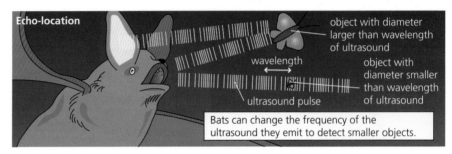

Figure 13

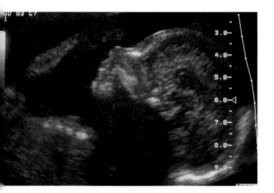

Ultrasound scans show doctors and the mother how her baby is developing.

Many bats use echo-location to hunt for insects as food, at night. They send out ultrasound wave pulses at regular intervals. The bats can tell when an object is in their path, how far away the object is and whether or not it is food from the waves that are reflected.

Echo-location can only be used to detect objects that are larger than the wavelength of the ultrasound. Bats use waves of 50 Hz when flying, but if they detect a small object which could be an insect they increase the frequency to 170 000 Hz. Bats can detect objects as tiny as gnats.

Ultrasound echo-location is used to observe unborn babies. Signals are sent into the mother's abdomen and are reflected back to a detector. Dense body tissue reflects sound more than softer tissue. Information about the signal's strength and how long it took to travel is collected by a transducer which changes the sound energy into electrical signals and sends them to a computer. A picture of the baby is created on a monitor.

20 Why do bats use high frequency pulses to detect small objects?

21 The speed of sound in air is about 330 m/s. What frequency of signal would a bat need to emit, to detect a strand of wire 1 mm in diameter?

22 What properties of ultrasound make it useful for examining unborn babies?

Summary of using sound

- Echo-location can be used to locate objects on the sea bed, and to examine unborn babies.
- Echo-location is used by many animals in their natural habitats, including bats.

- Ultrasound waves are suited to echo-location because their short wavelength means they are reflected by small objects rather than diffracted round them.

Light

Learning objectives

By the end of this chapter you should be able to:

- **recall** that light enables you to see
- **demonstrate** that light travels in straight lines
- **show** how light waves can be reflected or bent
- **describe** how light can pass through, be reflected by, or be absorbed by different materials
- **show** how white light can be split into different colours
- **explain** how lenses are used in optical instruments

24.1 Absorption and reflection

What is light?

Everything you can see is visible because light from it enters your eyes.

1 **a** List the light sources in the photos above.
  b Which objects are bright because they reflect light?
2 Which is the most important light source on Earth?

Light is a form of energy. Without it, you would not be able to see. Light sources, like stars, bulbs and glow worms, produce their own light. You see other objects, which are not light sources, because light bounces off them. Shiny surfaces such as polished metal reflect light in a regular way, so they produce a clear reflected image.

What causes shadows?

When light hits a surface, it can either be absorbed, reflected or refracted. If there is an **opaque** obstacle between you and an object, you cannot see the object. The light from the object travels in straight lines (see figure 1), and cannot pass through or bend around the obstacle to reach your eyes. Instead, the light is absorbed by the obstacle.

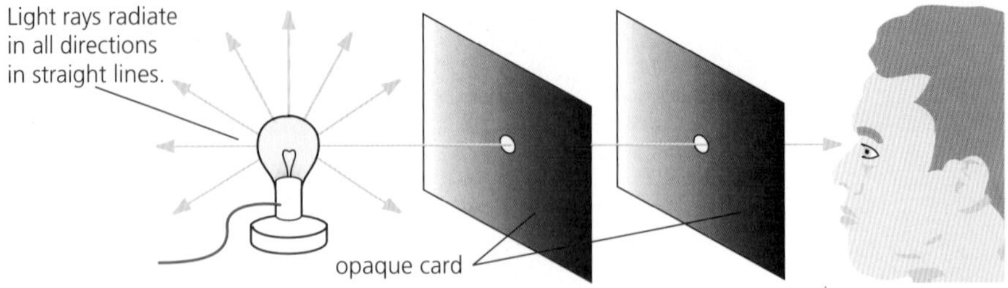

Figure 1 You can only see the light if the holes in the cards are lined up, because light travels in straight lines.

Light rays radiate in all directions in straight lines.

opaque card

Puppet theatre

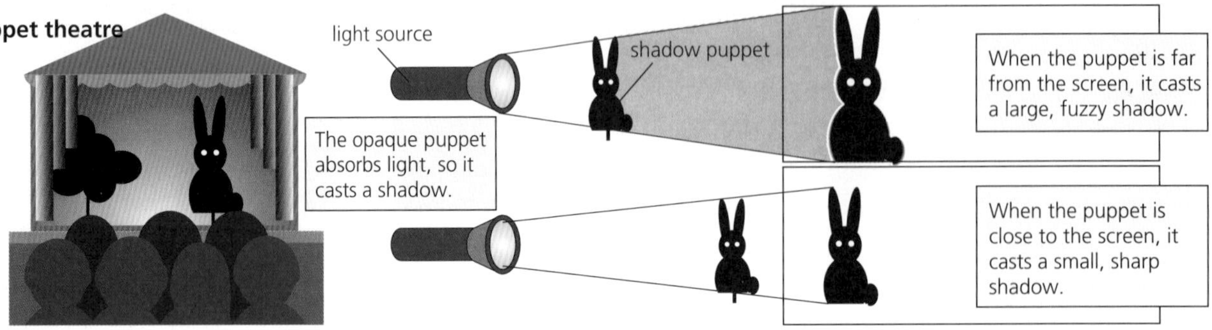

Figure 2 Opaque objects cast shadows. In this puppet theatre, the puppeteer can change the shadow size by moving the puppet.

light source

shadow puppet

The opaque puppet absorbs light, so it casts a shadow.

When the puppet is far from the screen, it casts a large, fuzzy shadow.

When the puppet is close to the screen, it casts a small, sharp shadow.

3 Explain, using a diagram, why your shadow is different in the winter and in the summer. (Hint: The Sun is low in the sky in winter.)

4 Use diagrams to explain how shadow puppeteers might make one character look big and frightening, and another character look small and scared.

How do mirrors make images?

When light falls on a surface, some is always reflected. Flat, smooth, shiny surfaces reflect the most light. Good reflectors produce a clear **image**. Bent and rough surfaces distort images.

Mirrors are made of a thin piece of glass with a silvered back. Mirrors reflect nearly all the light energy that falls on them, but a tiny fraction is absorbed. The image in a mirror is not really there. It just seems to be. You could not project the image onto a screen, for example. This kind of image is called a **virtual image** (see figure 3).

Mirror image

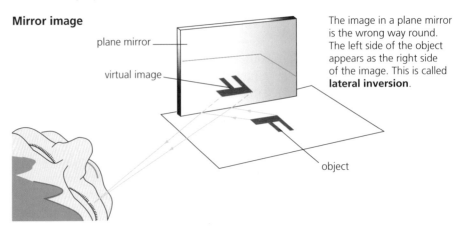

plane mirror

virtual image

The image in a plane mirror is the wrong way round. The left side of the object appears as the right side of the image. This is called **lateral inversion**.

object

Figure 3 A plane mirror forms a clear, laterally inverted, virtual image.

5 Copy the diagram below, and draw in rays to show how light is reflected from an object to your eyes through a periscope.

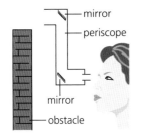

When drivers see this fire engine in their car mirrors, they will read the words Fire Rescue the right way round.

Periscopes contain two mirrors: the image from one mirror is reflected into the second and then into your eyes.

Are there rules about reflection?

Light rays hitting a reflecting surface at right angles reflect back along the same path. Light rays hitting the surface at an angle bounce off at an angle. To measure the angle you can draw an imaginary line called the normal. The normal is always at right angles to the surface (see figures 4 and 5).

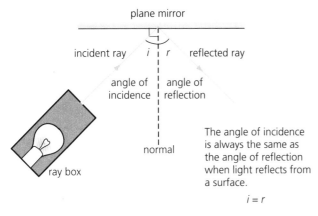

The angle of incidence is always the same as the angle of reflection when light reflects from a surface.

$$i = r$$

Figure 4

Light is reflected in a regular way from smooth surfaces, so you get a clear image.

Light is scattered from rough surfaces as it is reflected, so no clear image is produced. This is **diffuse** reflection.

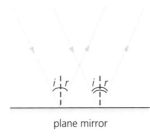

Figure 5

Polished surfaces reflect light in a regular way, so you get a clear image.

6 a Bhavyesh and Vinesh set up an experiment to measure the angles of incidence (*i*) and reflection (*r*) of rays reflecting from a plane mirror. What do their results tell you?

i	65°	59°	29°	23°	40°	15°	10°
r	65°		29°		40°	15°	

b Bhavyesh and Vinesh did not have time to complete their work. What do you think the missing angles of reflection would be?

7 Why do you get a better image in the surface of a polished car than in the surface of a dirty one?

173

Summary of absorption and reflection

- Light travels as transverse waves, which move in straight lines.

- When light waves hit a surface, they can be reflected or absorbed.

- We can see objects because light is reflected from them.

- When light is reflected, the angle of incidence is always equal to the angle of reflection.

- When a lot of light is reflected in a regular way, a clear, virtual image or reflection is formed.

- When light is absorbed by opaque objects, a shadow is formed.

24.2 Refraction

How can you bend light?

Glass and water refract light rays.

When you look at a person through water or bubbled glass their image is distorted. As light goes into a more **optically dense** material it slows down, which can make it change direction (figures 6 and 7). This is called refraction (see chapter 22, *Oscillations*). Materials that are more optically dense refract the light more. Glass, water and diamond all refract light passing in from the air.

Refraction of light

A light ray passing into a glass block at right angles (along the normal) slows down, but continues in the same direction. As it leaves the block, it speeds up again.

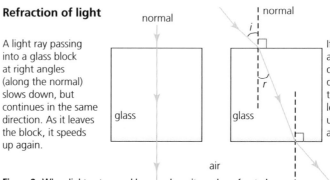

If the ray enters the glass at an angle, its speed and direction change. It slows down, and is bent towards the normal. As it leaves the block, it speeds up again, and is bent away from the normal.

Figure 6 When light enters and leaves glass, it can be refracted.

Explaining refraction

Imagine each wavefront as a row of particles. When all the particles are moving through the same medium, they all travel at the same speed, and the row is straight.

When the particles hit the glass, they slow down. Some particles in each row slow down before the others, if the ray is at an angle to the glass. The row bends.

In the glass, the particles all move at a slower speed than in air. The ray moves in a straight line, but its wavelength is shorter than in air.

As the ray leaves the glass and moves back into the air, some particles in each row escape first and speed up before those still in the glass. The row bends.

As the ray moves through the air again, it travels at the same speed as before it entered the block, with the same wavelength, and in the same direction (although it has been displaced).

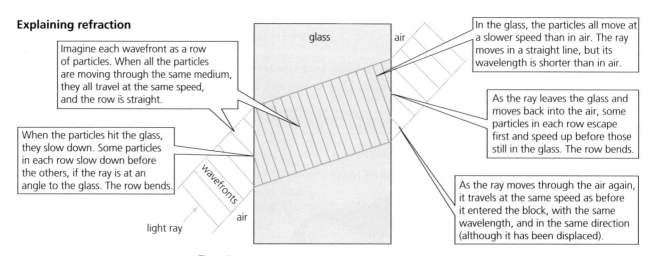

Figure 7

How much do different materials bend light?

Material	Speed of light (m/s)
Air	300 000 000
Glass	200 000 000
Water	225 000 000
Diamond	120 000 000
Perspex	200 000 000

Table 1 *The speeds of light through different materials.*

Light travels through different materials at different speeds (see table 1). You can work out how much a material will refract light from its **refractive index**, which is calculated from the ratio of the speed of light in air and the speed of light through the material. Optically dense materials have a large refractive index. The bigger its refractive index, the more the material refracts light.

$$\text{refractive index} = \frac{\text{speed of light in air}}{\text{speed of light in material}}$$

WORKED EXAMPLE

Find the refractive index of water:

$$\text{refractive index} = \frac{\text{speed of light in air}}{\text{speed of light in water}} = \frac{300\ 000\ 000}{225\ 000\ 000} = 1.33$$

8 Use table 1 to calculate the refractive index of: **a** glass **b** perspex **c** diamond

9 Which material in table 1: **a** refracts light the least, **b** is the most optically dense?

Why do pools seem shallower than they are?

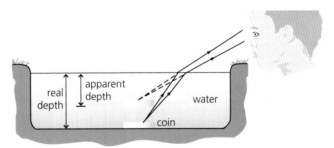

Figure 8 The coin seems higher up than it really is.

Light from the coin in figure 8 refracts as it leaves the water. The rays are bent, but your eye assumes all rays travel in straight lines, so they appear to have come from a point above the real position. It is an optical illusion. You can work out the real depth of the pool if you know the refractive index of water and the apparent depth of the coin on the bottom.

$$\text{refractive index} = \frac{\text{real depth}}{\text{apparent depth}}$$

WORKED EXAMPLE

Find the real depth of a coin in a bucket of water, if the coin appears to be 16 cm beneath the surface.

$$\text{refractive index} = \frac{\text{real depth}}{\text{apparent depth}}$$

real depth = 1.33 × 16 = 21.28 cm

10 Explain why spear fishermen do not aim at where the fish seems to be.

11 Archer fish catch insects above the surface by spitting water at them. Use a diagram to explain why the fishes aim just below the place where the insect seems to be.

Is light always refracted by a glass block?

Total internal reflection

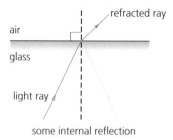

some internal reflection

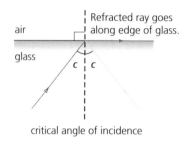

critical angle of incidence

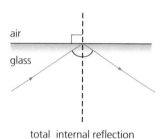

total internal reflection

Figure 9 If light travelling through a material hits a surface at a large angle of incidence, it can be totally internally reflected.

When light passes out of a glass block into the air, most of the light is refracted. A small amount of light is reflected back into the block. As you increase the angle of incidence, the angle of the refracted light to the normal also increases. When the angle of incidence reaches a **critical angle** the refracted light runs along the surface of the block (see figure 9). The critical angle for glass and perspex is about 42°. If the angle of incidence is greater than the critical angle, *all* the light is reflected back into the block. This is called **total internal reflection**.

What use is total internal reflection?

Total internal reflection makes emergency workers visible at night.

Reflectors

Bicycle reflectors are smooth on the outside but the plastic is angled on the inside. Light from a car's headlights goes straight through the smooth outside surface. When it hits the angled inside surface it undergoes total internal reflection. Nearly all the light from the headlights is reflected back into the plastic and then out through the flat outer surface (see figure 10). The driver of the car sees the reflected light, and knows the cyclist is there. The emergency services use the same principle in their safety equipment. Glass beads in reflective bands on jackets and vehicles reflect light so emergency workers can be seen when they deal with a crisis at night.

Bicycle reflector

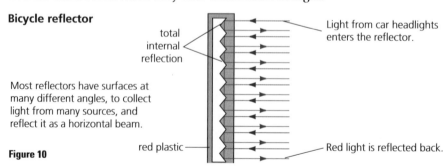

Most reflectors have surfaces at many different angles, to collect light from many sources, and reflect it as a horizontal beam.

Figure 10

12 Why do bicycle reflectors have angled inner surfaces?

13 Why do people use reflectors on bikes instead of plane mirrors?

An endoscope uses total internal reflection to provide surgeons with an image of a patient's internal organs.

Optical fibres

Optical fibres are glass threads about the thickness of a human hair. They have a pure glass centre surrounded by glass with a slightly lower refractive index (see figure 11). Light inside the fibre is totally internally reflected every time it hits the boundary between the pure glass core and the surrounding layer. So light entering at one end can be reflected the whole length of the fibre. Hardly any energy is lost. Optical fibres are used in underground telephone cables to carry vast amounts of information over long distances, literally at the speed of light. The messages are sent as pulses of light, which are used to code for voices, data, text or pictures (chapter 26, *Communication systems*).

Optical fibre

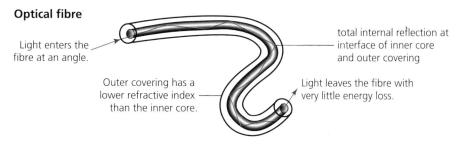

Light enters the fibre at an angle.

Outer covering has a lower refractive index than the inner core.

total internal reflection at interface of inner core and outer covering

Light leaves the fibre with very little energy loss.

Figure 11 Light can go round corners in an optical fibre.

14 Why does the outer layer of an optical fibre have a lower refractive index than the inside?

15 Suggest why an optical fibre can carry telephone messages as far as 200 km without the signal weakening.

Optical fibres allow surgeons to examine patients' internal tissues, and even operate on them, without lengthy and dangerous procedures. Fibres are inserted into tiny incisions in a person's skin, in an instrument called an endoscope. One fibre illuminates the area under examination, and another brings light rays back, which form an image of the tissue for the surgeon. Very small instruments can be manipulated through yet another tube. The patient recovers much more quickly from this kind of 'microsurgery', or 'keyhole' surgery, than from a normal operation.

Why do prisms split light?

16 Suggest why you sometimes see rainbow colours on a rainy day.

17 As the Sun sets below the horizon, light is refracted by the atmosphere. Try to explain why sunsets make the sky appear red.

A prism is a specially shaped glass block, which refracts light as it passes through. White light is split into different colours, which each have a different wavelength. For example, red light has a shorter wavelength than violet light. Short wavelengths are slowed down less than long wavelengths as they pass through an optically more dense medium. This means that short wavelengths are refracted less. Red light is refracted less than violet light. So as they pass into and out of the prism, the different coloured lights are bent by different amounts and get spread out.

Once people thought that prisms stained the light that passed through them. But in 1666, Isaac Newton did an experiment to prove instead that white light is made up of many different colours, which are split apart by a prism.

Summary of refraction

- Light travels at 300 000 000 m/s in a vacuum and in air, but is slowed down by optically dense materials such as water and glass.
- When light waves enter an optically more dense medium at an angle, they are bent or refracted. When they re-enter the original medium, they continue with the original speed, and direction.
- Total internal reflection is used in many devices, including road safety reflectors and optical fibres.

- When the angle of incidence at a boundary between two media of different optical densities exceeds a certain critical angle, total internal reflection occurs.
- White light is a mixture of different wavelengths, which we perceive as different colours.
- When white light enters a prism, each wavelength is refracted a different amount, so the ray spreads into a spectrum of coloured light. Red light is

24.3 Lenses

What is a lens?

Convex and concave lenses

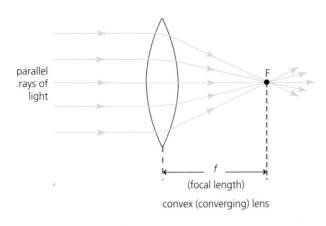

parallel rays of light

F

f (focal length)

convex (converging) lens

parallel rays of light

F

f (focal length)

concave (diverging) lens

Figure 12 Convex lenses make rays of light converge. Concave lenses make rays of light diverge.

The refraction of light can be very useful. Materials like glass can be shaped to make **lenses**, which bend light. You have lenses in your eyes. They are also used in cameras, telescopes, microscopes and projectors. The shape of the lens affects how the light is bent.

Convex lenses are thicker in the middle than at the edges. They make parallel rays of light come together or converge, so they are also called **converging lenses**. The point where the converging rays of light cross is called the **principle focus (F)** of the lens. Concave lenses are thinner in the middle than at the edges. They make parallel rays of light spread out or diverge, so they are also called **diverging lenses**. The rays of light appear to come from a point behind the lens. This is the principal focus (F) of a concave lens.

How can lenses be used to form an image on a screen?

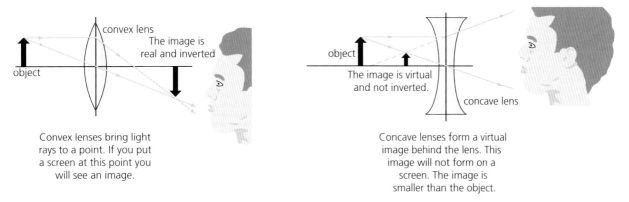

Convex lenses bring light rays to a point. If you put a screen at this point you will see an image.

Concave lenses form a virtual image behind the lens. This image will not form on a screen. The image is smaller than the object.

Figure 13

Convex lenses can be used to form images on a screen (see figure 13). The screen could be the back of your eyes, a camera film or a cinema screen. The image is **real**, and **inverted** (upside down). Concave lenses do not form an image on a screen. They form **virtual** images. The image appears to be behind the lens, but your eyes have been fooled. You cannot put the image on a screen. Concave lenses make the image smaller. If you look at this page with a concave lens the writing will look smaller, but it will be the right way up.

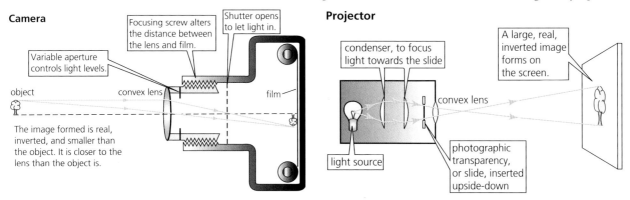

Figure 14

Figure 15

18 Why can't you use a concave lens in a camera, or a projector?

A camera is a light-proof box with an **aperture** (hole) at one end and a photographic paper (film) as a screen at the other (figure 14). A convex lens makes the image clear on the film. To form clear images of objects at different distances from the camera, you have to move the lens backwards and forwards using the focusing screw. Photographic film allows you to make a permanent record of the image. Light has a **photochemical** effect on chemicals in the film, which re-creates the shape and colour of the image when it is developed.

Some photographic film is designed to make transparencies (slides) that can be placed in a projector to produce an image on a screen (figure 15). The projector uses a convex lens to produce an image that is inverted, further from the lens than the slide, and larger than the picture on the slide. To see the image the right way up, you have to put the slide into the projector upside down.

How can your eyes see both near and distant objects?

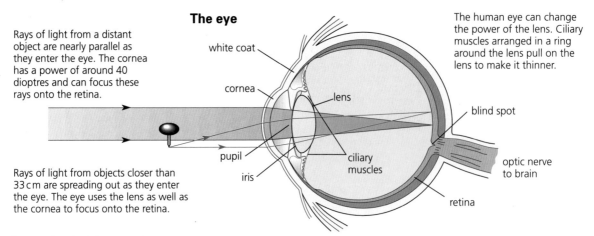

The eye

Rays of light from a distant object are nearly parallel as they enter the eye. The cornea has a power of around 40 dioptres and can focus these rays onto the retina.

The human eye can change the power of the lens. Ciliary muscles arranged in a ring around the lens pull on the lens to make it thinner.

white coat

cornea

lens

blind spot

pupil

ciliary muscles

optic nerve to brain

iris

retina

Rays of light from objects closer than 33 cm are spreading out as they enter the eye. The eye uses the lens as well as the cornea to focus onto the retina.

Figure 16 Your brain interprets the image formed in your eye.

Your eyes are like sophisticated cameras. The box is replaced by a tough white coat. The 'film' is a delicate tissue called the **retina**. The convex lens is made of a firm, jelly-like material. The **pupil** is like the aperture, which lets light in (see figure 16).

The convex lens in each of your eyes focuses light rays onto the retina at the back. The curved surface of the **cornea** also refracts light, and helps to focus the rays. In a camera, the lens has a fixed focal length, and must be moved backwards or forwards to focus rays from objects at different distances onto the screen. In your eyes, the lenses change shape to achieve this.

Thin and thick lenses

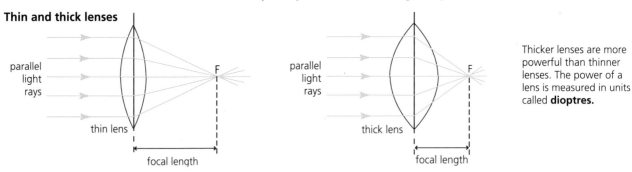

parallel light rays

F

thin lens

focal length

parallel light rays

F

thick lens

focal length

Thicker lenses are more powerful than thinner lenses. The power of a lens is measured in units called **dioptres.**

Figure 17 A glass lens can form a clear image of an object at one distance only.

Fat lenses have a shorter focal length than thin lenses. That means that fatter lenses bend light rays more (see figure 17). Light rays from a distant object are almost parallel and do not need to be bent very far to be brought to a focus on your retina. (In fact the refractive power of your cornea alone is often enough to focus light from a distant object.) So when you look at far off objects, the **ciliary muscles** in your eyes contract and stretch your lenses into a thinner, less powerful shape (see figure 16).

Light rays from close objects are spreading out at an angle as they enter your eye, and need to be bent much more in order to form a clear image on your retina. So when you look at close-up objects, the ciliary muscles relax and let each lens pull itself back into a fat, powerful shape. These changes happen automatically.

The sizes of your pupils alter automatically too. They get larger to let more light in if the surroundings are dim, so a clearer image is formed on your retina. If the surroundings are bright, your pupils become small, to prevent your retina becoming dazzled or damaged.

Light hitting the retina has a photochemical effect that makes a chemical split up, triggering electrical signals to your brain. The photochemical effect is temporary, because the chemical recombines and in a few seconds it is ready to work again. When a flash bulb goes off, too much light hits your retina. It takes longer for the chemicals to recombine, so you see an 'after image' of the flash.

19 In an old-fashioned pinhole camera you cannot move the lens to focus on objects at different distances. Instead you have to replace the lens.

    a What lens would you use to make a clear image of your friend at the other end of the room?

    b What would happen to the image if your friend moved towards you? Why?

    c How would you adjust your camera to take a close up photo of your friend?

What happens if your eyes cannot form clear images?

Short and long sight

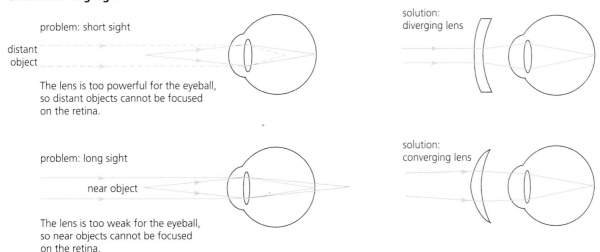

problem: short sight

distant object

The lens is too powerful for the eyeball, so distant objects cannot be focused on the retina.

solution: diverging lens

problem: long sight

near object

The lens is too weak for the eyeball, so near objects cannot be focused on the retina.

solution: converging lens

Figure 18

Some people can see near objects clearly but distant objects look blurred. This **short sightedness** is caused when the lens in each eye cannot be stretched thin enough, or the eyeball is too long. A clear image is formed in front of the retina, but the image on the retina is blurred (see figure 18). You need diverging lenses to correct short sightedness. The light rays are spread out more so they come to a point on the retina of each eye.

Long sighted people can see distant objects clearly but find it hard to read a book or use fine instruments. Long sightedness is caused by a short eyeball or a lens which cannot be squeezed up fat enough. A clear image would form behind the eyeball (if it could get through), but the image on the retina is blurred. You need converging lenses to correct long sight. These focus the light rays further forward, so a clear image is formed on the retina of each eye.

20 a A friend of yours finds it hard to read from the blackboard but can follow a work sheet. What is wrong with your friends eyes?

b What kind of glasses would you recommend for your friend?

21 Joshua wears diverging contact lenses. He has lost them and is on the way to the opticians. He is standing at the bus stop.

a What is wrong with Joshua's eyes?

b Will he find it easier to read the timetable on the bus stop or the number on the coming bus?

How do lenses make things look bigger?

Magnification

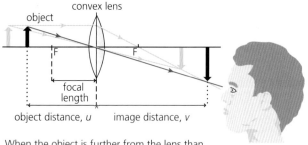

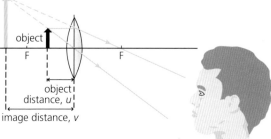

When the object is further from the lens than the focal length, the image formed is real and inverted. As the object is brought closer to the lens, the image becomes larger, and is formed further from the lens.

When the object is between the centre of the lens and its principle focus, the image is virtual, upright and magnified. This is how magnifying glasses work. When the image is virtual, the image distance, *v*, has a negative value.

Figure 19

Magnifying glasses have convex lenses.

Light rays from a distant object are parallel, and are focused by a converging lens to form a real, inverted image at the principle focus of the lens (see figure 12). As you bring the object closer to the lens, the image gets larger, and forms further from the lens (see figure 19). If you place the object between the principle focus and the centre of the lens, the image formed is upright, virtual and magnified. So convex lenses can be used as magnifying glasses, by placing the object to be examined right up close to the lens.

If you measure the distances between the object and the lens (*u*) and between the image and the lens (*v*), you can work out the focal length of the lens (*f*) using this formula:

$$\frac{1}{f} = \frac{1}{u} + \frac{1}{v}$$

WORKED EXAMPLE

When an object is placed 10 cm from a converging lens, a clear image forms on a screen 15 cm from the lens. What is the focal length of the lens?

$$\frac{1}{f} = \frac{1}{u} + \frac{1}{v}$$

$$\frac{1}{f} = \frac{1}{10} + \frac{1}{15} = \frac{15 + 10}{150} = \frac{25}{150} \qquad f = 6 \text{ cm}$$

22 Calculate the focal lengths of the two lenses in figure 20.

Telescopes and microscopes use converging lenses to make objects that are tiny to the naked eye look much larger. In both instruments, an objective lens (furthest from your eye) forms a real, inverted image of the object. This real image forms between the principle focus and the centre of a second lens called the eyepiece. This lens acts as a magnifying glass, and creates a large virtual image of the real image (see figure 20). It is this large virtual image that your eye looks at.

Microscope lenses

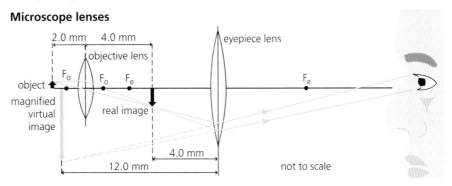

Figure 20 A microscope uses two converging lenses to create a magnified image of the object.

Summary of lenses

- A lens bends parallel light rays from a distant object to form an image at the principle focus (F).
- The distance between the principle focus and the centre of a lens is the focal length (*f*).
- A convex or converging lens makes parallel rays converge on the principle focus.
- A concave or diverging lens makes parallel rays spread out so they appear to come from the principle focus behind the lens.
- When an object is further from a converging lens than its principle focus, the lens forms a real, inverted image which can be shown on a screen.
- When an object is between a converging lens and its principle focus, the lens forms a virtual, upright, magnified image.

- Diverging lenses form virtual, upright images.
- Cameras, projectors, microscopes and telescopes use converging lenses.
- Fat lenses are more powerful than thin lenses. They bend light more, and therefore have shorter focal lengths.
- Your eyes contain converging lens that change shape.
- Short sightedness occurs when an eye's lens cannot be made thin enough, or when the eyeball is too long, to form a clear image of a distant object on the retina. A diverging lens improves short sight.
- Long sightedness occurs when an eye's lens cannot be made fat enough, or when the eyeball is too short, to form a clear image of a close object on the retina. A converging lens improves long sight.

Investigation

Investigate how the thickness of a lens affects its focal length. You can use a wire mesh in a ray box as an object and a sheet of white card as a screen upon which to project an image of the mesh.

Consider what measurements you have to take and how best to make them accurate. Consider how many times you need to repeat your measurements for accuracy. Choose a suitable method of recording your results. Choose an appropriate calculation to find the focal length.

Electromagnetic *spectrum* 25

Learning objectives

By the end of this chapter you should be able to:

- **recall** that there is a family of transverse waves
- **describe** the characteristics of waves
- **use** the terms wavelength, frequency, and amplitude correctly
- **understand** that waves with different characteristics have different effects
- **describe** the different jobs electromagnetic waves can be used for

25.1 Electromagnetic waves

What is the electromagnetic spectrum?

1 List some of the uses and effects of electromagnetic waves:

  a at home

  b at school

The **electromagnetic spectrum** is a family of waves. Like all waves they can be described by their wavelength and frequency. It is their differences in wavelength and frequency that give waves their different effects.

You come across most types of waves in the electromagnetic spectrum (EM spectrum) every day. You can see light waves, and feel **infra-red** radiation as heat on your skin. You cannot see or feel the other forms of electromagnetic radiation, but you can detect them by their effects. The energy in **microwaves** cooks food, and your skin darkens in **ultraviolet** light. **Radio waves**, **X-rays** and **gamma rays** can pass right through your body without you even noticing.

Electromagnetic spectrum

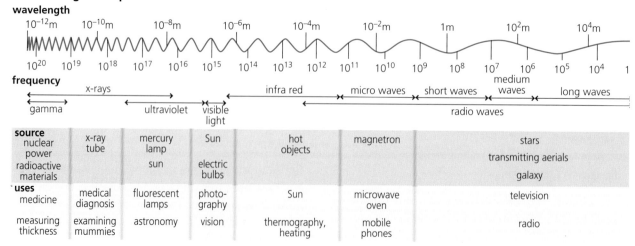

Figure 1 The electromagnetic spectrum is a continuous range of waves, split up according to their wavelengths, and the way they are produced.

Electromagnetic wave

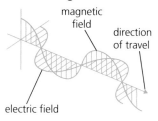

magnetic field

direction of travel

electric field

The electric and magnetic oscillations in an electromagnetic wave are at right angles to each other, and to the direction in which the energy travels.

Figure 2

Electromagnetic waves carry energy from one place to another. The shorter the wavelength the more energy the waves carry and the more harm they can do to living things. Like all transverse waves, electromagnetic waves carry energy along at right angles to the direction of the oscillations. The oscillations in electromagnetic waves are changes in electrical and magnetic fields. That is why the family is called the 'electromagnetic' spectrum.

2 How did electromagnetic waves get their name?

3 Which electromagnetic waves have the following wavelengths?
   a 10 m   **b** 0.01 m   **c** 10 000 m   **d** 10^{-10} m

4 a Which waves in the EM spectrum carry the most energy?
   b Which waves carry the least energy?

5 Which of these waves are the most dangerous to people?

How fast do electromagnetic waves travel?

Note

Remember:

1 micrometre (μm) = 0.000 001 m
                      (10^{-6} m)

1 nanometre (nm) = 0.000 000 001 m
                      (10^{-9} m)

1 m = 1 000 mm

1 km = 1 000 m

1 kHz = 1 000 Hz (10^3 Hz)

1 MHz = 1 000 000 Hz (10^6 Hz)

Waves radiate out from a source. The speed at which they travel (v) can be calculated from the wavelength (λ) and frequency (f) of the wave (see chapter 22, *Oscillations*).

$$v = f\lambda$$

WORKED EXAMPLE

A radio wave with a wavelength of 100 km has a frequency of 3 kHz. Calculate the wave's speed.

$v = \lambda f = 100\ 000$ m $\times$ 3 000 Hz

  $= 300\ 000\ 000$ m/s

Remember that the wavelength must be in m, and the frequency in Hz, to give the wave speed in m/s.

6 Calculate the wave speeds for each wave in the table. Use the Note in the margin to help you.

Wave	Frequency	Wavelength
Microwave	3000 MHz	100 mm
UHF	300 MHz	1 m
Medium wave	30 kHz	10 km
Red light	460×10^{12} Hz	650 nm
X-rays	3×10^{18} Hz	0.1 nm

7 What do you notice about the speed of all electromagnetic waves?

8 A VHF radio station transmits at 100 MHz. What is the wavelength of the waves it sends?

9 The average wavelength of green light is 0.52 micrometres. What is the frequency of green light?

What do electromagnetic waves have in common?

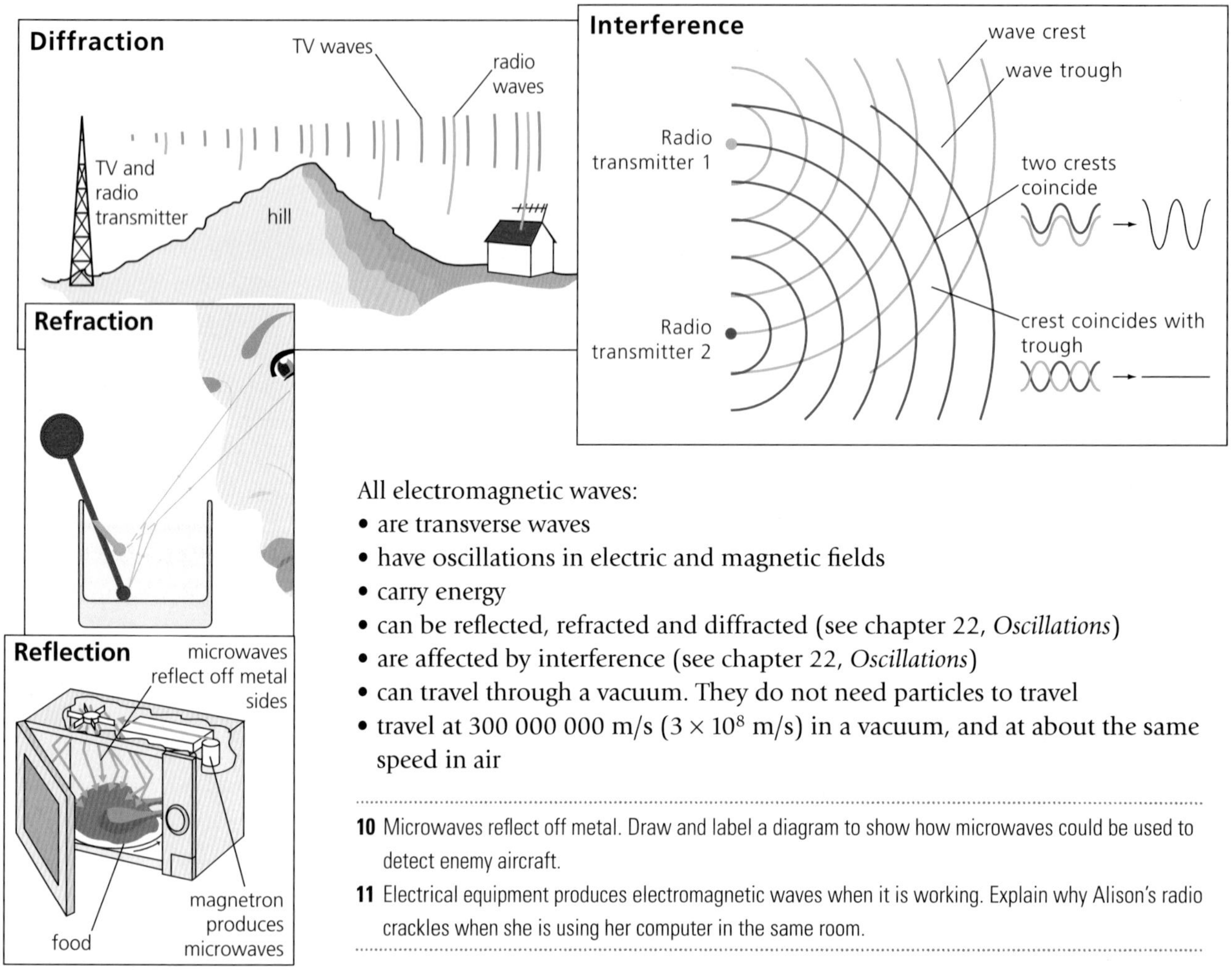

Diffraction

TV waves

radio waves

TV and radio transmitter

hill

Interference

wave crest

wave trough

Radio transmitter 1

two crests coincide

Radio transmitter 2

crest coincides with trough

Refraction

Reflection

microwaves reflect off metal sides

food

magnetron produces microwaves

Figure 3

All electromagnetic waves:
- are transverse waves
- have oscillations in electric and magnetic fields
- carry energy
- can be reflected, refracted and diffracted (see chapter 22, *Oscillations*)
- are affected by interference (see chapter 22, *Oscillations*)
- can travel through a vacuum. They do not need particles to travel
- travel at 300 000 000 m/s (3×10^8 m/s) in a vacuum, and at about the same speed in air

10 Microwaves reflect off metal. Draw and label a diagram to show how microwaves could be used to detect enemy aircraft.

11 Electrical equipment produces electromagnetic waves when it is working. Explain why Alison's radio crackles when she is using her computer in the same room.

Summary of electromagnetic waves

- The electromagnetic spectrum is a family of transverse waves.
- The spectrum includes radio waves, microwaves, ultraviolet light, visible light, infra-red, X-rays and gamma rays.
- Each member of the spectrum has a different wavelength and frequency.
- Wave speed can be calculated from speed (m/s) = frequency (Hz) × wavelength (m) or $v = f\lambda$.
- Electromagnetic waves carry energy from one place to another. The shorter the wavelength, the more energy is carried, and the more harmful the wave is to living things.

- Electromagnetic waves are made up of electric and magnetic fields oscillating at right angles to the direction of the wave.
- Electromagnetic waves can be reflected, refracted and diffracted, and are affected by interference.
- Electromagnetic waves can travel through a vacuum. They do not need particles to travel.
- All electromagnetic waves travel at 300 000 000 m/s (3×10^8 m/s) in a vacuum, and at about the same speed in air.
- Electromagnetic waves have many uses, including communication, broadcasting, medicine, cooking, photography, astronomy and food preservation.

25.2 Using electromagnetic waves

Why do objects appear different colours?

Mixing light

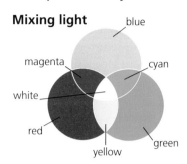

Figure 4

Filter

Figure 5

Visible light is a band of electromagnetic waves which human eyes can detect. Without visible light waves we would not be able to see the shapes or colours of anything around us. We detect different wavelengths of visible light as different colours. All the colours we see can be made by mixing three primary colours of light: red, green and blue. A mixture of all three primary colours gives white light. A mixture of two primary colours gives a secondary colour. For example, cyan is made from blue and green light (see figure 4).

The picture you see on a television screen is made up of millions of tiny dots of primary colour light. As different dots are made to light up, your brains 'mixes' them so that you see different colours on the screen, which together create a picture (see chapter 19, *Using electricity*).

An object looks a particular colour to our eyes, because of the colours of light it reflects. The colours it reflects depend on the colours in the light shining on it, and on the colours it absorbs. Filters absorb particular colours of light. Blue filters look blue because they absorb all colours except blue. So the only colour which passes through the filter into your eyes is blue (see figure 5).

All visible objects absorb some colours of light and reflect the rest. A person looking at a green T-shirt, during daylight, sees green light reflected from the dye: the other colours in daylight are absorbed. But if you shine blue or red light on the T-shirt, it looks black. The blue or red light is completely absorbed, so no light is reflected at all (see figure 6).

Absorbing and reflecting light

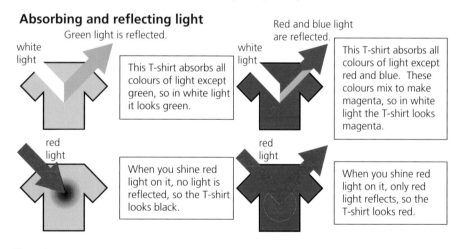

Figure 6

Stained glass behaves as a filter.

12 What colour will a blue sweat shirt look through a red filter?

13 What colour will a yellow dress appear viewed through a green filter?

14 Simone and Jamie are at a disco, where coloured spot lights shine onto the dance floor. Explain why Simone's white shirt and Jamie's cyan T-shirt both look red in the red spot light.

What are ultraviolet light waves used for?

Insects can see UV light from the Sun but we cannot, so flowers look different to insects and humans. The lower photo was taken using UV sensitive film. The other was taken using normal film.

Some chemicals **fluoresce**. They change ultraviolet light into visible light. Security marker pens contain chemicals that fluoresce in ultraviolet light. If you use a security pen to write your post code on valuables such as videos and cameras, the mark is invisible. But if the valuables are stolen, when the thief is caught the police can read the mark using a UV light, and return your belongings to you. Some discos use UV light to make your clothes fluoresce.

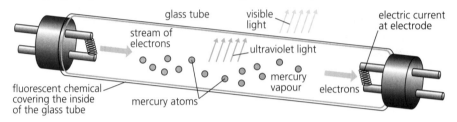

Figure 7 Fluorescent light tubes are covered in a chemical which fluoresces in ultraviolet light.

15 Some washing powders contain fluorescent chemicals called optical brighteners, which make your clothes look brighter. Explain to a customer whether this means the clothes are really cleaner or not.

16 Insects which visit yellow primroses might ignore yellow daffodils. Give a possible explanation for this behaviour.

How is infra-red radiation useful?

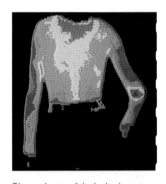

Diseased parts of the body give out extra heat. Thermal imaging is useful to identify problems like arthritis.

Particles in warm objects vibrate more energetically than those in cool objects, and give out infra-red radiation. In very hot objects, like light bulb filaments, the particles are vibrating so much, they give out visible light as well as infra-red. Infra-red rays are not hot themselves, but they make objects hot by transferring energy to particles and making them vibrate.

Some photographic films are sensitive to infra-red. This allows photographers to take pictures in the dark, and pictures that show how warm objects are. People trapped under rubble in an earthquake can be detected using an infra-red camera.

Many burglar alarms use infra-red beams to detect intruders. If an intruder breaks the beam, an alarm sounds. Hospital lifts use infra-red sensors to check there is no-one in the way when the doors shut. Infra-red beams carry signals from remote control units to televisions, video recorders and stereos.

What causes the greenhouse effect?

If visible light hits an object, it transfers energy to it, and heats it up. The energy is then radiated away from the hot object as infra-red waves, which have a longer wavelength than visible light. Usually the energy is spread out into the surroundings, but if the object is behind glass the heat gets trapped. Greenhouses get hotter because the glass lets short wavelengths of visible light in, but the longer wavelengths of infra-red radiation from heated objects inside cannot pass back out (see figures 8 and 9).

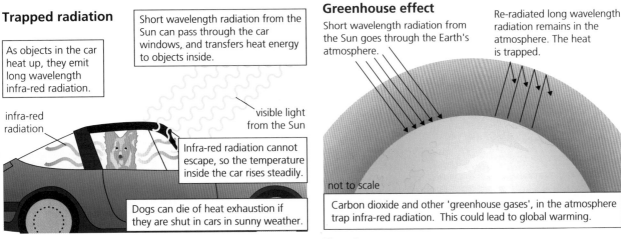

Trapped radiation

As objects in the car heat up, they emit long wavelength infra-red radiation.

Short wavelength radiation from the Sun can pass through the car windows, and transfers heat energy to objects inside.

infra-red radiation

visible light from the Sun

Infra-red radiation cannot escape, so the temperature inside the car rises steadily.

Dogs can die of heat exhaustion if they are shut in cars in sunny weather.

Figure 8

Greenhouse effect

Short wavelength radiation from the Sun goes through the Earth's atmosphere.

Re-radiated long wavelength radiation remains in the atmosphere. The heat is trapped.

not to scale

Carbon dioxide and other 'greenhouse gases', in the atmosphere trap infra-red radiation. This could lead to global warming.

Figure 9

17 Some snakes can detect infra-red. Why do you think these are successful night-time hunters?

18 How could infra-red cameras help:

   a to diagnose arthritis

   b architects to choose materials which reduce heat loss from houses

   c to rescue a person trapped in a collapsed building?

19 Explain why environmentalists are concerned about the build up of so-called 'greenhouse gases'.

What use are microwaves?

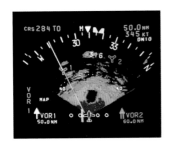

This is a radar weather map from an aircraft control panel.

Perhaps the most well known use for microwaves is for cooking or heating food in microwave ovens, but these waves are also used in mobile phones (see chapter 26, *Communication systems*) and in radar.

Radar uses echoes of microwaves to detect objects such as aeroplanes, war missiles or shoals of fish. Clouds reflect microwaves so radar can also be used to monitor the weather. The readings are sent to a computer which analyses them and generates pictures.

20 If enemy planes know the frequency they can block radar signals. How can radar signals be blocked?

Summary of using electromagnetic waves

- Visible light is a band of electromagnetic waves which human eyes can detect. We detect different wavelengths as different colours.

- All the colours we see can be made by mixing three primary colours of light: red, green and blue. A mix of all three primary colours gives white light.

- Different objects look different colours because they absorb and reflect different colours of light.

- Fluorescent substances change ultraviolet into visible light, and so appear bright in sunlight or UV.

- Infra-red sensitive cameras can be used to take thermal imaging photos, and to film in the dark. Infra-red sensors are used in burglar alarms, lift door detectors and remote control units.

- Microwaves are used in ovens, mobile phones and radar.

25.3 Electromagnetic waves and health

How do electromagnetic waves affect our health?

21 In what way is ultraviolet light
  a useful to people
  b harmful to people?

22 Give a possible reason why skin cancer is more common in Australia than in Europe.

23 Chemicals called CFCs destroy ozone. Why do some people want CFCs banned?

The ozone layer is a band of gas in the upper atmosphere. The purple areas in these satellite images show where the ozone layer has become very thin.

Ultraviolet light from the Sun is important for good health, as it helps your skin cells to make vitamin D. But too much UV can cause painful sunburn, and, over time, increases the risk of skin cancer. The ozone layer absorbs UV from the Sun, so it provides protection for living things on Earth.

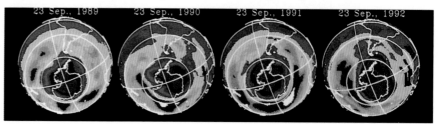

23 Sep., 1989   23 Sep., 1990   23 Sep., 1991   23 Sep., 1992

X-rays were discovered by a German scientist called Roentgen, in 1895. Within weeks of his discovery, X-rays were being used by doctors to see if bones were fractured or damaged. Unfortunately, the doctors did not know that X-rays are dangerous. They have short wavelengths, which means they carry a great deal of energy. A high dose of X-rays can cause cancer, so many of the early X-ray operators died of tumours.

Gamma rays have a very short wavelength. They carry more energy than any other electromagnetic radiation, and cause the most damage to living things. Exposure to gamma rays can cause cancer, genetic mutations and the destruction of cells. But a narrow beam of gamma rays, carefully focused, can be used to kill cancerous cells. This treatment is called radiotherapy.

X-rays pass straight through flesh, but are stopped by bone, so bones cast a kind of 'shadow'.

24 Gamma rays can both cause and cure cancer. How can this be?

25 Why are the gamma beams used in radiotherapy very narrow?

26 a Which electromagnetic waves are used in hospitals to check for bone fractures?

  b Think of as many other uses for electromagnetic waves in a hospital as you can. (They need not all be medical uses.) What risks does each use carry?

Summary of electromagnetic waves and health

- Ultraviolet light from the Sun is important for good health, as it helps skin cells to make vitamin D.

- Too much ultraviolet light can cause sunburn, and increases the risk of skin cancer.

- X-rays are short wavelength, high energy waves. A high dose of X-rays can cause cancer.

- X-rays pass straight through flesh, but are stopped by bone. So X-ray images allow doctors to see if bones are damaged.

- Gamma rays can kill healthy cells but they can also be used to destroy cancer cells. Firing gamma rays at unhealthy cells is called radiotherapy.

Communication systems

26

Learning objectives

By the end of this chapter you should be able to:

- **understand** that communication is the transfer of information and ideas across time and space
- **discuss** how communication systems have revolutionised human development
- **know** how information can be transmitted by waves

- **state** which systems are useful over short distances and which are best over long distances
- **use** systems diagrams to illustrate the flow of information
- **understand** that most communication systems involve coding and decoding information

26.1 Sending messages

How do people communicate?

Figure 1 All communication is a code which needs deciphering.

As soon as you were born you started to communicate. You cried. Your cries did not give very specific information. They just let people know you were unhappy or you wanted something. Your family had to guess what was troubling you. As you got older you learned a code – you learned to speak. There are many different codes, or languages, that people use. Some are spoken, some are written and some use signs. Most people are fluent in only one or two languages. Using language, you can now communicate all kinds of information about what you feel, what you know, and what you want to find out.

Sound waves are useful for communicating over short distances, using speech, music or other sound signals. To communicate with people over longer distances you need different systems. For example, telephone messages are carried by optical fibres or electric cables. Radio waves carry coded messages

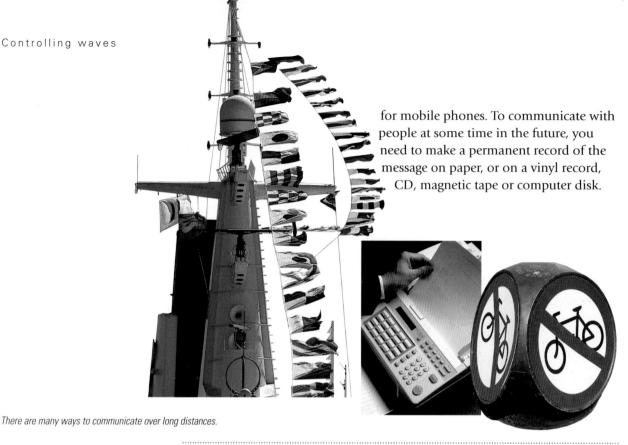

for mobile phones. To communicate with people at some time in the future, you need to make a permanent record of the message on paper, or on a vinyl record, CD, magnetic tape or computer disk.

There are many ways to communicate over long distances.

1 Write a list of all the ways of communicating that you can think of. Then draw and complete a table to show which methods of communication:

  a use light   **b** use sound

  c use radio waves   **d** use electricity

  e are temporary   **f** are permanent records

  g can carry messages over long distances (more than a few metres)

  h are only useful for distances less than a few metres

  i need special equipment.

2 List some advantages and disadvantages of language.

Are light signals better than sound?

If there are a lot of people talking at once, their messages can get confused. It is often hard to understand what people are saying in a crowded room, for example. Sound also travels quite slowly through the air, at only 330 m/s.

Light travels much faster than sound, at 300 000 000 m/s, so light signals can be a good way to send messages over long distances. But this is not always so. Normally light travels in straight lines, so if there are obstacles between you and the receiver, your message will not get through.

3 Give one advantage and one disadvantage of light signals over sound signals.
4 An ancient tribe of the South American rain forest used drum beats to send messages. Why do you think they used sound instead of light signals?

Lighthouses use light signals to warn ships about submerged rocks.

Summary of sending messages

- Both longitudinal and transverse waves help us to communicate. Communication allows us to share all kinds of information about what we feel, know, and want to find out.
- Sound waves are useful for communicating over short distances, using speech, music or other sound signals.

- Light signals can be used to communicate over quite large distances, as long as there are no obstacles between the sender and receiver.
- Permanent records of messages on paper, or on vinyl records, CDs, magnetic tapes or computer disks can be used to communicate with people at some time in the future.

26.2 Wires and cables

How can you send messages over long distances?

Sound and light messages travel through air. Energy from sound and light messages spreads out and gets harder to detect the further away you are from the sender. In order to send messages long distances without fading, you need to use a different **medium**. For example, you could send radio waves long distances through the air. Or you could use wires, or optical fibres, to carry signals long distances in cables. Many messages can be sent at once without becoming mixed up, using radio waves or cables.

How can you send messages through wires?

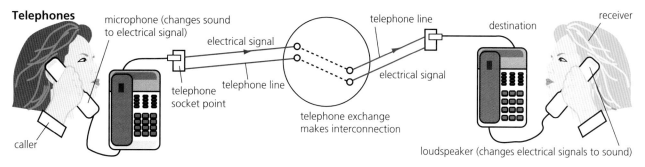

Figure 2 Alexander Graham Bell made the first long distance telephone call in 1892. He called Chicago from New York.

Telephones have a microphone in the mouthpiece, which changes the sound energy from the caller's voice into electrical energy. The electrical signals have the same frequency as the sound signals in your voice. In the earpiece, a loudspeaker changes electrical signals back into sound.

Telephones used to be linked by copper wires, and in some areas they still are. When you dial a number the exchange automatically connects your phone with the one you are dialling. The mouthpiece of your telephone acts as a **transmitter**, sending messages to the **receiver** (earpiece) in another telephone. It is relatively easy to 'tap' a telephone but it is hard to tell if someone else is listening to your conversation.

193

5 If you were going to connect a new town to the telephone exchange, and you had to use copper wires, would you use overground or underground cables? Why?

Most houses and work-places in the UK have telephones, and it takes millions of kilometres of cables to connect them all. When copper wires were used, one wire was needed for each message. It was cheaper to lay the electric cables overground, rather than burying them underground. Overground cables were cheaper to repair too, but they were more likely to be damaged by gales and vandals, and suffer electrical interference from power cables, storms and radio waves.

How can you send messages using optical fibres?

6 Give as many reasons as you can why optical fibres have replaced copper wires in telephone cables.

Optical fibres are thin, flexible strands of glass (see chapter 24, *Light*). The pure glass centre of the fibre is surrounded by a coat of different glass. Pulses of laser light are sent down the inner core of the fibre. (Laser light is light of one wavelength only.) Total internal reflection occurs when ever the light meets the boundary between the two layers, so very little light escapes. If the outer layer gets scratched more light can escape, so the fibres are coated in plastic to reduce the risk of damage.

Even when an optical fibre has a plastic coat, the pulse intensity does decrease slightly over long distances. The signal is reduced by the same fraction each kilometre. For example, if the signal is reduced by 10% in the first kilometre, only 90% remains. The next section loses 10% of that 90%, so the signal is reduced to 81% of the original intensity. To prevent total signal loss, booster stations along the route increase the signal intensity.

Sequences of laser pulses in optical fibres can be used to carry telephone messages and information for fax machines or computers, just like electrical signals in copper wires. Unlike overground copper wires, optical fibres are not affected by interference from power cables, lightning or radio waves. Fewer booster stations are needed for light signals in optical fibres than for electrical signals in copper wires, and if no light leaks out it is far harder to 'tap' an optical fibre line than a copper wire line.

Optical fibres can carry messages on a wide band of wavelengths, using lasers of different wavelengths. Each wavelength can carry a different message. So a single fibre can carry up to 10 000 messages at the speed of light. Almost all copper UK telephone cables have now been replaced by optical fibres.

Summary of wires and cables

- Wires and cables can be used to communicate over very large distances. Special systems are required to transmit and receive the messages.
- Copper wires can be used to transmit information along telephone lines as electrical signals.
- Optical fibres can be used to transmit information along telephone lines as sequences of laser pulses.
- Optical fibres are preferable to copper wires in telephone cables because:

1 they are not affected by interference from power cables, lightning or radio waves
2 fewer booster stations are needed to maintain signal intensity over large distances
3 it is far harder to 'tap' an optical fibre line than a copper wire line
4 a single fibre can carry up to 10 000 messages at the speed of light

26.3 Air waves

How can you send long distance messages without cables?

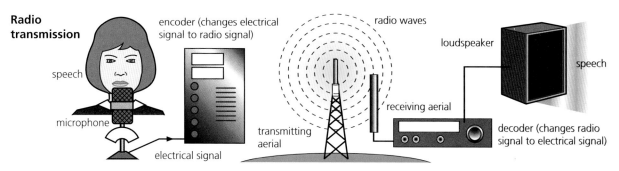

Radio transmission

speech

microphone

electrical signal

encoder (changes electrical signal to radio signal)

radio waves

transmitting aerial

receiving aerial

loudspeaker

speech

decoder (changes radio signal to electrical signal)

Figure 3 Radio waves can be used to send messages long distances through the air.

Radio waves are used to transmit messages over long distances. They can be sent through the air, from a transmitting aerial to a receiving aerial, so no expensive cables are needed.

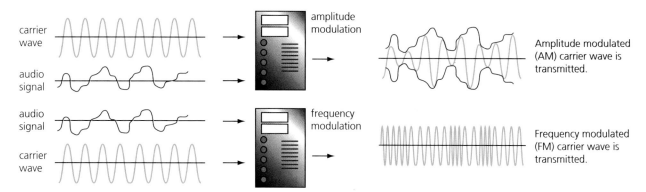

carrier wave

audio signal

amplitude modulation

Amplitude modulated (AM) carrier wave is transmitted.

audio signal

carrier wave

frequency modulation

Frequency modulated (FM) carrier wave is transmitted.

Figure 4 A carrier radio wave is used to carry the sound signal as a coded message.

7 Why does everyone have to apply to the same place to be given a frequency for transmitting radio programmes?

8 What is a pirate radio station? What problems can pirate stations cause?

9 What is a carrier wave?

10 What is the difference between frequency modulation and amplitude modulation?

To transmit sound messages using radio waves, the sound signals are superimposed onto a **carrier** radio wave, in a **modulator**. The modulated carrier wave is then transmitted from an aerial. The sound wave may be used to change the amplitude (height) of the wave. This is **amplitude modulation** (AM). **Frequency modulation** (FM) is more common now, as the signals are less prone to interference during transmission. Here the sound wave is used to alter the frequency (number of waves per second) of the radio wave. FM signals take up a wider band of frequencies than AM signals.

Radio waves have frequencies of between 3 kHz and 300 GHz. Each frequency range can carry separate signals, so many signals can be sent at once, but there are so many radio users, and the frequencies used are so close together, that there can be problems with messages getting mixed up. Radio stations have to apply to the Home Office for a licence to operate at a particular frequency, so that there is less risk of mixing up signals. The Home Office designates some frequencies for the emergency services. Each police station operates at its own frequency but they can change frequencies to talk to other stations.

Which wavelength is best?

Radio waves cannot go through tall buildings, hills or mountains (though long wavelengths can diffract around them). So radio transmitters are usually very tall, or sited on the top of hills or tall buildings so that signals are less likely to be interrupted. When there are no obstacles between the radio transmitter and the receiver, 'line-of-sight' transmission can be used. Microwaves (radio waves with very short wavelengths) are transmitted between relay stations which face each other (see figure 5). To transmit signals longer distances around the Earth, different methods and wavelengths are used (see figure 6).

Figure 5 This shows how a line-of-sight microwave transmission system is set up.

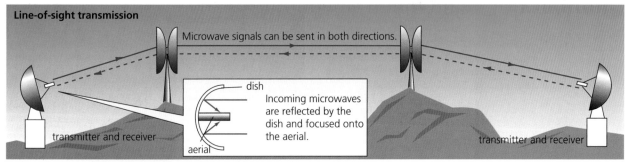

Line-of-sight transmission

Microwave signals can be sent in both directions.

dish

Incoming microwaves are reflected by the dish and focused onto the aerial.

aerial

transmitter and receiver

transmitter and receiver

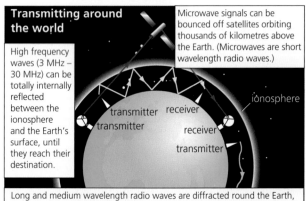

Transmitting around the world

High frequency waves (3 MHz – 30 MHz) can be totally internally reflected between the ionosphere and the Earth's surface, until they reach their destination.

Microwave signals can be bounced off satellites orbiting thousands of kilometres above the Earth. (Microwaves are short wavelength radio waves.)

ionosphere

transmitter   receiver
transmitter
receiver
transmitter

Long and medium wavelength radio waves are diffracted round the Earth, so they can be sent long distances without relay stations or satellites. Booster stations are required, though, to amplify the signal as it weakens with distance.

Figure 6 Radio transmissions can be local, national or international.

Television signals are also carried on radio waves. Both light and sound information is transmitted. Televisions use UHF waves, which have shorter wavelengths than those carrying radio signals. These waves are not diffracted very much around obstacles like hills, which means that houses in deep valleys cannot receive UHF waves from television transmitters. These houses are supplied with cable television instead.

11 Explain why radio transmitters are sited on hills rather than in valleys.

12 Explain why you can sometimes pick up long wave radio stations from other countries but you cannot pick up their VHF signals.

13 Why do people who live in valleys find it hard to pick up television stations?

What causes interference?

Radio waves are electromagnetic waves. They are formed by oscillations in electrical and magnetic fields. When a rapidly changing electric current is passed through a transmitting aerial the metal atoms vibrate. The vibrations produce a carrier radio wave. Electrical storms interfere with radio transmission by disturbing the electric current in the transmitting aerial, and so disturbing the carrier wave.

An oscillating electrical charge generates an electromagnetic wave. When you switch on the current in electrical equipment, it gives out electromagnetic waves. These waves may interfere with radio signals around the equipment, so you have trouble tuning into a station in the same room.

Can we use radio waves to carry telephone messages?

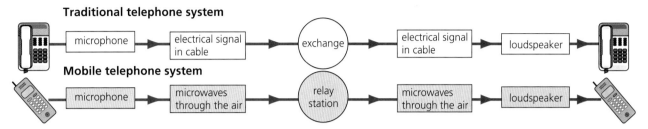

Traditional telephone system

microphone → electrical signal in cable → exchange → electrical signal in cable → loudspeaker

Mobile telephone system

microphone → microwaves through the air → relay station → microwaves through the air → loudspeaker

Figure 7

Traditional telephones send electrical or optical signals down cables. Cables above ground are ugly and get in the way. Underground cables are expensive to lay and repair, and digging trenches to do so can be disruptive for pedestrians, cause traffic delays or damage tree roots.

Mobile telephones use VHF radio waves (around 900 MHz) to transmit messages, which avoids many of the problems of traditional telephones. Speech is modulated onto a carrier wave which is transmitted on a single frequency for each phone, unlike radios which use a band of frequencies. This means that more telephones can send more messages simultaneously. There is not enough room for each telephone to be designated its own frequency permanently, because so many wavelengths are used for television and radio signals. When it is not in use, a mobile telephone does not have a designated frequency. The phone is given an available frequency each time a call is made.

The area is divided up into hexagonal sections or 'cells'. Each cell has its own frequency (see figure 8). Adjacent cells use different frequencies. The frequencies can be re-used in other areas. The relay stations send out messages using the correct frequency for the receiver phone.

Using radio signals for telephones in this way does have drawbacks. For example, UHF and VHF signals are blocked by hills and buildings. To help reduce this problem, each cell has a base station which relays messages short distances between obstacles. Base stations are sited every few metres in towns.

When you use a mobile telephone in a car, you might travel through many cells. Your call is automatically re-tuned to the base station with the strongest signal. You cannot tell that the call has been re-routed.

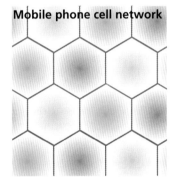

Mobile phone cell network

Figure 8 Cellnet is a mobile telephone operating system that uses a network of hexagonal cells. No two neighbouring cells use the same frequency.

14 Think of as many reasons as you can for the increasing popularity of mobile telephones.

15 What are the advantages and disadvantages of using high frequency waves for telephones?

16 Why do you think the cells in a mobile phone network are hexagonal instead of circular or square?

How are satellites used for communication?

A **satellite** is an object which orbits a planet. Our Moon is a natural satellite. Manufactured communication satellites relay signals around the Earth. They orbit the Earth above the equator, at a height of 35 900 km. At this height their speed exactly matches the speed of rotation of the Earth, so the satellite is always above the same place on Earth's surface. This is a **geostationary orbit** (see chapter 14, *Motion in two dimensions*). Only three satellites are needed to cover the whole Earth's surface, but in practice people use far more.

Geostationary satellites

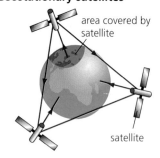

area covered by satellite

satellite

Figure 9 Satellites allow you to communicate with almost anyone in the world.

Satellites transmit information for telephones and televisions. There are also five geostationary satellites over the equator that collect and relay information about cloud cover around the world every half hour. Other non-geostationary satellites orbit much closer to the Earth's surface, and therefore send back information for a smaller area, but produce pictures that are far more detailed.

17 High frequency waves are used for satellite transmission. Why is this?

18 Explain why it is important to have satellites in geostationary orbit.

19 Draw a labelled diagram to show how a computer in Edinburgh could communicate with a computer in Glasgow by: **a** cable **b** microwave link **c** satellite

Your diagram should include transmission equipment and the names of the waves used.

What do all communication systems have in common?

All communication systems use an encoder to change the signal into a code for transmission, and a decoder to turn it back to a signal you can understand (see figure 10). A transducer changes the signal from one energy form to another. Messages are transmitted across a medium. For example, sound waves travel through the air, while electrical signals are sent through wires.

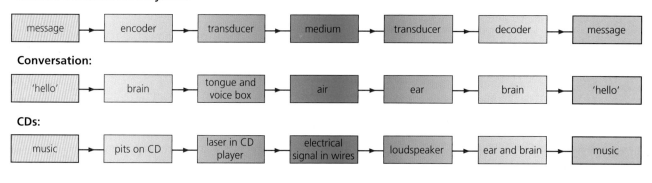

General communication system:

message → encoder → transducer → medium → transducer → decoder → message

Conversation:

'hello' → brain → tongue and voice box → air → ear → brain → 'hello'

CDs:

music → pits on CD → laser in CD player → electrical signal in wires → loudspeaker → ear and brain → music

Figure 10 All communication systems have certain features in common.

20 Draw a block diagram to show the stages in sending a radio message from a police station to a patrol car.

Summary of air waves

- To send messages over greater distances, the signal can be encoded onto radio or microwaves. You cannot detect these signals with your senses.
- Waves carrying signals can interfere with each other constructively or destructively.

- Communication satellites in geostationary orbits relay signals around the Earth.
- All communication systems use mechanisms to encode and decode signals.

Inside the **atom**

Learning objectives

By the end of this chapter you should be able to:

- **recall** that matter is made up of particles called atoms
- **understand** that atoms are themselves made up of smaller particles
- **describe** how changes in these particles change the nature of atoms
- **explain** what happens when atoms decay

27.1 Atomic structure

What are atoms?

Since 1932, scientists have used huge particle accelerators like this one at CERN in Geneva, Switzerland, to smash particles together at high speeds, to try to find out more about atomic structure. The atoms break up into particles even smaller than protons and neutrons.

All matter is made up of atoms. The properties of materials depend on the kinds of atoms they contain and how the atoms are combined. Scientists use their understanding of atomic structure to explain why reactions occur, what holds atoms together, why some chemicals react together and others do not, how electricity flows and how to release nuclear energy.

Atoms are too small to see directly – about 100 million atoms laid side by side would only measure 1 cm across. As scientists learn more and more about atomic structure, they make **models** which seem to fit their observations. Whenever new observations are made they are used to test the model. If the model does not fit the observations new models have to be developed (see figure 1).

In the model of the atom we use today, the **nucleus** is made of **protons** and **neutrons**, which are together known as **nucleons**. **Electrons** orbit the nucleus in areas known as **shells**. Protons and neutrons have about the same mass but electrons are about 2000 times lighter. In fact, they are so light we often ignore their mass and call it zero. Protons and neutrons are said to have a mass of 1. They are too small to measure in grams so the masses are just relative. Protons have a positive charge (+1) and electrons have a negative charge (–1). Neutrons have no charge. There are equal numbers of protons and electrons in an atom so the charges cancel out.

How our model of the atom developed

| 500 BC | Ancient Greeks suggested that materials are made of differently shaped solid particles, with hooks on to attach to other particles. |

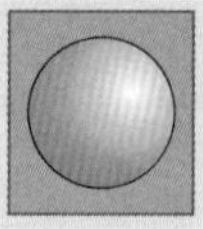

Billiard ball model
In 1804, John Dalton suggested that atoms are like tiny, solid billiard balls. He called them atoms, from the Greek word atomos, meaning indivisible.

| 1884 | Svante Arrhenius found that atoms could be charged |
| 1897 | J J Thomson passed electricity through a sealed tube of gas, and identified negatively charged particles. He called them electrons. |

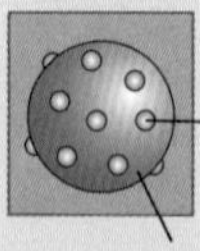

Current bun model
very light negatively charged electrons, embedded in a heavy positive mass

positive mass

| 1896 | Henri Becquerel found that uranium gave out electrons. |
| 1911 | Ernest Rutherford fired alpha particles at gold foil. Some particles were deflected, but others passed straight through. So gold atoms are not solid balls. |

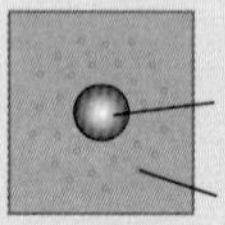

Rutherford's model
heavy positively charged nucleus in the centre

electrons in a cloud around the centre

| 1913 | Neils Bohr suggested that electrons are in orbits around the nucleus of an atom. Each orbit holds only a fixed number of electrons. |

Neils Bohr's model
electrons in orbit around a central positive nucleus

1919	Rutherford identified positive particles in the nuclei of atoms, and called them protons.
1922	Francis Aston found that some atoms of an element had different masses from others of the same element.
1932	James Chadwick discovered unchanged particles in the nuclei of atoms, and called them neutrons.

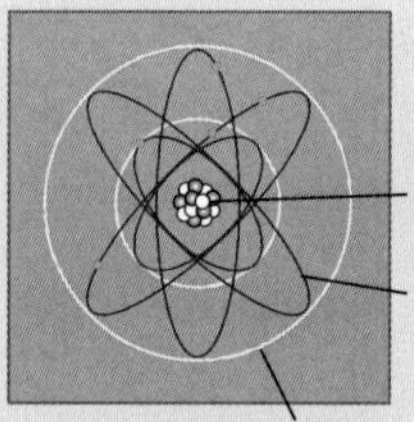

Nuclear atom model
protons and neutrons form a central nucleus

electrons move around nucleus in **shells**

electron shell

| 1972 | Very-high-speed electrons were fired at atoms in a linear particle accelerator in California, USA. This showed that protons and neutrons are made of even thinier particles, now called quarks. Similar experiments since since 1970s have identified many other subatomic particles. |

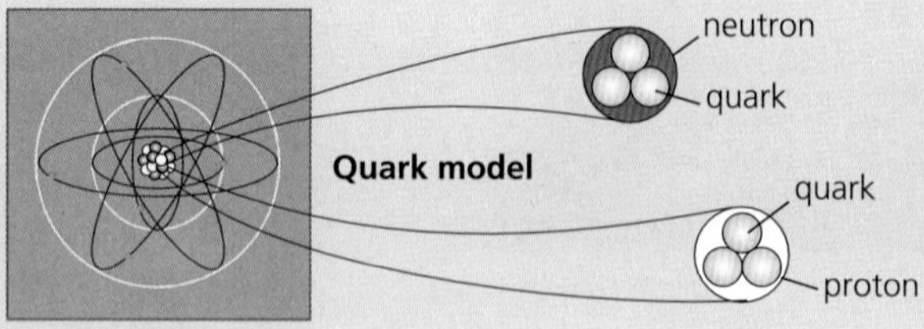

neutron
quark
Quark model
quark
proton

Figure 1 Many different scientists have helped to build models to explain atomic structure.

1 a Which particles are found in the nucleus?
   b Electrons are often referred to as having no mass. Why do you think this is?
   c Explain why atoms do not have an overall charge.
2 Look at figure 1. What changes did J.J. Thomson's evidence make to the Ancient Greeks' ideas on atomic structure?
3 How did Chadwick and Rutherford's discoveries change our ideas about atoms?
4 Does the existence of quarks suggest that the nuclear atom model is right, wrong or incomplete? Give reasons for your answer.

What makes chemicals different?

5 The atomic number of copper is 29. How many protons are there in a copper atom?

6 Sulphur atoms each contain 16 protons. What is sulphur's proton number?

There are about one hundred different types of atoms. Different atoms give chemicals different properties. The simplest chemicals, called elements, contain only one kind of atom, which all have the same number of protons. The number of protons in an atom is called the **atomic number** or **proton number**. Each element has a different atomic number.

The atoms of different elements also have different numbers of electrons arranged around the nucleus. This affects how the atoms combine together and how the elements behave in chemical reactions.

Are all the atoms in an element identical?

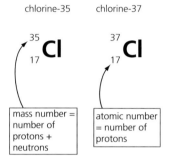

chlorine-35   chlorine-37

mass number = number of protons + neutrons

atomic number = number of protons

Figure 3 Chlorine has two isotopes – chlorine-35 and chlorine-37.

In 1922, a British physicist called Francis Aston discovered that for some elements there were some atoms that had a different mass from the others. This mystery was explained when another British scientist called Chadwick discovered neutrons in 1932. Atoms of the same element which have the same number of protons but different numbers of neutrons are called **isotopes**. They behave in the same way in chemical reactions but they have a different mass. The **mass number**, or **nucleon number**, gives the total number of protons and neutrons in an atom, and indicates its weight relative to other atoms (see figure 2). Symbols are used to represent all the information about isotopes in a short hand way (see figure 3).

Isotopes of hydrogen

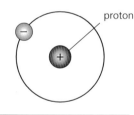

proton

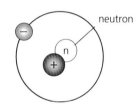

neutron

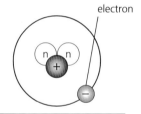

electron

A hydrogen atom has one proton and one electron. Its mass number is 1.

A deuterium atom is still the same element as hydrogen, but it has one neutron as well as a proton and an electron. Its mass number is 2.

Tritium is also a form of hydrogen. Its atoms have one proton, one electron and two neutrons. Its mass number is 3.

Figure 2 These are all hydrogen atoms but they have different numbers of neutrons.

7 Suggest a reason why water which contains a lot of deuterium atoms is often called 'heavy water'.

8 Copy and complete the table below for two of carbon's isotopes.

Isotope	Atomic (proton) number	Number of neutrons	Mass (nucleon) number
Carbon-12	6	6	?
Carbon-14	?	8	?

9 Magnesium atoms have 12 protons. The mass numbers of three of magnesium's isotopes are 24, 25 and 26. How many neutrons does each isotope have?

Summary of atomic structure

- Atoms are composed of a central nucleus containing protons and neutrons. The nucleus is surrounded by orbiting electrons.
- Protons have a positive charge, electrons have a negative charge and neutrons are electrically neutral.
- All atoms of an element contain the same number of protons.
- An atom has the same number of electrons as protons, so overall it has no charge.

- Protons and neutrons (together called nucleons) are made up of three tinier particles called quarks.
- Isotopes are atoms of an element which contain the same number of protons but have a different number of neutrons.
- The atomic number, or proton number, of an atom is the number of protons it contains. All atoms of a particular element have the same atomic number.
- The mass number, or nucleon number, is the total number of protons and neutrons an atom contains.

27.2 Radioactive decay

What is left when atoms decay?

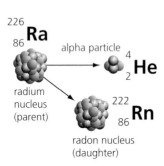

$^{226}_{86}$**Ra**

alpha particle

$^{4}_{2}$**He**

radium nucleus (parent)

$^{222}_{86}$**Rn**

radon nucleus (daughter)

Some isotopes are stable, and do not change. The nuclei of unstable isotopes break up and give out **radiation**. There are three sorts of radiation called alpha, beta and gamma.

Alpha decay

When a radium atom decays, it loses two protons and two neutrons. It becomes a new element called radon. The two protons and two neutrons make an **alpha particle (α)**. An alpha particle is the same as a helium nucleus (see figure 4).

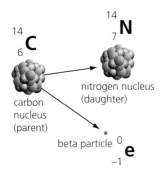

$^{14}_{6}$**C**

$^{14}_{7}$**N**

nitrogen nucleus (daughter)

carbon nucleus (parent)

beta particle $^{0}_{-1}$**e**

Figure 4

Beta decay

After about 5730 years, a 10 g piece of carbon-14 is reduced to about 5 g. The other 5 g is turned into nitrogen. One of the neutrons in the carbon-14 atom changes into a proton and an electron. Carbon atoms have six protons. The extra proton turns the carbon atom into a nitrogen atom which has seven. The nitrogen escapes as a gas. The electron is very fast moving and escapes as a **beta particle (β)** (see figure 4).

Gamma decay

Gamma radiation (γ) is not a flow of particles, like alpha and beta radiation. It is an electromagnetic wave like light or X-rays. High-energy gamma rays are released from the nucleus of some radioactive isotopes.

Some isotopes give out more than one kind of radiation. Uranium-238 emits alpha, beta and gamma radiation when it decays. Thorium-234 atoms are formed, which are also unstable so they decay too. It takes six changes for uranium-238 to change into a stable element.

Decay of uranium-238

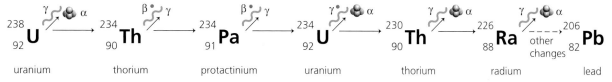

Figure 5 The radioactive decay of uranium-238 happens in several steps.

10 a Look at figure 5. What atom is formed when an atom of thorium-234 decays?

b What kind of radiation is emitted when thorium-234 decays?

c What is the difference in the radioactive decay of thorium-234 and thorium-230?

d What is the final product of the nuclear decay of uranium-238?

How long does radioactive decay take?

Some isotopes are more unstable than others. The more unstable an isotope is, the quicker its nuclei disintegrate. The amount of time it takes for half the atoms in any sample of an isotope to decay is called the **half-life** of the isotope. Strontium has a half-life of 28 years. That means that after 28 years about half the original strontium nuclei will have decayed. In another 28 years about half of what was left will have decayed (see figure 6).

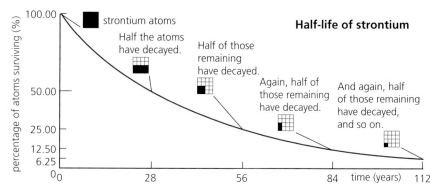

Figure 6 The number of atoms in a sample of strontium that are not yet decayed halves every 28 years.

You cannot tell when a particular nucleus will decay, just as you cannot predict whether a tossed coin will land on heads or tails, because these are chance or random events. But you can find the **probability** of a chance event. For example, when you toss a coin there is a one-in-two chance that the coin will land on heads. If you toss the coin often enough, it will land on heads 50% of the time overall, but you cannot be certain *when* it will be heads on any particular throw. The half-life of an isotope tells you how long it is likely to take for half the nuclei to decay, but you cannot predict when an individual nucleus will decay.

Note

The rate of most chemical reactions depends on temperature, concentration and which other atoms are present. The rate of nuclear decay is not affected by any of these things.

11 Look at figure 6. How much of a 10 g lump of strontium will still be strontium after 140 years?

12 a Copy and complete the bar chart on the right.

   b What is the half-life of americium-241?

   c Is americium-241 more or less stable than strontium? Give a reason for your answer.

13 A Geiger-Muller tube was used to find the half-life of protactinium (see chapter 28, *Radioactivity*). The number of counts was measured in successive 10s intervals. The table shows the results.

   a Plot a line graph of the results.

   b Explain why the graph is not perfectly smooth, but goes up and down.

   b What is the half-life of protactinium?

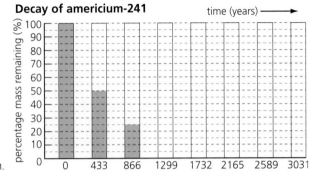

Decay of americium-241

Time from start (s)	5	15	25	35	45	55	65	75	85	95	105	115	125	135	145	155	165	175	185	195
Counts in 10 s	76	48	49	43	41	33	46	41	27	27	15	18	10	8	41	10	10	9	10	5

How can half-life help to date fossils?

Some rocks are thought to be over 50 million years old. The rocks contain radioactive thorium-232, which decays to produce lead-208. Thorium has a half-life of 13 900 million years. So young rocks will have a greater proportion of thorium-232 than lead-208. Old rocks will contain less thorium compared to lead. If you know the age of the rock in which you find a fossil, you can usually be sure the fossil is the same age.

Radiocarbon dating can be used to judge the age of fossils themselves. Carbon-14 is a naturally occurring isotope with a half-life of 5730 years. Living things take in radioactive carbon-14 from the air as carbon dioxide, or with their food, along with the normal isotope of carbon. All the time they are alive, the level of carbon-14 in their cells stays about the same. As soon as they die, the level starts to drop as carbon-14 decays to form nitrogen-14. The more time has gone by since the organism died, the less carbon-14 there will be in the remains. Since many fossils contain the remains of plants and animals, the carbon-14 levels in them can be used to indicate their age.

Summary of radioactive decay

- Radioactive elements have atoms with unstable nuclei. To become stable they emit alpha, beta or gamma radiation.
- Radioactive isotopes are also called radioisotopes.
- An alpha particle consists of two protons and two neutrons. It is the same as a helium nucleus.
- A beta particle is a fast moving electron.

- Gamma radiation is a high energy electromagnetic wave.
- When atoms emit radiation they change into another element. The time for half the atoms in a sample to decay is called the element's half-life.
- The decay of radioisotopes can be used to date rocks, fossils and other ancient organic materials.

Radio*activity* 28

Learning objectives

By the end of this chapter you should be able to:

- **describe** where radiation comes from
- **recognise** different forms of radiation from their properties
- **discuss** the benefits and disadvantages of radiation to living things

28.1 Ionising radiation

What does radiation mean?

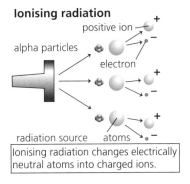

Ionising radiation

Ionising radiation changes electrically neutral atoms into charged ions.

Figure 1

Radiation is something that spreads out. Physicists think of radiation as energy spreading out from a source. Different kinds of radiation have different names. Electromagnetic radiation describes a family of waves with similar electrical and magnetic properties. Light, radio waves, X-rays and gamma rays all belong to this family (see chapter 25, *Electromagnetic spectrum*).

The radiation you will learn about in this chapter is **ionising radiation**. Ionising radiation transfers energy to atoms and molecules. It changes them into charged particles called ions (see figure 1). Ionising radiation is the result of the breakdown of unstable atoms. Materials which contain unstable atoms are sources of radiation. The three forms of radiation released from unstable nuclei are called alpha, beta and gamma radiation (see chapter 27, *Inside the atom*).

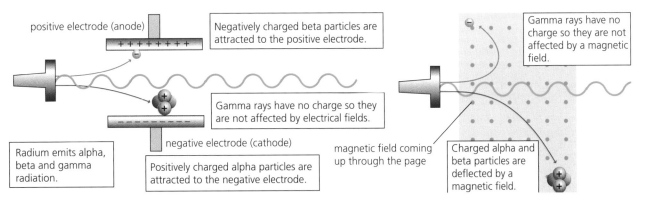

Radium emits alpha, beta and gamma radiation.

positive electrode (anode)

Negatively charged beta particles are attracted to the positive electrode.

Gamma rays have no charge so they are not affected by electrical fields.

negative electrode (cathode)

Positively charged alpha particles are attracted to the negative electrode.

magnetic field coming up through the page

Gamma rays have no charge so they are not affected by a magnetic field.

Charged alpha and beta particles are deflected by a magnetic field.

Figure 2 Charged particles are deflected by electric and magnetic fields, but gamma rays are not.

Types of radiation

Alpha particles are strongly ionising and soon transfer their kinetic energy to other particles as they bump into them. They can be stopped by just a few centimetres of air molecules. They travel at one tenth of the speed of light.

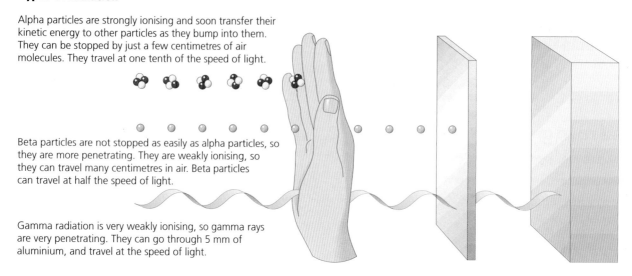

Beta particles are not stopped as easily as alpha particles, so they are more penetrating. They are weakly ionising, so they can travel many centimetres in air. Beta particles can travel at half the speed of light.

Gamma radiation is very weakly ionising, so gamma rays are very penetrating. They can go through 5 mm of aluminium, and travel at the speed of light.

Figure 3 Strongly ionising radiation can penetrate materials more than weakly ionising radiaton.

1 **a** What type of radiation is made up of particles each with a charge of +2?

   b If you wanted to stop this type of radiation in air, what could you use?

2 **a** What type of radiation is made up of waves?

   b Why is this type of radiation not deflected by an electric field?

3 **a** What type of radiation is made up of particles that are deflected towards the anode in an electric field?

   b Why is this type of radiation called 'weakly ionising' radiation?

As well as natural forms of ionising radiation, like alpha, beta and gamma radiation from decaying nuclei, there are X-rays. X-rays are similar to gamma rays. They are a member of the electromagnetic radiation family. X-rays are created when accelerated electrons hit a target in a vacuum.

How can you detect ionising radiation?

Photographic paper

You cannot detect ionising radiation directly, but you can detect its effects. Henri Becquerel was the first person to detect the effects of radiation. He discovered them by accident in 1895. He left some uranium on some unexposed photographic paper in a drawer. He developed the film the next day. There was a light patch where the uranium had been. In honour of his discovery radiation is now measured in units called **Becquerels**.

1 Becquerel = 1 nucleus decaying per second

Radioactive tracers can be used to study the movements of nutrients in plants.
The tracer is detected using photographic film.

Geiger–Muller tubes

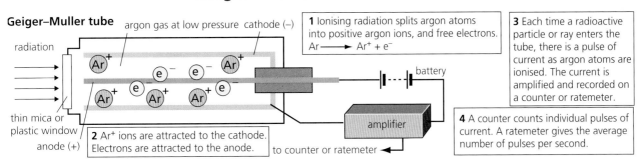

Geiger–Muller tube   argon gas at low pressure   cathode (−)

radiation

thin mica or plastic window

anode (+)

1 Ionising radiation splits argon atoms into positive argon ions, and free electrons.
$Ar \longrightarrow Ar^+ + e^-$

battery

amplifier

to counter or ratemeter

2 Ar^+ ions are attracted to the cathode. Electrons are attracted to the anode.

3 Each time a radioactive particle or ray enters the tube, there is a pulse of current as argon atoms are ionised. The current is amplified and recorded on a counter or ratemeter.

4 A counter counts individual pulses of current. A ratemeter gives the average number of pulses per second.

Figure 4

4   Why must the mica window be thin if the G–M tube is to be used to detect alpha particles?

Geiger–Muller tubes detect ionising radiation. When the probe is held near to a possible source, the amount of radiation present is shown on a counter in pulses per second. A G–M tube can detect beta and gamma radiation. If the mica window is thin enough it can also detect alpha radiation.

G–M tubes pick up background radiation (see page 208). The background count rate must be subtracted from the total to give the count rate for the test substance alone.

Cloud chambers

Alpha particles make straight thick trails in a cloud chamber. This photo was taken by C.T.R. Wilson in 1911.

Cloud chambers contain vapour which is kept very cool. When the vapour meets a particle, such as a speck of dust or an ion, it condenses. If you shine a light into the chamber the droplets of condensed vapour become visible. Trails of condensed droplets show where the particles have moved through the chamber, just like trails behind aeroplanes in a clear sky.

Alpha particles make thick trails because they ionise so many air molecules. Their trails travel in straight lines through the chamber. Beta particles are so small they get knocked off course by air molecules, so beta trails wander about. Beta particles do not ionise as many air molecules as alpha particles, so their tracks are thinner.

5   Why do you think gamma rays cannot be detected by a cloud chamber?

Summary of ionising radiation

- Ionising radiation transfers energy to atoms and molecules, changing them into charged particles called ions.
- There are three types of natural ionising radiation – alpha, beta and gamma.
- Alpha radiation cannot penetrate paper or skin.
- Beta radiation is stopped by a few millimetres of aluminium.

- A few centimetres of lead is needed to stop gamma radiation.
- Gamma rays are unaffected by electric and magnetic fields but alpha and beta particles are deflected by them.
- Radiation can be detected by cloud chambers, Geiger–Muller tubes and photographic film.

28.2 Radioactivity and people

How much radiation are you exposed to?

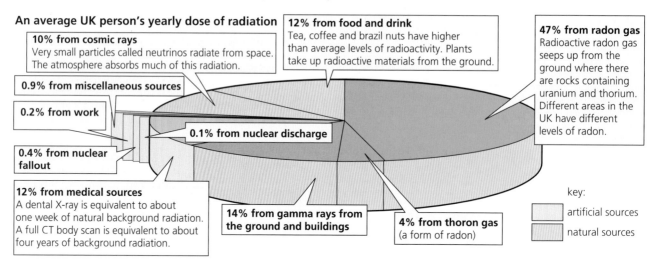

An average UK person's yearly dose of radiation

10% from cosmic rays
Very small particles called neutrinos radiate from space. The atmosphere absorbs much of this radiation.

0.9% from miscellaneous sources

0.2% from work

0.1% from nuclear discharge

0.4% from nuclear fallout

12% from medical sources
A dental X-ray is equivalent to about one week of natural background radiation. A full CT body scan is equivalent to about four years of background radiation.

12% from food and drink
Tea, coffee and brazil nuts have higher than average levels of radioactivity. Plants take up radioactive materials from the ground.

47% from radon gas
Radioactive radon gas seeps up from the ground where there are rocks containing uranium and thorium. Different areas in the UK have different levels of radon.

14% from gamma rays from the ground and buildings

4% from thoron gas
(a form of radon)

key:
artificial sources
natural sources

Figure 5 In the UK, people receive radiation from many different sources.

6 How much of the background radiation in the UK is due to:
  a natural sources
  b artificial sources?

7 What is the main source of background radiation in the UK?

8 List the artificial sources of radiation.

The vast majority of the radiation people are normally exposed to in the UK comes from natural sources. Granite rocks contain uranium, and release radioactive radon gas into the air. Cosmic rays from space shower ionising radiation onto the Earth. You get more cosmic radiation at higher altitudes than at sea level, because the radiation has to travel through less atmosphere to reach you. Everyone is exposed to these sources of **background radiation**.

Some radiation comes from artificial sources such as nuclear power stations, X-rays and nuclear weapons (see figure 5). The amount of radiation you are exposed to depends on where you live, your job and how many X-rays you have (see figures 6 and 7, and table 1).

Rock	Uranium concentration (ppm)
Granite	5–10
Slate	3–5
Chalk	0.5–1
Clay	1–3

Table 1 Uranium concentrations in different rock types.

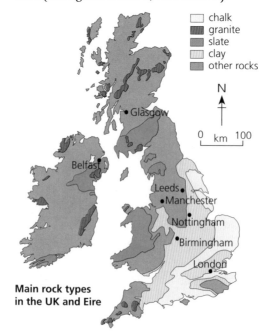

chalk
granite
slate
clay
other rocks

N

0 km 100

Glasgow
Belfast
Leeds
Manchester
Nottingham
Birmingham
London

Main rock types in the UK and Eire

Figure 6 The amount of radiation you receive depends on where you live.

Radiation and jobs

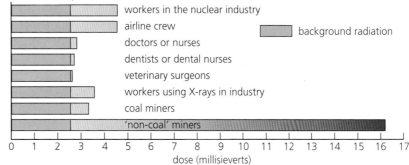

workers in the nuclear industry
airline crew
doctors or nurses
dentists or dental nurses
veterinary surgeons
workers using X-rays in industry
coal miners
'non-coal' miners

background radiation

dose (millisieverts)

Figure 7 Some people are exposed to additional radiation because of their work.

9 Why do doctors, nurses, dentists and vets receive more radiation than normal?

10 a Why are airline crew likely to receive higher doses of radiation than normal?

b How much more additional radiation do airline crew receive than workers in the nuclear industry?

11 a Use figure 6 to suggest which parts of the UK receive the highest dose of radiation.

b Would you expect to find high or low levels of radon in your area? Explain your answer.

What effect does radiation have on living tissue?

The amount of damage caused by radiation is different depending on which form of radiation you absorb. Human body tissues are damaged 20 times more severely by alpha radiation than by beta, gamma or X-rays. Some parts of your body absorb radiation more than others. Your ovaries or testes are most sensitive to radiation (see table 2). Lungs and bone marrow have a medium sensitivity. Bones and other organs are least sensitive.

Dose (mSv)	Effect
5	Annual maximum NRPB advisory limit
50	Annual legal dose limit for patients and workers
1 000	Radiation sickness
1 500	Reduced number of sperm or egg cells can cause sterility
2 500	Sterility lasts up to two years
4 000	Chance of death from exposure is 50%
10 000	Death

Table 2 The effects of radiation on humans.

If radiation penetrates your body it can damage or kill your cells. It is difficult for alpha particles to penetrate skin but they cause a lot of damage if they are swallowed or breathed in. Beta and gamma radiation can penetrate the skin, and cause damage to internal organs. Radiation particularly affects cells which are dividing, such as the cells in hair follicles and in your stomach lining. Victims of radiation sickness often loose their hair and vomit because of this.

Marie Curie and her daughter Irene (here seen as a little girl) studied radioactivity for many years. They both died of leukaemia .

Genetic material is very sensitive to radiation. Chemicals called DNA and RNA control your cell's activities and how they reproduce. Radiation can cause changes, or **mutations**, in these chemicals. Some mutations cause cancer. Survivors of the nuclear bomb dropped on Hiroshima in Japan, in 1945, had a greatly increased risk of getting leukaemia, because of the damage the radiation caused in their cells. Leukaemia is cancer of white blood cells.

Note

Radiation absorbed by objects is measured in **grays**. One joule of radiation energy absorbed by 1 kg of material is one gray. Radiation absorbed by people's bodies is measured in **sieverts** (Sv). A measurement in Sv takes into account the sensitivity of human tissues to the radiation, as well as the energy of the radiation itself. You multiply the number of grays of alpha radiation by 20 to get the value in Sv, and by one for beta radiation, gamma rays and X-rays. Sieverts are very big units – a single dose of 10 Sv would kill you – so millisieverts (mSv) are often used.

How can people protect themselves from radiation?

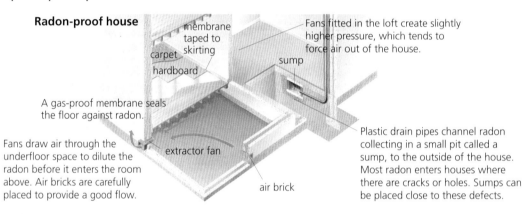

Radon-proof house

membrane taped to skirting

carpet

hardboard

Fans fitted in the loft create slightly higher pressure, which tends to force air out of the house.

sump

A gas-proof membrane seals the floor against radon.

Fans draw air through the underfloor space to dilute the radon before it enters the room above. Air bricks are carefully placed to provide a good flow.

extractor fan

air brick

Plastic drain pipes channel radon collecting in a small pit called a sump, to the outside of the house. Most radon enters houses where there are cracks or holes. Sumps can be placed close to these defects.

Figure 8

These workers are disposing of low level nuclear waste from a laboratory. The waste will be compacted, sealed in steel cans and stored in concrete vaults underground

People can protect themselves from radiation by creating barriers which radiation cannot penetrate. Many people living in Cornwall protect themselves from radon gas seeping up out of the granite rock by sealing their floors (see figure 8), and regularly having their houses tested for traces of excess radiation.

Workers in the nuclear industry wear protective clothing or use robot arms to work with radioactive material from the safety of another room. They wear special badges that contain photographic film. The intensity of the image on the film shows how much radiation the worker has been exposed to. The maximum dose a worker is allowed to receive in a year is 50 mSv. That is ten times higher than the maximum dose allowed for a member of the public.

Radiographers operate X-ray machines in hospitals from a separate room. Patients protect their internal organs with lead aprons.

12 The photographic material in a worker's badge is covered with lightproof material. Why?

13 The lead apron you wear when you have a dental X-ray covers your abdomen. Why must this area be protected in particular?

14 Why is it safe for you to stay in the room when you have an X-ray, while the radiographer has to go into another room?

How do we deal with nuclear waste?

Nuclear power stations, industry, hospitals and research laboratories all generate radioactive waste. It is not just the radioactive materials themselves which are a problem. Contaminated clothing and equipment have to be disposed of safely too.

Nuclear materials are transported around the world for disposal. Waste is packed in radiation-proof containers which are tested to make sure they will not break even in a severe crash or fire. The waste is eventually buried deep underground. In the UK there is a government rule which states that no-one should get more than 0.1 mSv a year from nuclear waste. That is about 4% of average background exposure.

Why do we risk using radiation?

Uses in medicine

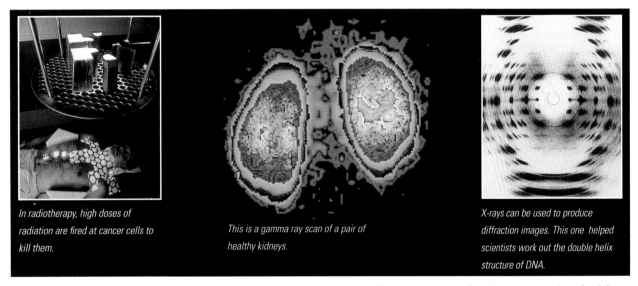

In radiotherapy, high doses of radiation are fired at cancer cells to kill them.

This is a gamma ray scan of a pair of healthy kidneys.

X-rays can be used to produce diffraction images. This one helped scientists work out the double helix structure of DNA.

Radiation has many uses in medicine. For example, X-rays are an invaluable tool for diagnosing damaged bones. About 35 000 000 X-rays are taken each year in the UK alone.

X-rays cannot be used to diagnose damaged kidneys, because X-rays go straight through soft tissue. Instead the patient is injected with a small amount of a **radioactive tracer** such as iodine-123. Iodine is absorbed by the kidneys in a few minutes, and after 20 minutes it should pass into the bladder in urine. A gamma camera counts the radiation given off by the kidneys and the blood. A computer converts the radiation count to an image on a screen. Doctors can then see if the kidneys are successfully removing waste. Radioactive tracers give off gamma radiation, which does not cause much ionisation so the risk of tissue damage is smaller than for alpha radiation.

Radioactive materials can be used to sterilise medical equipment. Metal instruments can be boiled to remove germs, but bandages and plastic syringes cannot, so instead this equipment is sealed in a plastic bag and irradiated with gamma rays. Both the equipment and package is then sterile.

Uses in industry

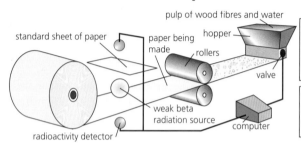

pulp of wood fibres and water

standard sheet of paper

hopper

paper being made

rollers

valve

weak beta radiation source

radioactivity detector

computer

> If the newly made paper is too thick, fewer beta particles will reach the lower detector than the upper detector. If the paper is too thin, the lower detector will receive more beta particles.

> The computer compares the readings from each detector and sends a signal automatically to the hopper valve. This adjusts the flow of pulp so that the paper thickness is corrected.

Figure 9 Beta particles can be used to measure the thickness of paper.

Gamma rays can be used to kill mould and bacteria so fresh food does not rot so quickly.

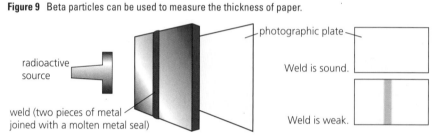

radioactive source

photographic plate

Weld is sound.

weld (two pieces of metal joined with a molten metal seal)

Weld is weak.

Figure 10 Gamma radiation can be used to check that welds are strong and safe.

Generating power

A small amount of nuclear fuel releases a large amount of energy, so it is an efficient fuel for generating electricity. Nuclear power stations do not produce gases which cause acid rain or global warming. Nearly every one in the UK lives less than 200 km from a nuclear power station.

These workers are replacing the fuel rods in a nuclear reactor.

15 a Why do doctors use radio tracers instead of X-rays to see if your kidneys are working properly?

b Explain why gamma sources are used as radioactive tracers instead of alpha or beta.

16 What are the advantages of using gamma rays to sterilise medical supplies?

17 Which form of radiation would you recommend for judging whether the soap boxes in the diagram are full enough? Why?

18 Radioactivity affects all our lives. Some effects are useful and some are harmful. In your opinion do the uses outweigh the disadvantages or are the risks too great? Explain your answer.

radioactive source

Detector reading is low.

box full

radioactive source

Detector reading is high.

box not full

Summary of radiation and people

- Radiation occurs naturally. This is known as background radiation. Radiation can also be produced artificially.
- Radiation has many uses in medicine, including X-ray photography, radiotherapy, radiotracing and sterilisation of equipment.

- Radiation has many uses in industry, including monitoring thicknesses of materials, and treatment of fresh foods.
- Radiation is harmful to living things, so it must be used carefully and waste must be disposed of securely, to minimise the risk of damage.

Earth in space 29

Learning objectives

By the end of this chapter you should be able to:

- **describe** the positions of the planets in the Solar System
- **distinguish** between the planets using their special features
- **know** that most planets have natural satellites

- **describe** how the Earth and Moon interact to produce tides and eclipses
- **describe** how the movement of the Earth relative to the Sun causes night and day, and the seasons
- **recognise** that the movement of the Earth and Moon control people's understanding of time

29.1 Solar System

What is the Solar System like?

Our Sun would look like a fairly ordinary star to a visiting alien.

Comets start in the Oort cloud – a region where rocks and ice orbit the Sun.

If alien beings approached our Solar System from deep space, they would see ahead of them a fairly small but stable star, which is our Sun. The alien visitors would cross the Oort cloud, which is made up of rocks and lumps of ice, with about the same total mass as the Earth. These rocks slowly rotate round the Sun, taking thousands of years to complete one orbit.

Occasionally some Oort cloud rocks fall towards the Sun, warming up as they do so. The gases locked inside vaporise, and form a 'tail', blown out by streams of particles from the Sun. Inhabitants of Earth see this as a comet. As comets orbit the Sun, at times they are very close to it (when they can be seen from Earth). At other times they move millions of miles off into space. The Sun is not at the centre of a comet's orbit, as it is for a planet. Debris from comets sometimes burns up in the Earth's atmosphere making sudden streaks of light across the sky. Many people call these 'shooting stars', although they have nothing to do with stars.

Next, the approaching aliens would see a family of planets, all orbiting the Sun in the same direction, and almost entirely in one plane (see figure 1). Only the outer planet, Pluto, orbits in a different plane. The orbits of all the planets are **elliptical** (like squashed circles), with the Sun close to the centre. Gravity holds all the planets in orbit, and keeps them from flying away from the Sun (see chapter 14, *Motion in two dimensions* for more about gravity and orbits).

Table 1 Data for the Solar System. *An astronomical unit is the average distance of the Earth from the Sun, which is 149 597 870 km.

Name	Diameter (km)	Mass (Earth masses)	Mean distance from Sun (millions of km)	Distance from Sun (astronomic units, AU*)	Year length (Earth days, d or Earth Years, y)
Sun	1 392 000	332 776	–	–	–
Mercury	4 840	0.054	57.91	0.31–0.47	87.97 d
Venus	12 300	0.815	108.21	0.72–0.73	224.70 d
Earth	12 756	1.000	149.60	0.98–1.02	365.26 d
Mars	6 790	0.107	227.94	1.38–1.67	686.98 d
Asteroids	varied		300 to 600		
Jupiter	142 800	317.89	778.34	4.95–5.45	11.86 y
Saturn	119 300	95.14	1427.01	9.01–10.07	29.46 y
Uranus	47 100	14.52	2869.6	18.28–20.09	84.0 y
Neptune	44 800	17.46	4496.7	29.80–30.32	164.8 y
Pluto	5 900	0.1	5907	29.6–49.3	248.4 y
Oort Cloud (10^{11} objects)		1			100 000 to 30 000

Figure 1 The Solar System is made up of nine planets and their moons, plus a band of asteroids, all orbiting the Sun.

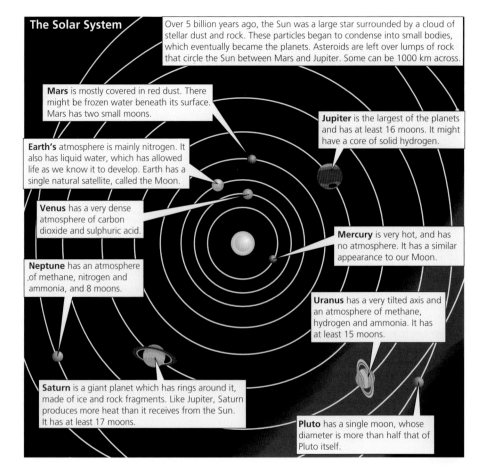

The Solar System

Over 5 billion years ago, the Sun was a large star surrounded by a cloud of stellar dust and rock. These particles began to condense into small bodies, which eventually became the planets. Asteroids are left over lumps of rock that circle the Sun between Mars and Jupiter. Some can be 1000 km across.

Mars is mostly covered in red dust. There might be frozen water beneath its surface. Mars has two small moons.

Jupiter is the largest of the planets and has at least 16 moons. It might have a core of solid hydrogen.

Earth's atmosphere is mainly nitrogen. It also has liquid water, which has allowed life as we know it to develop. Earth has a single natural satellite, called the Moon.

Venus has a very dense atmosphere of carbon dioxide and sulphuric acid.

Mercury is very hot, and has no atmosphere. It has a similar appearance to our Moon.

Neptune has an atmosphere of methane, nitrogen and ammonia, and 8 moons.

Uranus has a very tilted axis and an atmosphere of methane, hydrogen and ammonia. It has at least 15 moons.

Saturn is a giant planet which has rings around it, made of ice and rock fragments. Like Jupiter, Saturn produces more heat than it receives from the Sun. It has at least 17 moons.

Pluto has a single moon, whose diameter is more than half that of Pluto itself.

Space probes like Voyager 2 have visited other planets in our Solar System, and have sent back incredible pictures.

As you look into the night sky, to the naked eye the planets look like tiny dots of light quite similar to stars. However, they appear this way because they reflect light from the Sun, not because they produce light as stars do. If you keep watching a planet over time, you will notice that it moves in the sky relative to the stars. Because of the huge distance between the stars and Earth, the stars appear fixed relative to one another, and seem to rotate together across the sky as the Earth spins on its axis. Because they are much closer, the planets' movements in their own orbits are clearly noticeable against this background.

A space probe called Mariner 10 sent this image of Mercury back to Earth.

1 Which is the largest planet in the Solar System?

2 Using the idea of an orbit, describe what is meant by 'a year'.

3 **a** Which planet takes longest to orbit the Sun?

   b What pattern do you notice in the distances of the planets from the Sun, and the time they take to complete one orbit?

4 Why is the sentence 'My Very Energetic Maiden Aunt Just Swam Under North Pier' useful?

Summary of Solar System

- The Earth is one of a family of nine planets in the Solar System, each with its own special features.
- The planets move around the Sun, in elliptical orbits, with the Sun almost at the centre.
- The further the planet is from the Sun, the longer it takes to complete one orbit.
- Many of the planets have natural satellites or moons, orbiting them.
- The orbits of the planets and moons are maintained by the force of gravity.

- Comets move round the Sun in highly unsymmetrical orbits.
- Comets are made up of rocks and frozen gases, originating in the Oort cloud. As a comet nears the Sun, the gases vaporise producing the comet's characteristic tail.
- Asteroids are pieces of rock and ice orbiting the Sun in a band between Mars and Jupiter.

29.2 **Earth and Moon**

How does the Earth move in space?

5 As the Earth travels round the Sun, you travel at about 30 000 m/s. Why do you not just fly off into space, as you would if you let go on a spinning roundabout or Wurlitzer?

If alien beings visited our part of the Solar System, the Earth and its Moon would appear to them to be so similar in size that they would look like a double planet system rather than a planet and satellite. The system swings round and round as it orbits the Sun (see figure 2). It is like a fairground Wurlitzer, but travelling over a thousand times faster. As the Earth rotates round the Sun once a year, it carries everyone on it at a speed of nearly 30 000 m/s (about 2.6 million km each day).

As the Earth rotates around the Sun and swings around the Moon, it also spins on its own axis.

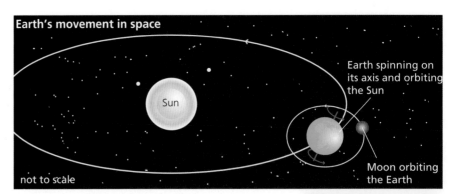

Earth's movement in space

not to scale

Sun

Earth spinning on its axis and orbiting the Sun

Moon orbiting the Earth

On a Wurlitzer, each car swings around on the end of a long arm. At the same time, all the cars rotate around the centre. In a similar way, the Earth and Moon swing around each other, and also rotate around the Sun.

What causes day, night and the seasons?

6 Greenland was once called The Land of the Midnight Sun. Why do you think it got such a name?

The Earth spins on its axis, so the half of it that faces towards the Sun, and so experiences daylight, keeps changing. As a place moves into the half facing the Sun, it becomes light and experiences day. As the place moves into the dark, shaded half of the Earth's surface, it experiences night.

The axis around which the Earth spins is tilted compared to the plane of its orbit. This means that sometimes the half of the Earth nearest the North Pole (the northern hemisphere) points towards the Sun and receives more direct sunlight, while the southern hemisphere points away, and receives less direct sunlight. In the northern hemisphere, it is summer when this happens, while in the southern hemisphere, it is winter. Six months later, the Earth has moved round to the opposite side of the Sun, but has kept its axis of rotation pointing in the same direction. This means that the situation is reversed, and the northern hemisphere experiences winter, while the southern hemisphere has summer (see figure 3).

Figure 3

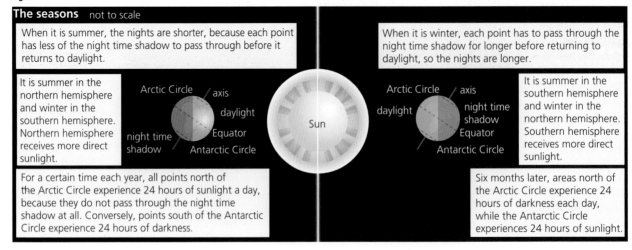

The seasons not to scale

When it is summer, the nights are shorter, because each point has less of the night time shadow to pass through before it returns to daylight.

It is summer in the northern hemisphere and winter in the southern hemisphere. Northern hemisphere receives more direct sunlight.

Arctic Circle / axis

daylight

night time shadow

Equator

Antarctic Circle

Sun

For a certain time each year, all points north of the Arctic Circle experience 24 hours of sunlight a day, because they do not pass through the night time shadow at all. Conversely, points south of the Antarctic Circle experience 24 hours of darkness.

When it is winter, each point has to pass through the night time shadow for longer before returning to daylight, so the nights are longer.

Arctic Circle / axis

daylight

night time shadow

Equator

Antarctic Circle

It is summer in the southern hemisphere and winter in the northern hemisphere. Southern hemisphere receives more direct sunlight.

Six months later, areas north of the Arctic Circle experience 24 hours of darkness each day, while the Antarctic Circle experiences 24 hours of sunlight.

What is the Moon like?

The Moon provides no light of its own, but is visible because it reflects about 7 % of the sunlight which strikes it. As the Moon moves round the Earth, we sometimes see all of the side which is lit by the Sun, and sometimes only part of it. This effect produces **phases of the Moon**, such as the Full Moon, New Moon and Crescent Moon.

The Moon spins on its own axis as it orbits the Earth, at just the right speed to keep the same face towards us all the time. A full orbit takes 27.3 days, but because the Earth moves round the Sun during this time, it takes 29.5 days before the Moon appears in the same place in the sky relative to the Sun. So the time between Full Moons is 29.5 days. This interval is called a **lunar month**, and is the basis of our present length for one calendar month.

What causes tides?

Because the Moon has mass, it produces a gravitational force on other masses. Fluids on the Earth are pulled towards it, so the Earth's oceans and atmosphere bulge out towards the Moon. As the Earth spins, different parts of the oceans are pulled towards the Moon. On Earth this pull is experienced as a high tide. Meanwhile, on the other side of the Earth, the water bulges out in another high tide. Water on this side of the Earth is furthest away from the Moon, so it does not feel such a strong force of attraction in the direction of the Moon as water elsewhere. The tides are affected by the position of the Sun, as well as the Moon (see figure 4).

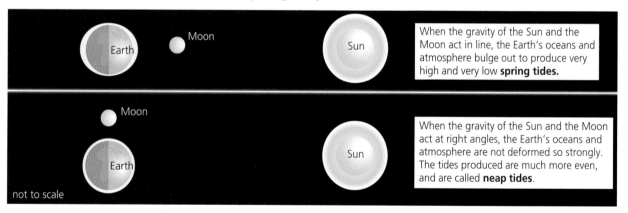

When the gravity of the Sun and the Moon act in line, the Earth's oceans and atmosphere bulge out to produce very high and very low **spring tides.**

When the gravity of the Sun and the Moon act at right angles, the Earth's oceans and atmosphere are not deformed so strongly. The tides produced are much more even, and are called **neap tides**.

Figure 4 The gravity of the Sun and Moon pull on the Earth, and make the oceans and atmosphere bulge out.

What causes eclipses?

The plane of the Moon's orbit is tilted compared to the Earth's. When the orbit is tilted in a certain direction, it is possible for the Moon to cast a shadow over the Earth, creating a **solar eclipse** (see figure 5). Sometimes only part of the Sun is covered by the Moon. This is a partial eclipse. Solar eclipses are rare because the Moon is very rarely in the right position, and because the Moon casts such a small shadow. **Lunar eclipses** are more common. A lunar eclipse is when the Moon passes into the Earth's shadow, which is relatively large (see figure 5).

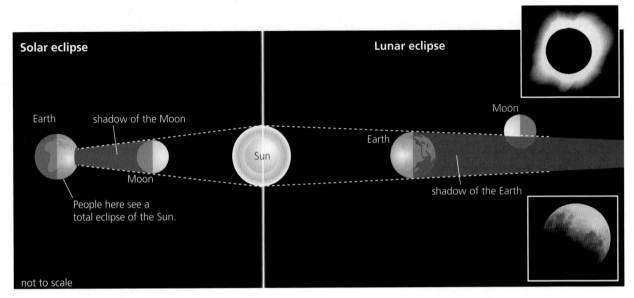

Figure 5 A solar eclipse occurs when the Moon casts a shadow on the Earth. A lunar eclipse occurs when the Earth casts a shadow on the Moon.

Earth	Moon	
Mass (kg)	5.98×10^{24}	7.35×10^{22}
Diameter (km)	12756	3476
Gravity strength (N/kg)	9.81	1.62
Maximum surface temperature (°C)	74 (Death Valley USA)	110
Minimum surface temperature (°C)	−57 (Antarctic winter)	−180

Table 2 *Data for the Earth and the Moon.*

7 Table 2 shows that the Earth experiences a smaller range of temperatures than the Moon.
  a How does the Earth's atmosphere reduce the range of temperatures we experience?
  b What other features on Earth make the temperature range less extreme than on the Moon?
8 There are many craters on the Moon, but very few on the Earth. What two reasons are there for that difference?

Summary of Earth and Moon

- The time taken for the Earth to orbit the Sun is one year.
- The time taken for the Moon to orbit the Earth is approximately one month.
- Phases of the Moon are due to the Moon moving around the Earth.
- Tides are caused by the gravity of the Moon and the Sun.

- When the Moon blocks the view of the Sun from the Earth, there is a solar eclipse.
- When the Earth blocks sunlight to the Moon, there is a lunar eclipse.
- The spinning of the Earth causes night and day.
- The facts that the Earth's axis is tilted, and that the Earth orbits the Sun with the axis always pointing in the same direction, give rise to the seasons.

Cosmology
Cosmology
Cosmology
ogy Cosmology Cosmology
Cosmology
Cosmology
smology
Cosmology
Cosmology Cosmology

30

Learning objectives

By the end of this chapter you should be able to:

- **explain** what a star is, and why it glows
- **describe** the differences between the various types of stars in our galaxy
- **describe** the life cycle of a star, and how it depends on the mass of the star

- **describe** emission and absorption nebulae
- **describe** what a galaxy is, and the evidence for the view that all the galaxies in the Universe are generally moving apart
- **describe** the evidence for the Big Bang theory and the theory of the expansion of the Universe

30.1 Stars

What is a nebula?

Note

The distances involved in discussions about the Universe are huge. One of the most convenient units to use is called a **light year**. This is the distance that a beam of light would travel in a year. One light year is equal to 9.46×10^{12} km.

Interstellar travellers moving through our galaxy would see a huge variety of stars of different sizes and colours. They would also see mysterious clouds of gas, with strange shapes and colours, called **nebulae**.

Being Earth-bound, our experience of the Universe is very limited. Nevertheless, scientists have managed to describe the exact positions of stars and nebulae, explain why they shine, describe what they were like a million years ago, and estimate how much longer they might 'live'.

An **emission nebula** is a volume of gas and plasma which is so hot that it emits light. The colour of the light emitted depends on how hot the gas is, which elements are in the gas, and whether they are ionised or not. The nebula might have been formed when a star exploded, throwing hot gas into space. Or it could be that the gas is gathering together due to gravity, and might eventually form a new star. Our own Sun formed from material that was probably thrown out by old, exploded stars.

An absorption nebula is a volume of gas and plasma which is too cool to emit light. You can only see this sort of nebula when it absorbs light trying to pass through it, so it appears as dark patches against the light of emission nebulae behind it.

The material in an absorption nebula is called **dark matter**. Because it does not give out light, it is impossible to say how much dark matter there is in the Universe. Scientists believe the Universe is currently expanding. If there is very little dark matter in it, the Universe will continue to expand forever. If there is a great deal of it, there will be enough gravity to stop the present expansion, and the Universe will eventually start to collapse.

Note

Plasma is a state of matter in which electrons, protons and neutrons separate, forming a 'gas' of charged particles.

The Orion Nebula is an emission nebula, which will probably form a star one day.

The Horsehead Nebula is an absorption nebula. It was once thought that the dark areas were gaps in the stars, so you could see right through to the space beyond.

How do nebulae form stars?

Newly forming star

light pressure pushes atoms outwards   gravity pulls atoms inwards

Figure 1 If a newly formed star is to last, the light pressure pushing atoms of gas *out* must balance the force of gravity pulling them *in*.

Large volumes of gas and plasma gradually get pulled together into a nebula, by their own gravity, getting hotter and more dense as they do so. The amount of light emitted also increases, which exerts **light pressure** on the atoms in the star. This light pressure acts against the force of gravity pulling the gas inwards (see figure 1).

If the pressures and temperatures inside the gathering gas become high enough, hydrogen atoms in the gas could begin to undergo nuclear fusion, and join together to become helium atoms. This releases large amounts of energy, so the gas becomes much hotter and brighter and is now called a **star**.

The Sun is a typical example of one type of star. It converts 500 million tonnes of hydrogen to helium by nuclear fusion every second. Even at this rate, the Sun is so massive that it should last for 10 000 million years before it runs out of hydrogen. The fusion reaction requires very high pressures and temperatures: the temperature of the Sun's core is around 14 000 000 °C, though the surface is much 'cooler' at around 5500 °C.

What happens when the hydrogen runs out?

1 Describe the differences between an emission nebula and an absorption nebula.

2 The Sun will one day become a red giant. Should humankind be concerned? Explain your answer.

Once a star has run out of hydrogen, the light pressure reduces. There is nothing to act against the force of gravity pulling its atoms in together. The centre of the star therefore shrinks, getting hotter as it does so. The outer layers of gas move out to make the star a hundred times larger. The outer part is now cooler, and glows red, so the dying star is called a **red giant** (see figure 2).

In smaller stars, as the outer material drifts further out, it cools to become a dim sphere lit by the light from the central core. This is called a **planetary nebula**. The centre gets hotter as it shrinks, allowing helium atoms to combine by nuclear fusion to make carbon and oxygen. The central star is now brighter than before, but as it runs out of helium, its fuel, it again becomes cooler and shrinks to become a **white dwarf**. Gradually it becomes dimmer and dimmer, and eventually it goes out.

Life of a star

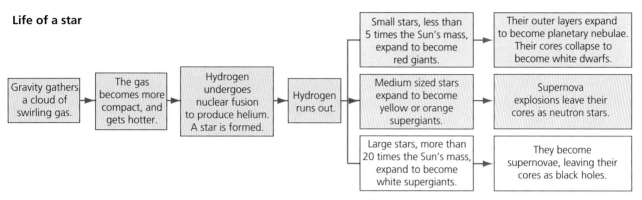

Figure 2 When the hydrogen runs out, a star turns into something else. What it turns into depends on the star's size.

What is supernova?

In large stars, when the hydrogen runs out, and the core collapses in on itself and becomes much hotter, the nuclear reactions do not stop at the conversion of helium atoms to carbon and oxygen. The extra size means the temperatures in its core are high enough to convert carbon atoms to silicon, and silicon atoms to iron. But the iron is unstable. It cannot be converted to heavier elements. The iron breaks down into helium, and the core begins to collapse in on itself, triggering a huge explosion. This blows the rest of the star outwards, making it expand at a rate of 15 000 km/s, and making it shine brighter than a thousand million stars. From the Earth, the sudden burst of light is seen as a **supernova** – an event only observed once every several hundred years. The forces inside the remaining core can be so high that atoms are crushed forcing protons and electrons together to form neutrons. The material is incredibly dense. A matchbox-full would have a weight of several thousand tonnes. A **neutron star** has been formed.

What is a black hole?

A black hole is a star so massive, with gravity so strong, that not even light can escape from it. According to Albert Einstein's theory of general relativity, the strength of its gravity means the space-time around a black hole could be warped so much, that it could link up with the space-time of other parallel Universes, or other parts of our own Universe (see figure 3). So, assuming you do not get crushed into neutrons as you approach, it might be possible to travel through a black hole into other Universes!

Figure 3

How space-time can be warped

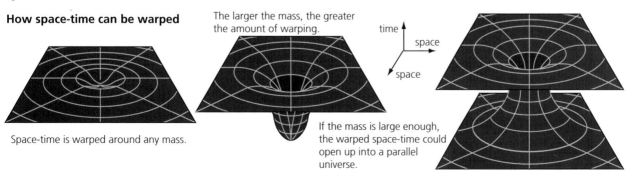

Space-time is warped around any mass.

The larger the mass, the greater the amount of warping.

If the mass is large enough, the warped space-time could open up into a parallel universe.

Summary of stars

- Stars contain hot gas and plasma, which produce light. They are held together by gravity, and pushed out by light pressure.
- The source of heat and light energy in a star is nuclear fusion.
- Material from dying stars is pulled together by gravity to form new stars, in a life cycle.

- At the end of its life, a star becomes a red giant. Some then become white dwarfs, others may collapse to form a black hole or a neutron star. What happens to a star depends upon its mass.
- Emission nebulae produce their own light, while absorption nebulae are only visible if they block light from behind.

30.2 The Universe

What is a galaxy?

Note

Most stars in our galaxy are double or triple star systems, rather than single stars like our Sun. People used to think this meant 'Solar Systems' like ours must be rare. But data collected in 1994 on 110 stars, using the Hubble Space Telescope, indicated that about half of the stars seem to have 'proto planetary discs' around them.

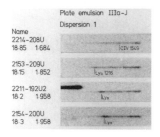

In 1929, Edwin Hubble published values for the red shift shown by a range of galaxies. His data showed that the galaxies are moving apart.

This spiral galaxy is very similar to our own.

If interstellar travellers moved further and further away from our Solar System, they would see that the Sun and millions of other stars around it form a huge spiral structure. This is slowly turning around a massive centre where the stars are closer together than at the edge. This spiral structure is called a **galaxy** and it contains around 100 000 000 000 (a hundred thousand million) stars. The Solar System is around 33 000 light years from the centre of our galaxy, which is about 100 000 light years across altogether.

Our galaxy is certainly not alone in space. Indeed, many scientists think there are probably more galaxies in the Universe than there are stars in our own galaxy. The galaxies vary in size and shape, and are usually categorised as spiral, barred or planetary, or described using a mixture of these terms.

Galaxies are not fixed in the Universe, but instead seem to be moving away from us, and each other. The further away from the Earth they are, the faster they are moving. The evidence for this is that the light we receive from these distant galaxies is much redder than you would expect if the galaxies were fixed. Light emitted by each element has a certain colour, but the wavelengths are stretched if the object is moving away rapidly, making the light closer to the longer red wavelengths (see chapter 24, *Light*). This is known as **red shift**.

According to work based on data collected by the American astronomer Edwin Hubble, objects at the edge of the Universe must be travelling at close to the speed of light, which is the fastest speed possible, but if they are, their red-shift will be so great that they will be invisible.

Hubble's red shift data suggest that all the matter in all of the galaxies in the Universe must have been together at some stage, and been thrown out by some tremendous explosion. This 'Big Bang', occurred between 8 and 12 billion years ago. If there is enough matter in the Universe, gravity will gradually slow this expansion down, and the Universe will start to collapse, eventually crushing itself in the 'Big Crunch'. If there is not enough matter, the Universe will continue expanding, but at a slower and slower rate.

Are the galaxies all moving at the same rate?

At one time, cosmologists thought that the Universe was expanding smoothly, and that galaxies were spread fairly evenly, all moving apart at the same rate. It now seems that galaxies form groups, or **clusters**, and these clusters affect each other's motion. Our local cluster includes our galaxy, the Andromeda galaxy, and about 30 smaller galaxies. Our galaxy is carrying us towards the Andromeda galaxy at a speed of about 300 km/s.

By measuring variations in the background radiation left over from the Big Bang, scientists have worked out that our whole local cluster is also moving, at about 600 km/s, towards the southern constellation of Antila. It is being pulled across space by the gravity of some really vast systems in that direction.

Around our local cluster, there are about 12 others, forming a supercluster in the shape of a very long, thin cylinder, 50 million light years long and 5 million light years wide. The supercluster contains over a hundred galaxies. Other superclusters contain many more: our nearest supercluster, the Virgo supercluster, contains almost a thousand galaxies.

Even the Virgo supercluster is small compared to the Great Attractor – a supercluster containing about 7500 galaxies, with a total mass 50 000 times that of our own galaxy. The Great Attractor lies 300 million light years away, and is pulling our supercluster towards it.

Our supercluster is also attracted, at a speed of 370 km/s, in the direction of Canis Minor. Scientists have detected at least 550 galaxies in that direction, over a billion light years away. Perhaps a supercluster even larger than the Great Attractor lies in that direction. Beyond that, there could be an even larger one. When you think that the Universe is estimated to be 12 billion light years across, and expanding at about the speed of light, just about anything is possible!

Note

Quasars are 'quasi stellar objects'. They have huge red shifts, which implies that they are further away than any other known object. However, they appear to be very bright – much brighter than such distant objects should seem from Earth.

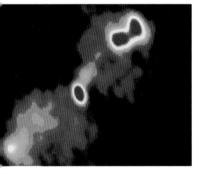

Scientists have yet to work out a good theory to explain what quasars really are.

3   In 1994, the Hubble Space Telescope detected evidence of vast amounts of helium gas between the galaxies, thought to be left over from the Big Bang. What two other pieces of evidence are there to support the Big Bang theory?

4   Some stars in our own galaxy are moving towards our Solar System. How might their light appear different to stars which are not moving relative to us?

5   90% of the material in the Universe is thought to be dark matter, which does not give out light. How could dark matter ever be detected?

Summary of the Universe

- The Universe began with the Big Bang, when all matter was created, and it has been expanding ever since.
- If there is not enough matter (not enough gravity) the Universe will continue to expand forever. If there is enough matter, gravity will cause the Universe to collapse, in the Big Crunch.
- The light from many galaxies shows a red shift, which shows they are moving away from us.
- Quasars, or 'quasi stellar objects', seem to be further from the Earth than any other objects, but appear far brighter than expected at that distance.
- A black hole is a star so massive that nothing can escape its gravity, not even light.

Natural gas

This spread brings together ideas about *Controlling matter*, from chapters 5 to 9 in this book.

At the Brent oil and gas field in the North Sea, the water is over 300 m deep. To reach the gas, engineers have drilled many holes into the sea bed, to depths of 5–8 km. The gas comes to the surface at 195 times atmospheric pressure, and 0 °C. The gas is carried along a 450 km pipeline, to join up with the main gas grid system on the UK mainland. The grid reaches over 17 million customers, and is over 240 000 km long in total – that is over six times the circumference of the Earth. People in the UK use over 130 000 million litres of gas every day.

When it reaches customers' homes, the gas is almost pure methane with a small amount of 'odorant' added so that you can smell the gas if there is a leak. But when the gas comes out of the ground it is far from pure. The gas from some wells is even dissolved in oil.

Because natural gas is such a useful and valuable fuel, for heating, cooking and generating electricity, companies go to great trouble to get it.

Processing natural gas

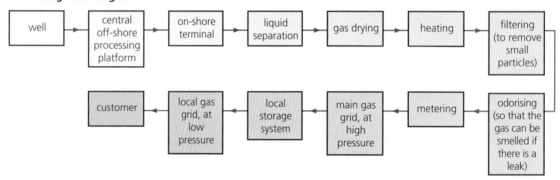

Figure 1 This flow chart shows the stages in processing the gas from the Morecambe Bay gas field in the Irish Sea.

Gas	Composition (%)
Carbon dioxide	1.6
Ethane	4.3
Nitrogen	7.7
Propane	1.0
Methane	84.0
Other gases (mainly heavy hydrocarbons) plus small amounts of sulphur, water and solid materials	1.4

Table 1 Composition of natural gas from Morecambe Bay gas field. (Source: British Gas and Shell UK.)

Processing stage	From well	At on-shore terminal	During gas drying	During filtering	During metering and in main gas grid	At customer
Pressure (× 100 000 N/m²)		75			70	0.035
Temperature (°C)	36	10	−23	6	2	

Table 2 *Data for processing of gas from Morecambe Bay gas field. (Source: British Gas and Shell UK.)*

1 The temperature of the 450 km steel pipeline in the Brent field varies with the seasons. By how much will it expand when its temperature rises by 4 °C, if the linear expansivity of steel is 0.000 015?

2 A device called a 'pig' is fitted snugly inside the gas pipes, and is pushed along by the gas pressure. As it goes along the pig cleans the pipe and records information about possible leaks in an on-board computer, to be analysed later.

If the gas pressure is 70 times atmospheric pressure (atmospheric pressure = 100 000 N/m²), calculate the maximum forces on pigs designed to fit into pipes of diameter:

a 0.20 m **b** 0.60 m **c** 1.05 m

The intelligent pig

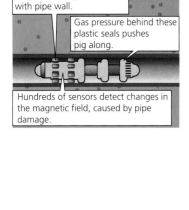

Flexible steel brushes ensure magnets have good contact with pipe wall.

Gas pressure behind these plastic seals pushes pig along.

Hundreds of sensors detect changes in the magnetic field, caused by pipe damage.

3 As the gas comes towards the shore, it cools, and water vapour in it condenses. What happens to the saturated water vapour pressure as the gas comes to the shore?

4 The gas laws apply to ideal gases.

a Use the pressure law, and some of the data from table 2, to see whether natural gas behaves like an ideal gas. (Hint: remember to convert °C into K. What assumptions are you making?)

b Estimate the gas pressures at the drying and filtering stages using the same law.

c Why are such high pressures used in the gas processing system? (Hint: think of Boyle's Law.)

5 The diagram below shows the metering system used to measure how much gas is passing into the main gas grid.

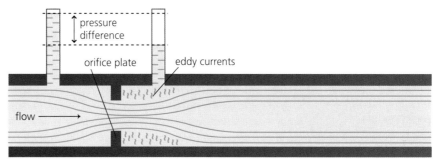

pressure difference

orifice plate   eddy currents

flow

a Why is the pressure of the gas lower just after the orifice plate, than before it? (Hint: who's principle is being used here?)

b How will the reading alter to show that more gas is passing through the system?

c What other systems could be used to measure the flow rate?

6 When fluids flow through a pipe, there must be a pressure difference between the ends of the pipe. The graph shows how the pressure drop of natural gas varies with the diameter of the pipe.

a Describe in words what the graph shows.

b Use your knowledge of fluids to explain the shape of the graph.

7 A typical gas storage tank is a cylinder 65 m in diameter, containing gas at a pressure of 3500 N/m² above atmospheric pressure. What is the total upward force on the roof of the tank?

8 Natural gas is exported to many countries in liquefied form, at −161 °C.

a Why is it liquefied?

b Why would it be dangerous if the cooling system failed, and the liquefied gas warmed up?

c Why is it not transported as 'solid gas'?

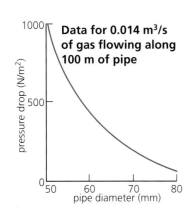

Data for 0.014 m³/s of gas flowing along 100 m of pipe

pressure drop (N/m²)

pipe diameter (mm)

Forces in a Fender *Stratocaster*

This spread brings together ideas about *Controlling movement*, from chapters 10 to 14 in this book.

A Fender Stratocaster is a well known model of electric guitar, used by many famous guitarists. It was invented in the late 1950s by the American Leo Fender. Like all guitars, a Stratocaster is designed to withstand many different sorts of forces.

body

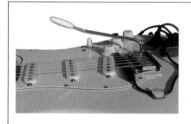

1 The strings pass over a 'bridge', which has a 'tremolo' on this guitar. When you press the tremolo arm, the strings slacken, and the pitch of the sound they make falls. When you release the arm, five springs pull the bridge back, and pull the strings back to the correct tension.

bridge

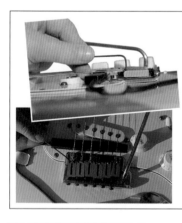

2 The height of the strings above the fingerboard is adjusted using screws which pass through each bridge section. When making the adjustment, the bridge section must be moved while the string is still stretched tightly. The bridge piece therefore needs a large force to move it.

tremolo arm

Data	
Tension in a string	60 N
Number of strings	6
Height of string above fingerboard	2 mm
Depth of truss rod below fingerboard	3 mm

1 Look at the photo with label 3.
  a In which direction does the string try to move the tuning machine?
  b In which direction does the string tree feel a force due to the strings?
  c In which direction does the nut feel a force due to the strings?
2 **a** Read label 1. If two of the tremolo springs are removed, do you think this will affect how easy it is to move the bridge with the tremolo arm?
  b How is the tremolo arm designed so you can move the bridge by applying a small force?
3 **a** Use label 5, and the data in the table, to estimate the force the truss rod must provide.

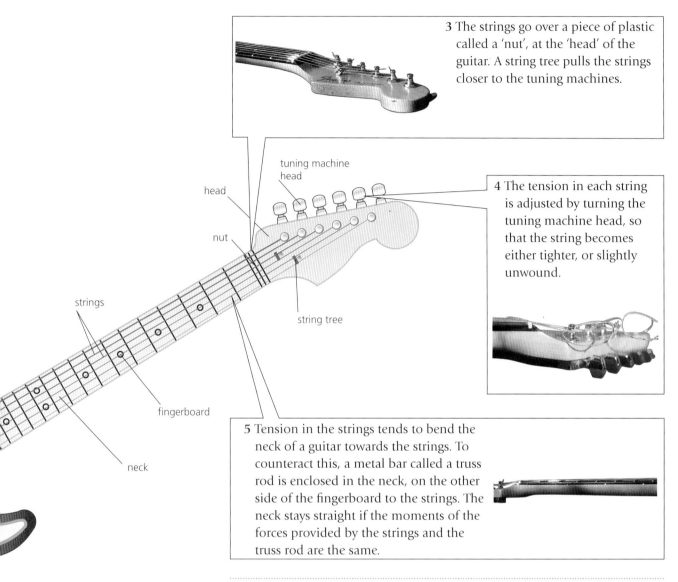

3 The strings go over a piece of plastic called a 'nut', at the 'head' of the guitar. A string tree pulls the strings closer to the tuning machines.

head

tuning machine head

nut

strings

string tree

fingerboard

neck

4 The tension in each string is adjusted by turning the tuning machine head, so that the string becomes either tighter, or slightly unwound.

5 Tension in the strings tends to bend the neck of a guitar towards the strings. To counteract this, a metal bar called a truss rod is enclosed in the neck, on the other side of the fingerboard to the strings. The neck stays straight if the moments of the forces provided by the strings and the truss rod are the same.

b When the strings are changed, the force on one side of the fingerboard is reduced. Which way will the neck tend to bend while this happens?

c If you were designing a 12 string version of this guitar, what would you have to do to stop the neck from being damaged?

4 Look at label 2. In what two ways does the design of the instrument make it easier to adjust the height of the strings correctly?

5 When the guitar is free to hang from its strap, it hangs as shown on the left.

a Look at the photo, and suggest where the centre of mass of the guitar is.

b Why do you think Leo Fender designed the guitar so that the centre of mass is in this position? (Imagine playing the instrument.)

c If the body of the guitar was made smaller, or the head made larger, what problems might there be (if any)?

d If the body of the guitar was made larger, or the head made smaller, what problems might there be (if any)?

Car *electrics*

This example brings together ideas about *Controlling electrons*, from chapters 15 to 21 in this book.

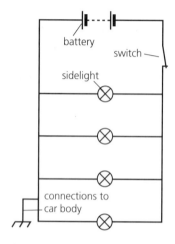

Modern cars rely on electricity to make the engine run efficiently, to provide lighting, and for many safety features such as sensing ice, and sensing when the brakes are worn.

1 As a car moves along a road, parts of the tyres rub on the ground, so the car can build up a static electrical charge.

   a When are you most likely to notice that a car has a large static charge?

   b What can be done to reduce the problem?

2 The sidelights on a car are connected in parallel, with one side of each lamp wired to the metal body of the car, as shown on the left.

   a Why are the lights not joined in series?

   b Suggest a reason why the body of the car is used as one of the electrical connections.

3 A car uses a 12 V battery.

   a Each sidelight is rated at 21 W. What is the total current flowing to the sidelights, when they are switched on?

   b Each headlight is rated at 60 W. How much current flows in the headlights when they are on?

   c The starter motor is rated at 0.7 kW. How much current flows in it, when the car starts up?

   d The fuses available are 7.5 A, 10 A, 15 A, 20 A, 25 A and 30 A. Which fuse (if any) would you use for: **i** the sidelights,   **ii** the headlights,   **iii** the starter motor?

   e The car battery is rated at 36 amp hours (Ah). That is to say it can provide 36 A for 1 hour, or 18 A for 2 hours and so on. Estimate how long takes to run the battery flat, if the headlights and sidelights are accidentally left on.

4 The amount of fuel in the tank can be measured using a variable resistor wired as a potential divider. The sliding connection of the variable resistor is moved by a float which rises and falls as the fuel level varies (see diagram below). Design a complete circuit to show the driver how much fuel remains in the tank. State what sort of meter you would you use.

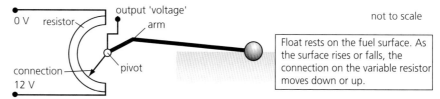

5 The car engine is cooled by water, which must never boil. So the driver must be able to check the temperature from a display on the dash board. Suggest a suitable method of monitoring the water temperature. What type of sensor would you use, and how could you display the value on the dash board? (Hint: you may find it useful to look at chapter 5, *Matter and temperature change*.)

6 Many cars have a central locking system. Each door contains a pair of solenoids. When one of the solenoids in the pair is activated, it becomes a magnet, so it pulls the armature across, locking the door. Activating the other solenoid pulls the armature back, releasing the door lock.

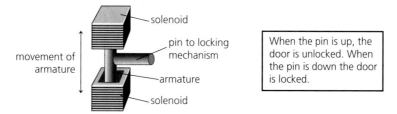

a Suggest a suitable material for the armature. Explain your choice.

b Suggest how the solenoids are designed to produce a force large enough to move the armature.

7 Electric motors are used at several places on a car, such as on the windscreen wipers and in the water pump for the windscreen washers. But the starter motor has to provide the largest turning force of all. Describe how the starter motor must be designed to produce a force large enough to start the engine.

8 To keep the battery charged, older cars used dynamos which generated DC, but modern cars use alternators which generate AC.

a Suggest some advantages of using an alternator rather than a dynamo.

b The alternator is driven by a belt forced round by the engine. The size of the pulley wheel on the alternator is small so that it makes the alternator turn rapidly. Why is this a good idea?

9 To ignite the fuel inside the engine, a high voltage is needed. This is produced by a device called a 'coil'. This is actually two coils – a primary and a secondary coil – wrapped around each other. A current is passed through the primary coil producing a large amount of magnetism. This current is then switched off quickly, and a high 'voltage' is generated in the secondary coil. Describe how the 'coil' must be designed so that a really high 'voltage' is produced.

10 To inform other road users that the car is about to turn, the driver activates flashing indicator lights on the left or right side of the car. Design an electronic system to achieve this.

11 When any of the doors is opened, the courtesy light should come on. To activate the light, microswitches are placed in each door. Design an electronic system to activate courtesy lights in a car.

12 To ensure that the driver and passengers fasten their seat belts, a warning light is shown on the dash board if one of the seat belts is not clicked into its socket, and there is someone sitting in the seat. Draw a diagram for the circuit that operates this system.

Colonising Mars

This example brings together ideas about space, from chapters 29 and 30 in this book.

NASA and the Russian Space Agency have developed plans for a mission to take astronauts to Mars, with the aim of one day building a space station on the planet. Some scientists have suggested that, in the longer term, it might be possible to increase the atmosphere on Mars, and produce oceans as the planet warms up. Eventually, it might be possible for people to colonise the planet.

Mars is smaller than Earth, with a very thin atmosphere, and two moons called Phobos and Deimos. The planet has a dusty surface, but there is evidence of frozen water locked beneath it. There are 'ice caps' made of solid carbon dioxide at the poles. Use the data from the table opposite, and ideas that you have read about in this book, to answer the questions.

This image, from the Viking space probe, shows a giant extinct volcano called Olympus Mons on the surface of Mars.

	Earth	Moon	Mars	Phobos	Deimos
Distance from Sun (AU)	0.98–1.02		1.38–1.67		
Distance from planet (km)		384 400		9350	23 490
Mass (Earth masses)	1	0.012	0.11	0.000 000 001 6	
Radius (km)	6378	1738	3397	Not a sphere (approx. 27 × 19 × 21)	Not a sphere (approx. 15 × 12 × 15)
Atmospheric pressure (compared to Earth)	1	0	0.007	0	0
Tilt of axis	23°		24° (varies)		
Strength of gravity (N/kg)	9.81	1.65	3.80		
Magnetic field strength (compared to Earth)	1		0.002		
Period of orbit (Earth days, d, Earth hours, h)	365.25 d	27.3 d	687 d	7.65 h	30.46 h
Time for one spin (Earth days, d, Earth hours, h)	24 h	27.3 d	24.62 h	7.65 h	
Maximum surface temperature (°C)	74	110	20		
Minimum surface temperature (°C)	−57	−180	−100		

Table 1 *Data on Earth, Mars and the moons of these planets.*

1 If people colonise Mars, the colonists will face many hardships and dangers which people on Earth do not. Suggest what some of these could be.

2 Light and radio waves take 8 minutes to reach the Earth from the Sun.

a How long would a radio signal take to reach Mars from the Earth when they are:

i at their closest   **ii** at their furthest distance apart?

b What problems might this cause for communications between Earth and the colonists?

3 The colonists might want geostationary satellites around Mars (see chapter 14, *Motion in two dimensions*). The geostationary orbit for Mars would be 17 196 km above the surface, compared to 35 900 km on Earth.

a What use might such satellites have for the colonists?

b What two factors make the distance of this orbit above the surface different on Mars than it is on Earth.

4 The Earth's Moon causes several events on the Earth. Explain whether or not the events below are likely to happen on Mars.

a solar eclipse

b lunar eclipse

c tides (assuming the scientists could make oceans)

5 The Earth's motion relative to the Sun causes several events on Earth. Explain whether or not the events below might happen on Mars.

a night and day

b seasons

6 Mars is sometimes over 400 million km from the Earth. In what ways will the night sky appear different to a Mars colonist, compared to the view a star gazer gets on Earth?

7 **a** Explain whether or not moving to Mars will save the human race from extinction when the Sun becomes a red giant.

b Suggest some other reasons for attempting to colonise Mars.

Glossary

Absolute Zero   The lowest possible temperature, at which particles do not vibrate: −273° C, or 0 K.

Acceleration   Rate of change of a velocity, involving a change of speed or direction of travel. Measured in metres per second squared (m/s/s or m/s^2).

Adhesive forces   Forces between particles in a liquid and those in a nearby solid.

Alpha particle   Particle containing two protons and two neutrons, emitted from a radioactive source.

Alternating current (AC)   A current which repeatedly changes direction, usually at a regular rate with a wave pattern.

Alternator   Device which converts kinetic energy into electrical energy. The current produced is AC.

Ampere   Unit of electric current, used to measure how rapidly electric charge is flowing. 1 ampere = 1 coulomb per second.

Amplitude   Maximum deflection of a wave from the base line.

Atomic (proton) number   Number of protons in the nucleus of an atom.

Becquerel   Unit of radioactive decay. 1 becquerel = one nucleus decaying per second.

Beta particle   Fast moving electron emitted from a decaying nucleus.

Binary   Coding information as series' of 'high' and 'low' electrical signals, which can be used to represent numbers and letters.

Bistable   Electrical device with two stable output states, 1 or 0, onto which it can be 'locked'.

Black hole   Star which is so massive that its gravitational attraction is great enough to pull the light it emits back into itself.

Boiling point   Temperature at which all of a liquid becomes a gas.

Capacitor   Electrical component which stores electrical charge.

Capillarity   Tendency for a liquid to rise up a narrow tube.

Centre of mass   Position where the mass of an object can be thought to be concentrated.

Centripetal force   A 'centre seeking' force which acts to push or pull an object towards the centre of a circular path.

Chemical energy   Energy associated with the bonds between atoms and molecules.

Cohesive forces   Forces which act between particles in a liquid.

Compression   Effect of squeezing a material. Part of a longitudinal wave where particles are squeezed together.

Conduction   Heat transfer from particle to particle in a solid, or the transfer of electrical energy through an object by the movement of charge.

Conductor   Material that allows electricity or heat to pass through it with little resistance.

Constructive interference   Merging two waves to form a stronger wave.

Convection   Heat transfer in fluids where hotter particles rise relative to colder particles.

Coulomb   Standard unit for an amount of electrical charge.

Couple   Two equal forces acting in opposite directions to cause a turning effect.

Crest   Highest part of a wave.

Critical angle   Angle at which light is totally internally reflected at a boundary with a more optically dense material.

Current gain   Ratio of the base current to the collector current which flows through a transistor.

Dark matter   Matter in interstellar space which does not emit light, but can absorb it.

Decibels   Measure of the loudness of sounds.

Density   The mass of a 1 m^3 of a material. Density = mass/volume.

Destructive interference   Combining two waves so that the resulting wave is weaker.

Diffraction   Bending of wavefronts as they pass an obstacle of similar or larger size than one wavelength.

Diffusion   Fluids mixing purely because of the random movement of the particles.

Dilitant fluid   Fluid whose viscosity increases as its speed or the force applied increases.

Displacement   Measurement of how far an object is from a starting position, which takes into account the direction as well as the distance.

Dynamo   Device for converting rotational kinetic energy into direct current electricity.

Earth connection   Electrical link which allows current to flow from a device, through the earth wire and into the ground.

Efficiency   Proportion of available energy used for a useful purpose.

Elastic limit   Point at which an elastic object is deformed so much that permanent deformation is caused.

Elastic potential energy   Energy contained in a stretched material such as rubber.

Electric current   Co-ordinated movement of electric charge.

Electric field   Region around a charged object where other charged objects feel a force.

Electrode   Conductor that releases or receives electrons, often from a liquid. Positive electrodes (which receive electrons) are called anodes. Negative electrodes (which release electrons) are called cathodes.

Electrolysis   Separation of positive and negative ions by passing an electric current through an electrolyte.

Electromagnetic induction   Production of an EMF when the amount of magnetism contained in a circuit changes.

Electromagnetic spectrum   Family of waves which are made up of vibrations in electrical and magnetic fields.

Electromotive force (EMF)   The cause of an electric current, measured in volts.

Electron   Negatively charged particle in an atom.

Energy reserve   Fuel humans can extract from the Earth's crust at an economic price.

Energy resource   Total amount of fuel in the Earth's crust.

Energy source   Material or physical event which provides energy.

Epicentre   Point on the Earth's surface immediately above the place where an earthquake starts.

Evaporation   Molecules at the surface of a liquid become a gas.

Fluid   Gas or liquid: a material capable of flowing.

Fluid pressure   Force per unit area produced by a fluid, which acts in all directions equally.

Frequency   Rate at which an event occurs e.g. the number of waves made in a second.

Friction   Process due to contact between surfaces, which causes a force restricting the movement of objects.

Gamma rays   Short wavelength electromagnetic waves emitted from a radioactive atom.

Geostationary orbit   Path of an object travelling around the Earth at the same speed as the Earth rotates, so that it remains above the same part of the surface at all times.

Geothermal energy   Heat energy derived from radioactive decay of materials in the Earth's crust.

Gravitational potential energy   Energy an object has due to its raised position.

Gravity   Pulling force between two massive objects.

Half-life   Average time taken for half the radioactive atoms present in a material to decay.

Heat energy   Energy resulting from vibrating particles in a material.

Hydraulic   System that transmits force using a liquid.

Impulse   A force multiplied by the time it lasts for. Impulse = Ft.

In parallel   Way of connecting electric components so that current separates into two or more routes before recombining.

In phase   When the pattern of crests and troughs of more than one wave is the same.

In series   Way of connecting electric components so that current passes through each component in turn.

Infra-red   Long wave electromagnetic wave just beyond the human visible spectrum.

Insulator   Substance which does not conduct an electric current (electrical insulator), or which does not conduct heat (heat insulator).

Ionising radiation   Radiation that makes atoms or molecules become charged particles called ions.

Isotope   Atoms of the same element, with the same number of protons but different numbers of neutrons.

Joule   Unit used to measure energy.

Kelvin scale   Temperature scale with units the same size as $°C$, called kelvins, K.

Kinetic energy   Energy associated with movement.

Laminar flow   Smooth movement of a fluid, where there is no mixing of layers.

Latent heat of fusion   Energy required to melt 1 kg of a substance when it is already at its melting point.

Latent heat of vaporisation   Energy required to evaporate 1 kg of a substance when it is already at its boiling point.

Lateral inversion   Reversal of an image left to right, compared to the object.

Lens   Shaped glass or plastic that bends rays of light.

Light-dependent resistor (LDR)   Electrical component, whose resistance varies with light intensity.

Linear expansivity   Proportion by which a material changes its length for each $°C$ change in temperature.

Live   Wire which varies in potential relative to zero.

Logic gate   Electrical device that responds to a combination of input signals, and produces a high output or no output in response.

Longitudinal waves   Waves vibrating in the same direction as the movement of the wave energy.

Machine   Device that allows a small force exerted at one place to produce a larger force elsewhere.

Magnetic field   Region of space where a magnetic material (such as iron), or another magnetic field feels a force.

Mass (nucleon) number   Number of protons and neutrons in the nucleus of an atom.

Melting point   Temperature at which all of a solid becomes a liquid.

Microwaves   Short wave radio waves belonging to the electromagnetic spectrum.

Moment   Turning effect of a force. Moment = force x distance from pivot.

Momentum   Mass of an object multiplied by its velocity.

Monostable   Electrical device with only one stable state. If moved from this state, it returns to it after a delay.

Motor   Device for converting electrical energy into kinetic energy.

Nebula   Region of thinly spread gas in space which can emit light (emission nebula) or absorb light (absorption nebula).

Net force   Resultant force produced by the combination of several other forces.

Neutral   Wire in a mains electrical cable which is at zero potential.

Neutron star   Star which has collapsed due to its gravity. The forces are so high that electrons and protons are forced together to make neutrons.

Newtonian fluid   Fluid with constant viscosity regardless of the speed at which it flows.

Non-renewable   Fuels that cannot be replaced once they have been used up.

Nucleus   Central part of an atom which contains protons and neutrons.

Ohm   SI unit of electrical resistance.

Optical fibres   Thin strands of glass used to carry signals on pulses of laser light.

Optically dense   Material through which light moves more slowly.

Oscillation   Vibration.

Parabola   Special sort of curve which gradually gets steeper and steeper. It is the path followed by a projectile.

Period   Time taken for one complete oscillation in a wave.

Pivot   Point around which an object can rotate.

Plasma   State of matter where atoms have become separated into protons, neutrons and electrons.

Pneumatic   System that transmits force using air pressure.

Potential divider   Two or more resistors in series which 'share' an overall potential in proportion to their resistances.

Power   Rate at which energy is transferred, measured in joules per second, or watts W.

Pressure   Force exerted per unit area.

Principle focus   Point to which parallel rays are converged by a lens, or from which they appear to diverge.

Projectile   Object that is moving sideways, but is also affected by the pull of gravity.

Proton   Positively charged particle found in the nucleus of an atom.

Pulsar   Star whose brightness varies at a regular rate, due to its rotation.

Quark   Extremely small particle which makes up protons and neutrons.

Quasar   'Quasi-stellar' object which appears to be extremely compact, and distant, and yet extremely bright.

Radio waves   Long wave members of the electromagnetic spectrum, used to carry signals.

Rarefaction   Area of low air pressure in a longitudinal wave.

Reaction   Force which occurs in response to another force. Forces always come in pairs: an action and a reaction.

Real image   Image which can be formed on a screen.

Reflection   Effect of a wave hitting an object and bouncing off.

Refraction   Bending of a wavefront as it enters another material, at an angle, because the wave speed is changed.

Refractive index   Measure of how much a material will bend light, calculated by comparing the speed of light through the material with the speed of light through air.

Relay   Electromagnetic device, which allows a small current to control a higher current or 'voltage'.

Renewable   Fuel which can be replaced after it has been used up.

Resistance   Property of a conductor which limits how easily electricity flows through it.

Resistivity   Electrical resistance of a 1 m^3 block of material.

Satellite   Object which orbits a planet.

Scalar   Any variable with size but no direction.

Seismic waves   Waves which originate in an earthquake.

Sievert   Unit used to measure a dose of radiation.

Specific heat capacity   Energy needed to raise the temperature of 1 kilogram of a material by 1 °C.

Star   Vast amount of gas which is so hot and dense that at the centre, nuclear reactions occur and light is emitted.

States of matter   Way of classifying materials as solid, liquid, gas or plasma.

Static electricity   Imbalance of electric charge at rest.

Streamlined   Shape that provides minimum resistance to movement through a fluid.

Supernova   Stage in a star's lifecycle when it explodes.

Surface tension   Forces that make the surface of a liquid behave like an elastic skin.

Terminal velocity   Steady speed attained by a falling object when the accelerating force is matched by the resistive forces.

Thermionic emission   Process by which electrons are released from a hot wire.

Thermistor   Electrical component whose resistance varies with temperature.

Thixotropic fluid   Fluid with a viscosity that reduces when a force is applied.

Transducer   Device which transfers energy.

Transformer   Device which 'steps up' or 'steps down' AC voltages.

Transverse waves   Waves vibrating at right angles to the direction in which the wave energy is travelling.

Trough   The lowest point in a wave.

Turbulent flow   Chaotic motion of a moving fluid.

Ultrasound   High frequency sound waves which humans cannot hear.

Ultraviolet   Short wavelength light, just beyond the human visible spectrum.

Vapour pressure   Force per unit area produced by a vapour. (Vapour is a gas that cannot be compressed into a liquid by force alone.)

Vector   Any quantity which has a direction as well as a size.

Velocity   Vector quantity that indicates the speed and direction of a moving object, measured in m/s.

Virtual image   Image that can be seen but cannot be formed on a screen.

Viscosity   Friction within a fluid which causes it to resist flowing.

Volt   Unit used to measure potential difference. 1 V = 1 joule per coulomb.

Wavelength   Distance between two crests (or troughs) in a wave.

Weight   Force resulting from the action of gravity on a mass.

White dwarf   Very compact star which emits white light.

Work   Transfer of energy.

X-rays   Short wave member of the electromagnetic spectrum.

Index

absolute zero 37, 58

acceleration 81–83, 88, 94, 97, 99,

action and reaction 67, 90–92

adhesive forces 52–53

aerogenerator 33

alpha particle 202–203, 205, 207, 209, 211

alternating current (AC) 123

alternator 140–141

ampere 107, 122

amplifier 130, 149, 167

amplitude 152, 153, 162, 164, 167, 168, 169

amplitude modulation (AM) 195

analogue 144

angle of incidence 173

angle of reflection 173

anode 108

asteroids 214

atomic (proton) number 201

atoms 37, 116, 199–204, 205

auditory nerve 166

battery (see *cell*)

Bernoulli's principle 57

beta particle 202–203, 205, 207, 209, 212

Big Bang 214, 222

biofuels 31–32

bistable 147

black hole 221

Boyle's Law 60–61

braking distance 86

buffer 149

buzzer 136, 150

capacitor 148

capillarity 53

catapult field 137

cathode 108

cathode ray oscilloscope (CRO) 130, 163

cell (electrochemical) 3, 112

centre of mass 72–74

centripetal force 97–99

Charles's Law 62–63

ciliary muscles 180

circuit

    parallel 110, 111, 113, 118–121, 127

    series 111, 113, 118–121

circular motion 97–99

cochlea 166

cohesive forces 51–52

collisions 89–90

colour 187

comets 213

compression 163

conductor

    electrical 103, 106

    thermal 12, 14

convection current 12–13, 108

cornea 180, 181

coulombs 107, 122

count rate 207, 211

critical angle 176

crust 159

deceleration 81

density 12, 13, 41, 48, 164

diffraction 157, 165, 186

diffusion 36

digital 144–145

displacement 75–76, 80

drift speed 106

dynamo 140

ear 166

earth connection 103, 104, 105, 126–127

echo-location 169–170

eclipse 217–218

efficiency 5, 24, 26, 35

elastic 68

electric

    charge 102–105, 106–110

    current 106–110

    field 102, 130, 185, 205

    motor 138–139

    bell 136

electrical resistance 113–117

electricity

    cost 127–128

    generator 25, 34, 140

    production 25, 26, 31, 32–34, 140–141

    safety 124–127

    static 102–105

electrolysis 108–109

electromagnet 25, 136

electromotive force (EMF) 112, 140

electron 37, 102–108, 110, 112, 115, 116, 128, 129, 130, 131, 134, 188, 199, 200, 201, 202, 205, 221

electron beam 128–131

electron gun 129

energy (see also *potential energy*)

    crisis 28, 35

    geothermal 26–27

    internal 10, 11

    kinetic 1, 4, 6, 10, 17, 20, 21, 24, 30, 33, 86, 89, 206

    reserve 28

    resource 28

    source 23

eye 180

fault 159

fluid flow 54–57

fluid pressure 48–50

fluorescence 188

focal length 178, 180, 182

force

    and extension 68–69

    and gravity 94–95

    and motion 85–86

    mass and acceleration 88–89

fossil fuels 28

freezing 37, 38

frequency 152, 153, 155, 160, 162, 164, 166, 168, 169, 170, 184, 185, 193, 195, 197

frequency modulation (FM) 195

friction 19, 64–65

fuses 124–125

fusion 30, 220

galaxy 222–223

gamma rays 184, 190, 202, 205, 211

Geiger–Muller tube 207

geostationary orbit 99, 100–101, 197–198

gradient 77–78, 82

gravity 3, 17, 30, 65, 83, 85, 91, 94–95, 97, 100–101, 213, 217–222

grays 210

greenhouse effect 188–189

half-life 203–204

heat

    conduction 11

    convection 11–12

    expansion 41–43

    radiation 11

hertz 152

Hooke's Law 69

hydraulics 49–50

image

    inverted 179, 182, 183

    real 179, 182, 183

    virtual 172, 179, 182, 183

impulse 92–94

induction 103

infra-red 184, 188, 189

inertia 88

insulator

    electrical 103, 106, 124

    thermal 12, 14

inverse square law 100

interference 158, 186, 194, 195, 196

ions 116, 205

isotopes 201–204

joule 2, 122

Kirchhoff's First Law 107

latch (see *bistable*)

latent heat

    of fusion 38–39

    of vaporisation 40

Newton's Laws of Motion 87, 88, 90
lateral inversion 172
lens 178–183
    converging (convex) 178, 179, 180, 182
    diverging (concave) 178, 183
lever 19, 70
light-dependent resistor 117, 146
lightning 105
linear expansivity 43
logic gates 147
long sightedness 181
loudspeaker 136, 150
machine 18–19
magnet 131, 132–135, 137, 138, 139, 140, 141
magnetic field 126, 129, 130, 131, 132–141, 185, 196, 205
magnification 182
mantle 159
Mars 214, 230–231
mass (nucleon) number 201
melting 37–38
microwaves 184, 186, 189, 196
miniature circuit breaker (MCB) 125
modulator 195
moment 70–72
momentum 87, 88–90, 91, 92, 93
monostable 148
Moon 163, 215–218
natural gas 224–225
nebula 219–220
neutron star 221
neutrons 37, 102, 199, 200, 201, 202, 221
noise 167–168
non-renewable energy 28, 33
nucleus 199, 200, 202, 203
ohm 113
Ohm's Law 114
optical fibres 177, 191, 193, 194
optical instruments 179, 182–183
orbit 100–101, 196, 197–198
oscillations 152, 154, 158, 163, 185, 186
period 152
pitch 153, 162, 163, 164
planet 213–215
plasma 37, 219
plastic 68
pneumatic 49–50
potential difference 110–111, 113, 114, 118, 120, 121, 122, 123
potential divider 120–121, 145–146
potential energy 1, 4
    elastic 3, 4, 18, 21
    gravitational 3, 4, 18, 21

power 22
    electric 122
    of lens 180
power stations
    coal-fired 25
    combined heat and 26
    hydroelectric 32–33
    nuclear 25, 208, 211, 212
    thermal 25
pressure 46–47
    in fluids 48–50
    in gases 58–61
    law 59–60
principle focus 178, 182
projectiles 96–97
protons 37, 134, 199, 200, 201, 202, 221
pulley 19
pupil 180
radar 189
radiation
    background 207–209
    electromagnetic 184–190, 196, 202
    gamma 202–203, 205, 207, 209, 212
    ionising 205–207
radio waves 154, 184, 186, 191, 193. 194, 195, 196, 197, 205
radioactive
    decay 202–204, 205–212
    tracer 211
radiocarbon dating 204
ramp 19
rarefaction 163
receiver 192, 193, 195, 196
red giant 220–221
red shift 222, 223
reflection 156, 171–174, 186, 187
    total internal 176, 177, 194
refraction 156, 159,174–178, 186
refractive index 175
renewable energy 29, 31, 34
residual current device (RCD) 126
resistors 120
resonate 158, 166
respiration 2
retina 180, 181
ring main system 127
satellite 100–101, 196, 197–198, 215
semiconductor 116, 144
sensors 146
shells 199, 200
short sightedness 181
sieverts 210
sonar 169
specific heat capacity 7, 9
speed 20–21, 76–77, 78, 79–80, 86, 93, 98, 100, 155, 164, 169, 174, 185, 186

stability 73–74
stars 219–222
states of matter 36–37, 219
Sun 13, 29–31, 132, 155, 184, 188, 190, 213–218, 220, 222
surface tension 51–52
telephones 177, 191, 193, 197
television 131, 187, 196
tension 66
terminal velocity 94–95
thermistor 146
three-pin plug 126–127
tides 217
timebase 130
transducer 198
transformer 141–143
transmitter 186, 193, 195, 196
truth table 147
ultrasound 169–170
ultraviolet 184, 188, 190
universe 221, 222–223
Van der Graaf generator 104
vapour 44–45
velocity 20, 80–84, 87, 88, 89, 90, 95, 97
viscosity 54–56
visible light 154, 171–183, 187, 188, 192, 193, 194
volt 110, 122
wave
    carrier 195, 197
    crests 153, 158, 186
    electromagnetic 184–190, 196, 202, 205
    longitudinal 154, 163, 164
    seismic 159
    speed 155, 164, 174, 175, 185, 186
    transverse 154, 163, 185, 186
    troughs 153, 158, 186
wavelength 153, 155, 157, 163, 164, 165, 168, 169, 170, 177, 184, 185, 187, 188, 189, 194, 196, 197
weight 17–18, 20, 65, 71, 72–73, 85, 91
work 16–20
X-rays 131, 154, 184, 190, 202, 205, 206, 208, 210
y-gain 130